BO4

D0531227

BlackpoolCo

BUILDING A BETTER COMMUNITY FOR ALL

13 MAR 2013

- 3 APR 2013

1 0 FEB 2014

- 4 JAN 2017

- 6 FEB 2017

25 Feb.

Please return/renew this item by the last date shown.
Books may also be renewed by phone or the Internet.

Tel: 01253 478070
www.blackpool.gov.uk

Which? Books are commissioned and published by Which? Ltd,
2 Marylebone Road, London NW1 4DF
Email: books@which.co.uk

British Library Cataloguing in Publication Data
A catalogue record for this book is available from the British Library

Picture credits:
Microsoft product screen shot(s) reprinted with permission from Microsoft Corporation, Microsoft, Encarta, MSN, and Windows are either registered trademarks or trademarks of Microsoft Corporation in the United States and/or other countries.
Adobe product screenshot(s) reprinted with permission from Adobe Systems Incorporated.
All other pictures courtesy of Digital Visions except for page 24: courtesy of Shutterstock, and page 196: courtesy of Lynn Wright

ISBN 978 1 84490 125 8

1 3 5 7 9 10 8 6 4 2

Disclaimer: Although the publishers endeavour to make sure that the information contained in this book is both accurate and up to date this is not guaranteed and the book is intended as a general guide only. You should conduct your own research into the suitability of software before installing or using it and you are responsible for checking that your computer and software equipment are compatible with the information contained in this book. The publisher will not be responsible for any data loss that may be incurred as a result of you following the information in this book. It is the responsibility of the user to back up any information contained on their computer and neither the author nor the publisher can accept liability for any loss or damage suffered as a consequence of relying on any of the information contained in this book.

The publishers would like to thank Sarah Kidner, Matt Bath and the Which? Computing team for their help in the preparation of this book.

Consultant editor: Lynn Wright
Project manager: Emma Callery
Designer: Blanche Williams, Harper Williams Ltd
Proofreader: Sian Stark
Indexer: Lynda Swindells
Printed and bound by Charterhouse, Hatfield
Distributed by Littlehampton Book Services Ltd, Faraday Close, Durrington, Worthing, West Sussex BN13 3RB

Essential Velvet is an elemental chlorine-free paper produced at Condat in Périgord, France using timber from sustainably managed forests. The mill is ISO14001 and EMAS certified.

For a full list of Which? Books, please call 01903 828557 or access our website at
www.which.co.uk, or write to Littlehampton Book Services.

which?

USING YOUR PC
MADE
EASY

OFFICE 2010 AND MORE

Contents

⊳ EXCEL

⊳ POWERPOINT

⊳ PDFs

⊳ PHOTOS & VIDEOS

⊳ RESOURCES

INTRODUCTION

Your computer is your passport into new ways of working, having fun and managing your home and hobbies. But it can sometimes feel that getting the most out of your PC is a daunting journey. With this book, its step-by-step lessons and advice are designed to make you a more confident computer user, making your computer work for you, and helping you to perform tasks that save you time and effort.

From getting the most from Microsoft Windows 7 so you can personalise your PC to suit your needs, to using your computer for day-to-day activities, *Using Your PC Made Easy* will help you quickly discover the skills and steps you need for success.

Written in plain English and with a handy jargon buster, using your computer for everyday tasks, such as creating family newsletters, managing home finances, editing photos and videos, and even creating professional presentations, is explained in clear, easy-to-follow steps. It shows you how to get more from Microsoft's popular Office 2010 software, helping you learn the ropes of Microsoft Word, Excel and PowerPoint. It also shows you how to successfully edit and manage video and photos, and even share them with friends and family using Microsoft's free video and photo-editing software.

If you get stuck, you can contact the Which? Computing Helpdesk. Simply go to www.which.co.uk/computinghelpdesk and input code USINGYOURPC1 where it asks for your membership number.

EDITORIAL NOTE

The instructions in this guide refer to the Windows 7 operating system and Microsoft Office Home and Student 2010.

Screenshots are used for illustrative purposes only.

Windows 7 and Microsoft Office Home and Student 2010 are American products. All spellings on the screenshots and on the buttons and boxes in the text are therefore spelled in US English. The rest of the text remains in UK English.

All technical words in the book are either discussed in jargon busters within the text and/or can be found in the Jargon Buster section on page 214.

When asked to click on something, note that this means a left click unless specified otherwise.

WINDOWS

By reading this chapter you'll learn how to:

 Find and open files, folders and programs

 Create individual user accounts

 Personalise your computer settings

▶ Windows

YOUR WINDOWS DESKTOP

The desktop is the screen you see as soon as you start your Windows computer. Here you find icons linking to documents, programs or specific areas of your computer.

The taskbar

Running across the bottom of the desktop is a blue strip called the taskbar. From here you can open programs, switch between programs, and access the main Windows functions. And when you shrink – or minimise – a window, you can quickly reopen it by clicking on it in the taskbar.

THE WINDOWS 7 START BUTTON
Click to open the main Windows menu.

TASKBAR SHORTCUTS
These icons allow you to easily open programs that you use regularly.

TASK BUTTONS
These show the programs that are currently open. Move your cursor over an icon to see a preview of the windows that are open in that program.

NOTIFICATION AREA
This area shows the time, speaker volume and information about any network you're connected to. Other icons will appear when Windows is performing different tasks. For example, when you're printing, an icon appears that shows you the printing progress.

TIP
You can close a program by right-clicking on it in the taskbar and clicking **Close window**.

Reposition and resize the taskbar

You don't have to keep the taskbar at the bottom of the screen, you can move it to the sides or top of the screen. You can also resize it to suit.

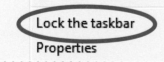

Toolbars   ▶

Cascade windows
Show windows stacked
Show windows side by side
Show the desktop

Start Task Manager

Lock the taskbar
Properties

1 Right click on an empty space on the taskbar

2 A small window appears. If Lock the taskbar has a tick mark next to it, the taskbar is locked

3 Unlock it by clicking **Lock the taskbar**. This removes the tick

4 To reposition the taskbar, click on the taskbar and hold down the mouse button, then drag the taskbar to the left, right or top of the screen to change its location

5 To resize the taskbar, hover your cursor over the edge of the taskbar until the cursor changes into a double-headed arrow, click and drag to move the border up or down

Pin items to the taskbar

You can also choose what you have on your taskbar in the 'Taskbar Shortcuts' section next to the 'Start' button.

1 Click

2 Right click on any program

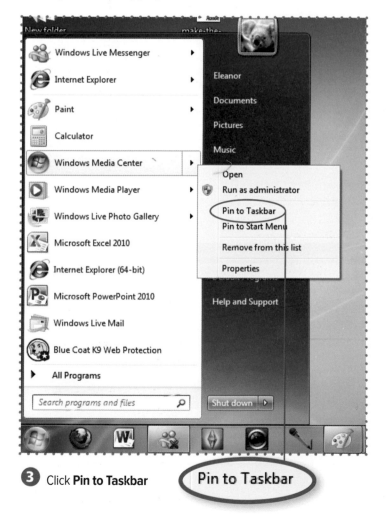

3 Click **Pin to Taskbar**

▶ Windows

HOW TO HANDLE WINDOWS

When you open a program or a web page, it will open as a window on your desktop. You can have more than one window open at once and you can resize them to suit your preferences.

To change the size of a window, move your cursor over the edge or corner of the window until the pointer changes into a double-headed arrow, then click and drag the border up or down, or diagonally to the size you want.

MINIMISE ICON
Click this to make the window disappear from the desktop. It is now accessible from the relevant icon in the taskbar.

MAXIMISE ICON
Click this to make the window occupy the whole of the screen. Click again and your window returns to its original size.

CROSS ICON
This will close the window and you'll have to open the program afresh if you want to use it again. Depending on which program you're using, you may see two crosses – one for the file you're working on and one for the program as a whole. For example, in Microsoft Word, you will have the option to close either the document or close Word completely.

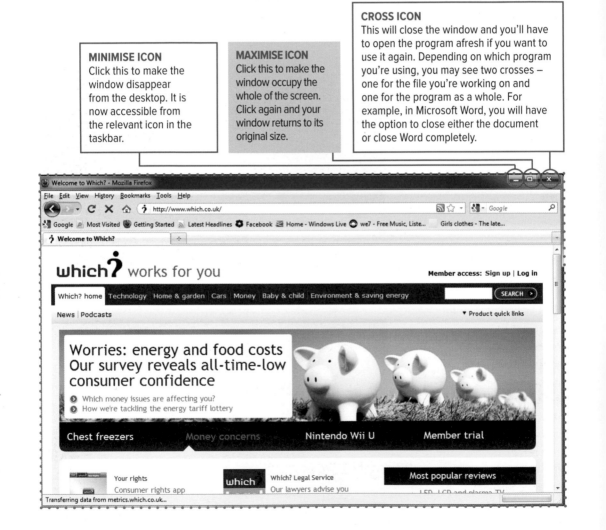

Deal with desktop clutter

Opening files and folders can result in a cluttered desktop that makes it hard to find and use the program or document you want. Windows 7 has three useful features that let you quickly cut through the clutter and take control of your desktop.

Shake If you've a lot of windows open and you want to focus on just one, simply shake that window (click on the bar at the top of the window with the mouse and, holding down the mouse button, quickly move the mouse cursor back and forth, shaking the window). All of the other windows on screen are minimized. Shake the window again and the other windows return.

Peek To look at your desktop even if it's buried beneath several open windows, hover the cursor over the transparent rectangle in the bottom corner of the taskbar. This makes all the windows on your screen transparent, so you can easily see gadgets and icons on your desktop. Click on the rectangle to switch back to your open windows.

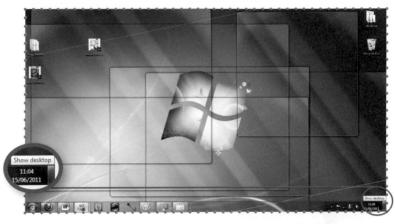

Snap This feature lets you resize and rearrange two windows to view them side-by-side. To do this, simply drag one window off screen to the left, and the other window to the right. Each window will expand to take up half the screen.

OPEN PROGRAMS

You can open a program one of two ways. If you can see the program icon on the desktop, double click it with the mouse and the program will open on the screen ready to use. Another way is to click the **Start** button, and then choose a program from the menu list. If you can't see the program you want, click the arrow next to **All Programs** to bring up a full list of all the programs stored on your computer.

When you use Windows for the first time, you'll see some program icons already on the desktop. These will be for commonly used programs, and are known as desktop shortcuts. It's easy to add a desktop shortcut for another program.

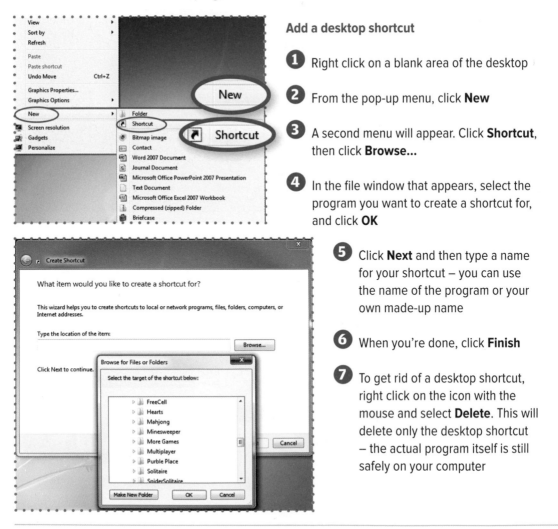

Add a desktop shortcut

1 Right click on a blank area of the desktop

2 From the pop-up menu, click **New**

3 A second menu will appear. Click **Shortcut**, then click **Browse...**

4 In the file window that appears, select the program you want to create a shortcut for, and click **OK**

5 Click **Next** and then type a name for your shortcut – you can use the name of the program or your own made-up name

6 When you're done, click **Finish**

7 To get rid of a desktop shortcut, right click on the icon with the mouse and select **Delete**. This will delete only the desktop shortcut – the actual program itself is still safely on your computer

SEARCH FOR FILES AND FOLDERS

You can use the 'Start' menu's search box to find files, folders and even email messages on your hard drive.

1 Click

2 Start typing into the search box

3 As you type, any items that match your text will appear on the 'Start' menu

4 Click on a search result to open the file

If you're looking for a file in a specific folder, such as 'Documents', use the search box at the top right of the open folder window to narrow the search to just this folder. This saves time searching for an elusive file if you've lots of files and folders.

Control Panel (2)
- Windows Defender
- Scan for spyware and other potentially unwanted software

Documents (4)
- break from acts
- Encolpedia
- Your Majesty Queen Elizabeth
- History henry 8th

Eleanor (6)
- Windows Defender
- break from acts
- Encolpedia
- 01 Laptops and netbooks
- Your Majesty Queen Elizabeth
- History henry 8th

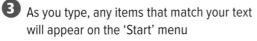

Windows

Jargon buster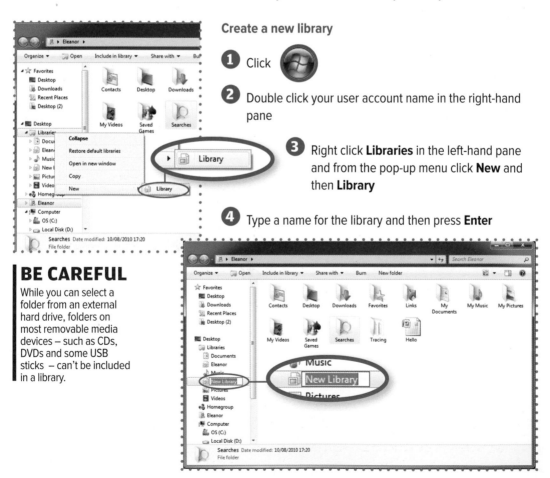

External hard drive
A storage device that plugs into your PC. Useful for saving copies of important files or creating additional storage.

MANAGE YOUR FILES

In older versions of Windows, organising your files meant placing them in different folders and subfolders. With Windows 7, you can use libraries to manage your files. These work by gathering together files, such as pictures or documents, from different locations on your hard drive and displaying them as a single collection – or library.

The files themselves aren't moved from where they're stored – they are just displayed in one location. So for example, if you have photos in various folders on your hard disk and also on an external drive, you can look at all of them at once using the Picture library.

Windows 7 comes with four default libraries – Documents, Music, Pictures and Videos – but it's easy to create a new library should you want to.

Create a new library

1 Click

2 Double click your user account name in the right-hand pane

3 Right click **Libraries** in the left-hand pane and from the pop-up menu click **New** and then **Library**

4 Type a name for the library and then press **Enter**

BE CAREFUL

While you can select a folder from an external hard drive, folders on most removable media devices – such as CDs, DVDs and some USB sticks – can't be included in a library.

Add a folder on your computer to a library

To save files to a library, you first need to add a folder to the library. This becomes the default save location for the library.

1 Click then your user name

2 In the left-hand pane of the pop-up window, find and click the folder you wish to add to the library

3 In the toolbar click **Include in library** and click a library – either your new library or an existing one, such as Pictures

Add a folder from an external hard drive to a library

You can add a folder from an external hard drive to your library so that each time you connect the drive the selected files appear in the designated library.

1 Connect the hard drive to your computer

2 Click then your user name

3 Click **Computer** in the left pane, then find the folder on your external hard drive that you want to include

4 In the toolbar, click **Include in library**

5 Then click the library you want to use

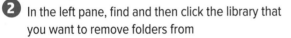

Remove a folder from a library

By removing a folder from a library, you're just deleting the connection – the folder and its contents remain safe in their original location.

1 Click then your user name

2 In the left pane, find and then click the library that you want to remove folders from

3 In the library pane, next to 'Includes', click **Location(s)**. In the dialog box, click the folder you want to remove. Click **Remove** and then click **OK**

▶ Windows

UNDERSTAND THE CONTROL PANEL

From Windows 7's Control Panel you can make changes to your computer, including the appearance of your desktop, your security settings and the programs that are on your computer.

Open the Control Panel

1 Click

2 Click **Control Panel** in the right-hand column

SYSTEM AND SECURITY
View your computer's specifications and carry out tasks, such as backing up your files and checking your computer's security status.

USER ACCOUNTS AND FAMILY SAFETY
Add and remove user accounts, as well as change user account settings and passwords.

APPEARANCE AND PERSONALIZATION
Customise the look of your desktop and make changes to the 'Start' menu or Taskbar.

NETWORK AND INTERNET
Set up an internet connection or network and set preferences for sharing files and computers.

HARDWARE AND SOUND
Make changes to devices such as printers and speakers.

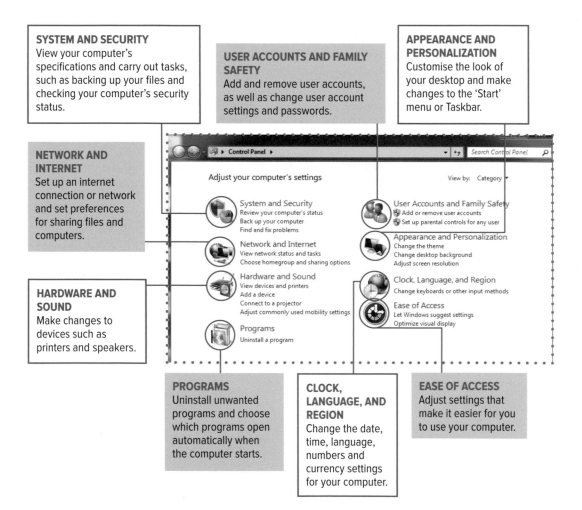

PROGRAMS
Uninstall unwanted programs and choose which programs open automatically when the computer starts.

CLOCK, LANGUAGE, AND REGION
Change the date, time, language, numbers and currency settings for your computer.

EASE OF ACCESS
Adjust settings that make it easier for you to use your computer.

CREATE DIFFERENT USER ACCOUNTS

When you first set up your computer, Windows creates an 'Administrator account'. This gives you full control of the computer so you can change settings and add programs. However, anyone else using the computer with this account can do the same. This means others can make fundamental changes to your computer setup, read private files or even install programs without your permission.

So, it's a good idea to restrict other people's level of access by creating a Standard user account for each person. When someone logs on using their individual user account, Windows knows which folders and files they're allowed to open. It also knows how they like their screen and desktop to look and what changes they are allowed to make. If they try to make changes they're not allowed to, they will be asked to provide the Administrator password.

Create a Standard user account

1 Click

2 Then click **Control Panel**

3 Click on **User Accounts and Family Safety**, then click **Add or remove user accounts**

4 Click on **Create a new account**

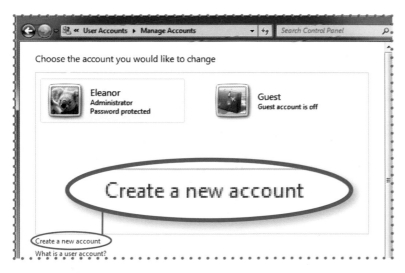

▶ Windows

TRY THIS

You can use your own photograph as a picture icon. Click on **Browse** when presented with the picture choices (in step 8) and select a photograph saved on your computer.

5 Type in a name for the user and select **Standard User**

6 Click **Create Account**

7 You can add a password to this account by clicking **Create a password**

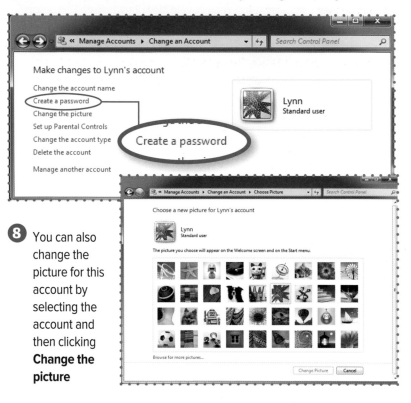

8 You can also change the picture for this account by selecting the account and then clicking **Change the picture**

TRY THIS

You can switch users by pressing **Ctrl, Alt + Delete** simultaneously, and then selecting **Switch user** from the menu that appears on screen.

Switch between users

To switch between users while you're using your computer:

1 Click

2 Click on the **arrow** icon next to 'Shut down'

3 From the drop-down list, click **Switch user**. Your programs won't be closed down; when you switch back to your user account everything will be as you left it

4 Select the user account that you want to switch to

PARENTAL CONTROLS

Parental controls help you to manage your child's computer and internet use. You can ensure your child only visits approved websites, set limits for how long a child can use the web, and prevent them from running programs such as games, chat programs and file-sharing tools. You can also get up-to-date reports on their online activities.

Windows 7 includes parental controls, though you will need to download the free Windows Live Family Safety tool for the maximum control. It can be downloaded from http://explore.live.com/windows-live-family-safety.

TRY THIS

Also included under 'Web restrictions' are activity reports so you can keep tabs on what your children are up to online, along with tools that monitor who they can contact online using instant messaging software.

Set up parental controls

Parental controls can only be applied to Standard user accounts, so make sure you have set one up for your child. You have to do this from the Administrator account.

1 Click

2 Then click **Control Panel** and then **User Accounts and Family Safety**. Click **Set up parental controls for any user**

3 Click the account name you want to apply parental controls to and click **On, enforce current settings** to switch it on

4 Adjust the individual settings as required for the account, such as 'Time Limits', and click **OK** to take you back to the 'User Controls' panel. Either adjust other settings, such as 'Games', or click **OK**

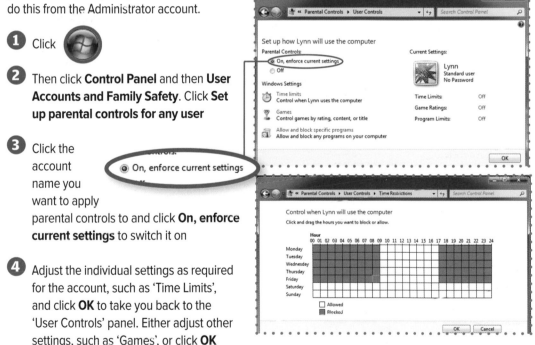

Set web restrictions

1 Next to 'Web Restrictions', click **Windows Live Family Safety**

2 Click **Web filtering**, then move the slider to the appropriate settings for your child. Click **Save** to save your changes

PERSONALISE YOUR DESKTOP

Changing the appearance of your desktop is a quick and easy way to make using your computer more enjoyable. To change the appearance of the desktop:

1 Right click anywhere on the desktop

2 Click **Personalize**

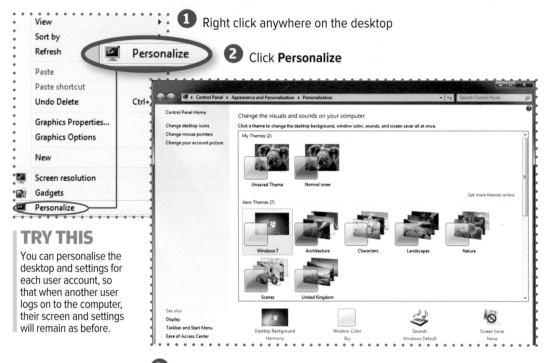

TRY THIS

You can personalise the desktop and settings for each user account, so that when another user logs on to the computer, their screen and settings will remain as before.

3 From this menu you can change how your screen looks. You can choose to change individual screen elements – the background image (also called wallpaper), window colour and a screen saver

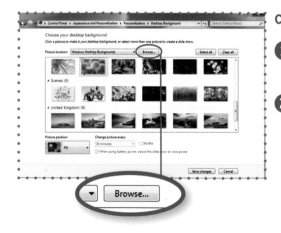

Change the desktop background

1 On the 'Personalization' window, click **Desktop Background**

2 Click the picture or colour that you want to use for your desktop background. If a picture isn't listed, click on the arrow in the 'Picture location' drop-down menu, to choose from a collection of images, including ones from your 'Picture' folder or click **Browse...** to find one elsewhere on your hard drive

When you've chosen an image, simply click it to preview the new desktop background

 Under 'Picture position', click the arrow and choose whether to crop the picture to fill the screen, fit the picture to the screen, stretch the picture to fit the screen, tile the picture – use multiple small versions of the image arranged in a grid – or centre the picture on the screen, and then click **Save changes**

5 Click **Save changes**

Change the screen saver

1 On the 'Personalization window', click **Screen Saver**

2 You can either choose a screen saver from the drop-down menu or create one using your own photos:

▶ To use an existing screen saver, click the one you want to use, and then click **OK**

▶ To create a new screen saver from a photo, select **Photos**. Click **Settings** and then **Browse**. Choose the folder that contains the photos you want to use and then click **OK**

3 Click **Preview** to see what your new screen saver will look like – your images will be displayed in sequence

Adjust screen saver settings

1 To change the length of time your computer is inactive before the screen saver starts, select a time in the 'Wait' box

2 A screen saver can be deactivated by using the keyboard or mouse. Tick the **On resume** box next to the 'Wait' box if you want to make sure that your password must be entered to access the computer at that point

3 To customise your screen saver further, click on **Settings**. When you're happy with your choices, click **OK**

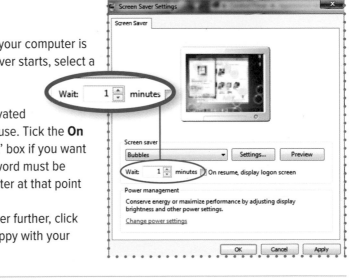

TRY THIS

For a quick way to make any picture on your computer the desktop background, right click the picture, and then click **Set as Desktop Background** from the pop-up menu.

BE CAREFUL

You can download screen savers from the internet but watch out. Some may contain viruses that slow down your computer. Only download from reputable sources – for example, sites that you're familiar with and know you can trust.

▶ Windows

TRY THIS

Windows 7 comes with several accessibility focused themes designed to help users with visual impairments or special conditions. These 'High Contrast' themes heighten the colour contrast of text and images on the screen, making them more distinct and easier to see.

Apply a theme

A theme is a combination of desktop background, screen saver, window border colour, and computer sounds. Themes are a quick way to change these settings in one go so they all share a common subject such as arctic landscapes, fireworks or space.

Windows comes with several themes and there are hundreds more to download online from Microsoft's website. You can even create your own theme and share it with others.

To change your current Windows theme, just click on one of the themes listed in the centre panel of the 'Personalization' window (see page 20). Windows immediately applies the new theme, and you can start using it.

Make Windows easier to use

Windows has several options that make your computer easier to use – helpful if you suffer from poor vision or other physical impairments. These options are found in the 'Ease of Access Center'. To launch this, you:

1 Click

2 Then click on **Control Panel**

3 In the screen that appears, click on **Ease of Access**, and then click on **Ease of Access Center**

Here you'll find various settings that make using your computer more comfortable. For example:

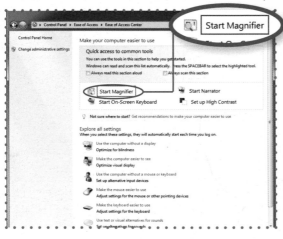

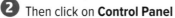

- ▶ **Magnifier** is a virtual magnifying glass that's great for tasks such as typing a document or reading a news story online
- ▶ **Narrator** reads aloud text on screen as you navigate
- ▶ **Make the computer easier to see** has a number of options. For example, you can make all the items on screen larger by adjusting the screen display and changing the colour of windows
- ▶ **Make the mouse easier to use** allows you to increase the size of the mouse cursor to make it easier to see on screen

WORD

By reading this chapter you will get to grips with:

▶ **Creating different document layouts**

▶ **Positioning and formatting text**

▶ **Importing and editing images**

▶ Word

TRY THIS

OpenOffice at www.openoffice.org is a good alternative choice for anyone wanting a full-featured office suite free of charge. It's what's known as open source software, so you can download and install the software at no cost. The website encourages you to contribute to the ongoing development of the software, donating time or money to help it progress.

OFFICE SUITES

For many people, the ability to create professional looking office documents is one of the main reasons they bought a computer. Whether it's using a word processor to write a letter or a spreadsheet to calculate household finances, these tasks are made easier by using suitable software.

While your computer may have come with a very basic word processor, such as Wordpad (which comes built into Windows), investing in an office software suite is something that most users should consider if they are going to make the most of their computer.

An office suite is a bundle of computer programs for doing common tasks such as writing letters and managing budgets. Originally, office suites were designed with professional office workers in mind. However, with the growing trend towards working from home and the increasing use of the computer at home in general, software manufacturers now create versions of office suites with the home user in mind.

The best-known office suite on the market is Microsoft Office, which is available in several versions to suit different needs and budgets. It contains familiar Microsoft programs such as Word (word processor), Excel (a spreadsheet program) and PowerPoint (a presentations package).

GET STARTED WITH WORD

Before creating your first document, it's worth spending a little time getting to know Word's workspace. The key tools and commands you need can be found on the Backstage view, the Quick Access Toolbar or on the Ribbon.

Backstage view

Here you'll find various options for opening, saving, printing or sharing a document. To get to the Backstage view:

1 Click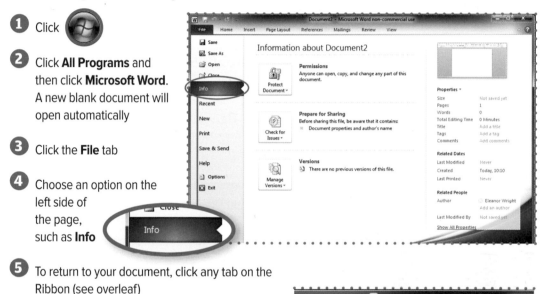

2 Click **All Programs** and then click **Microsoft Word**. A new blank document will open automatically

3 Click the **File** tab

4 Choose an option on the left side of the page, such as **Info**

5 To return to your document, click any tab on the Ribbon (see overleaf)

Quick Access Toolbar

This sits above the Ribbon (see overleaf), and offers fast access to common commands such as 'Save', 'Undo' and 'Repeat'. You can also add other commands to make working in Word easier.

1 Click the drop-down arrow to the right of the Quick Access Toolbar

2 Select the command you want to add from the drop-down menu and it will appear in the Quick Access toolbar

3 If the command you want to add isn't there, click **More Commands...** to see more listed

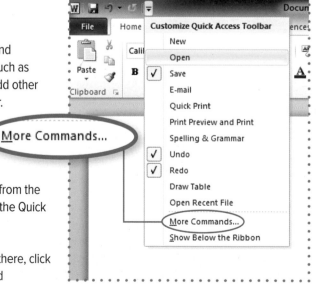

Word

THE RIBBON

The Ribbon that appears at the top of your Word window features all the commands you need to make changes to your document. It contains multiple tabs, each with several and related groups of commands. You can also add your own tabs containing your favourite commands. Some groups have an arrow in the bottom-right corner. When you click the arrow, you can get access to even more commands.

The Home tab

This houses the basic formatting tools. From here, you can change the style, size and colour of your text, create bulleted and numbered lists and more. Find out how to use these on pages 42–50.

The Insert tab

Insert other elements into your document such as pictures and shapes (see pages 56 and 66). You can also add headers and footers or the date and time (see pages 52–3).

The Page Layout tab

Change the orientation of your page from vertical (portrait – usually the default setting) to horizontal (landscape), create multiple columns of text or add borders to your page.

The References tab

A great tab full of tools that are useful for anyone writing long research documents or papers. Tools include ones for inserting endnotes and footnotes into long documents or creating a table of contents.

The Mailings tab

Create labels and envelopes, or do a mail merge (see pages 78–80).

The Review tab

Check the contents of your document using the spellchecker or access the thesaurus. You can also 'Track Changes', which lets you see the changes that you or others have made to a single document.

The View tab

Zoom in or out on documents to make them easier to view. You can also see how your document will look when printed or published online as well as when displayed in draft mode – plain text with no formatting.

CUSTOMISE THE RIBBON

You can change the Ribbon to suit the way you work in Word. For example, you can create new tabs with the commands you use most often on them. Commands are housed within a group, and you can create as many groups as you need to keep your tab organised. You can also add commands to any of the default tabs, provided you create a custom group in the tab.

1 Right click the Ribbon and select **Customize the Ribbon...**

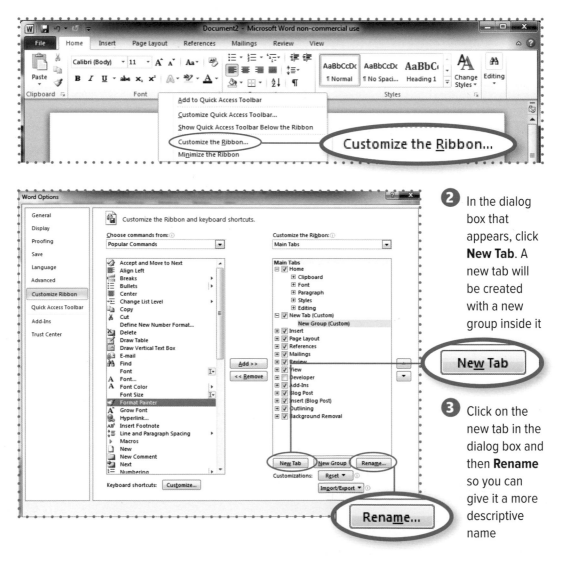

2 In the dialog box that appears, click **New Tab**. A new tab will be created with a new group inside it

3 Click on the new tab in the dialog box and then **Rename** so you can give it a more descriptive name

Under the new renamed tab, click **New Group (Custom)**

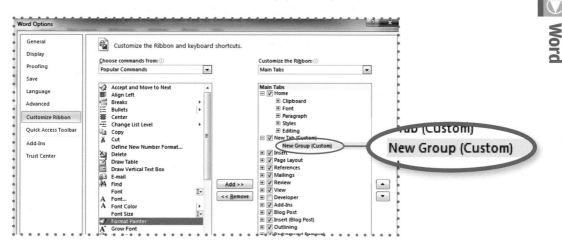

 Select a command from the list on the left, then click **Add**. You can also drag commands directly into a group

 If you can't see the command you want, click on the arrow below 'Choose commands from', and click **All Commands**

 Use the arrow keys to order your commands exactly the way you want them to appear on the Ribbon tab. In this case, up means left and down means right

 When you have finished adding commands, click **OK**

Shrink the Ribbon
If you find that the Ribbon is taking up too much screen space you can choose to minimise it.

 Click the arrow in the upper-right corner of the Ribbon to minimise it

 To maximise the Ribbon, click the arrow again

TRY THIS

When the Ribbon is minimised, you can make it reappear by clicking on a tab. However, the Ribbon will disappear again when you're not using it.

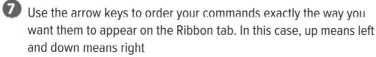

▶ Word

CREATE AND OPEN A DOCUMENT

To create a new, blank document in Word:

1 Open Microsoft Word – there may be an icon on the desktop or taskbar. If not, search for it by clicking on **Start**

2 A new blank document will open automatically. If you already have a document open and want to create a new document, click **File**

3 This shows the Backstage view (see page 25). Here are the commands you use to manage and apply changes to your document. Click **New**

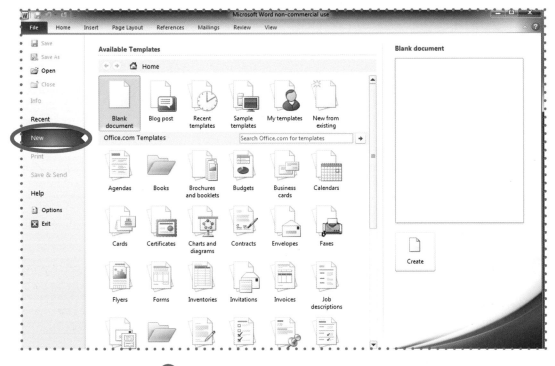

4 The Blank document option under 'Available Templates' will be highlighted by default

5 Click **Create**

6 A blank document, which looks like a white sheet of paper, will appear taking up most of the window. Above this document sits the Ribbon

7 You can start typing

Open an existing document

1 Click **File** to go to the Backstage view

2 Click **Open**. The 'Open' dialog box will appear showing folders and files on your computer hard drive

3 Select a document and then click **Open**

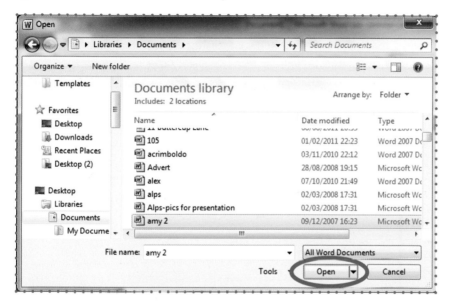

4 If you've opened a file recently, you can access it from the **Recent Documents** list. Click on the **File** tab and select **Recent**

31

USE A TEMPLATE

A template is a pre-designed document that lets you quickly create documents without worrying about page layout and text formatting. Word comes with a range of sample templates that can help save time and effort. Whether you want to create a letter, a flyer, newsletter or form, you can usually find a template to suit.

Open a template

1 Open Word and click the **File** tab to go to the Backstage view

2 Select **New** to open the 'New Document' pane

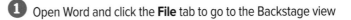

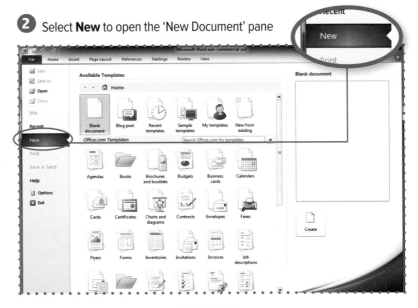

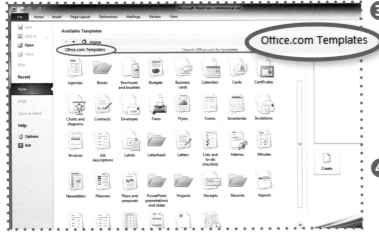

3 Click **Sample templates** to choose a built-in template, or select an 'Office.com Template' category, shown here, to select and download a template from Microsoft's website

4 Select a template and click **Create**. A new document will appear using the template you've chosen

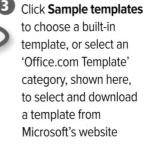

Insert text into a template

Most templates use placeholder text – sometimes shown surrounded by square brackets – which you replace with your own text.

1 Click on the text you want to replace. The text will appear highlighted

TRY THIS
Instead of placeholder text within brackets, some templates use ordinary text. If so, simply delete the text and type in your own.

2 Enter your text. It will replace the placeholder text

Jargon buster

Placeholder text
Also known as dummy text. A piece of text – sometimes nonsense text such as lorem ipsum – designed to show the position, font, size and format of text in a layout.

Word

SAVE A DOCUMENT

1 Click **File**, then click **Save**. If this is the first time you've saved your document, the 'Save As' dialog box will open

2 'Save As' lets you choose a name and location for your document. The default location for saving files is the Documents folder. By default too, Word will suggest a file name for your document based on the first few words in your document

3 Click **Save** if you're happy with these default settings

4 If, at step 2, you wish to save your document to a different location, use the shortcuts on the left-hand side of the 'Save As' dialog box to select a new location

5 If, at step 2, you want to name your document yourself, click in the **File name** box to highlight the default name and type the name of your choice

6 Click **Save**. If you've saved your document previously but want to give it a new name, select **Save As** from the drop-down list

Save as an older format

You can share your documents with anyone using Word 2010 or 2007, as they use the same .docx file format. However, older versions of Word use a different file format. To ensure your documents can be opened and read using a previous version of Microsoft Word, you need to save it as a Word 97-2003 Document. Here's how:

1 Click **File**

2 Click **Save As**

3 In the 'Save As' dialog, click on the down arrow next to the 'Save as type' box

4 From the drop-down menu, select **Word 97-2003 Document**

Jargon buster

File format
File format refers to the specific way that information is stored within a computer file. The type of file format is shown by the letters that appear after the file name, and these indicate what type of file it is and what type of program will open it – for example, a Microsoft Word file will end in .docx, while a Microsoft Excel file will end in .xlsx

5 Click **Save**

Word

RECOVER AN UNSAVED DOCUMENT

It's important to regularly save your document by clicking **File** and then **Save**. Or you can press the keys **Ctrl** and **S** at the same time (indicated by pressing **Ctrl + S**) on your keyboard to perform a save.

Word can automatically save your document at regular intervals using the AutoRecover feature, so should something unexpected happen – such as power outage – or you accidently close a document without saving, a version of your file will be saved.

Enable AutoRecover

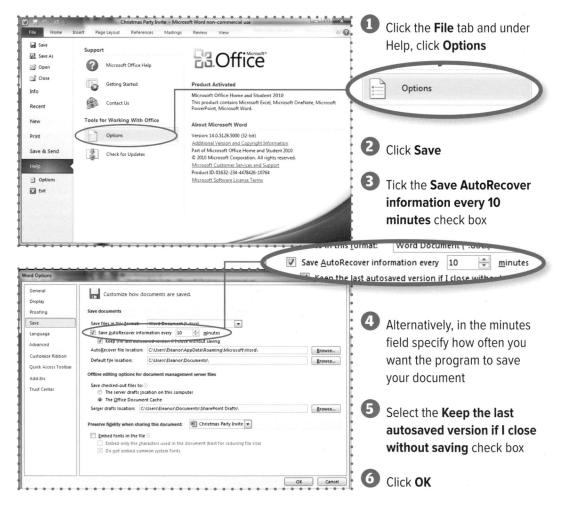

1 Click the **File** tab and under Help, click **Options**

2 Click **Save**

3 Tick the **Save AutoRecover information every 10 minutes** check box

4 Alternatively, in the minutes field specify how often you want the program to save your document

5 Select the **Keep the last autosaved version if I close without saving** check box

6 Click **OK**

Open an autosaved version of your document

1 Open the document that was previously closed without saving

2 Click **File**

3 In Backstage view, click **Info**

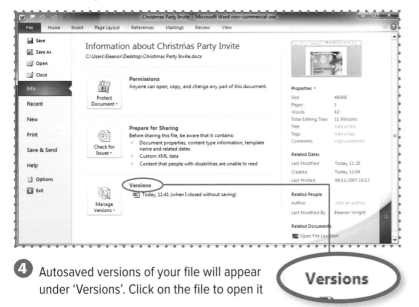

4 Autosaved versions of your file will appear under 'Versions'. Click on the file to open it

5 To keep this version, click **Restore**

6 A dialog box appears with a warning that you are about to overwrite the last saved version of that file with the selected version. Click **OK**

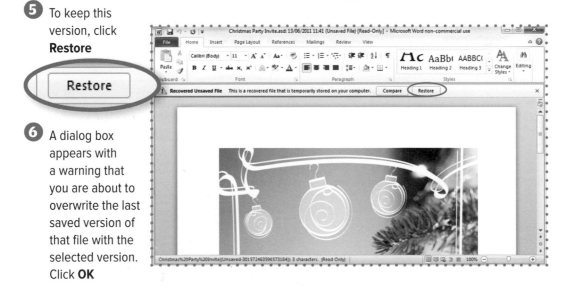

Word

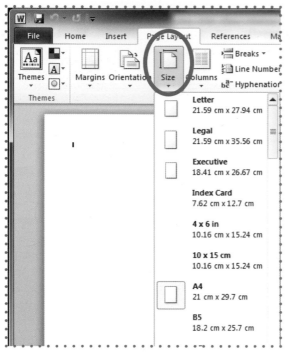

CHANGE THE PAGE LAYOUT

When you create a new document, the blank page that appears uses Word's default page layout settings. These may not work for the document you wish to create. For example, you may need to change your document's page size to match the size of paper when printing or you may wish to change the page orientation or margins.

Change the page size

1 Click the **Page Layout** tab

2 In the 'Page Setup' group, click **Size**. A drop-down menu appears with the current page size highlighted

3 Click the page size you want and the document will change accordingly

Change page orientation for the entire document

1 Click the **Page Layout** tab

2 In the 'Page Setup' group, click **Orientation**

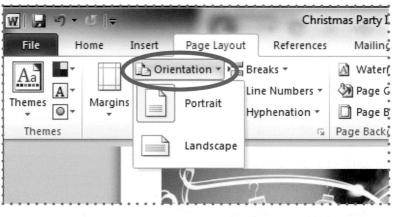

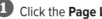

TRY THIS

You can use both portrait or landscape pages in the same Word document. On the **Page Layout** tab, in the 'Page Setup' group, click **Margins**. Then click **Custom Margins**. On the **Margins** tab, click **Portrait** or **Landscape**. Then in the 'Apply to' drop-down menu, click **Selected text**.

3 Click either **Portrait** or **Landscape** to change the page orientation

CHANGE THE PAGE MARGINS

Page margins are the blank areas around the edges of a page. In most page layouts, text and graphics appear inside these page margins. By changing a document's page margins, you can change where text and graphics appear on each page. You can do this either by selecting one of Word's default settings or by creating your own custom margins.

Change page margins settings

 Click the **Page Layout** tab

 In the 'Page Setup' group, click **Margins**. The Margins gallery appears – with 'Normal' selected by default

 Click the margin size you want

Create custom page margins

 Click the **Page Layout** tab

 In the 'Page Setup' group, click **Margins**

 At the bottom of the 'Margins' gallery, click **Custom Margins**

 In the 'Page Setup' dialog box that appears, enter new values for the margins. Then click **OK**

View page margins

When designing a page layout, it's useful to see the text area. Word can display lines in your document that represent the page margins.

 On the **File** tab, click **Options**

 Click **Advanced**, and then under 'Show document content' select the **Show text boundaries** check box

 The page margins will appear in your document as dotted lines

---

BE CAREFUL!

Most printers require a minimum margin width, because they can't print to the edge of the page. If your margins are too narrow, you may see the following message 'One or more margins are set outside the printable area of the page.' To avoid text from being cut off, click **Fix to automatically increase the margin width**. Check the manual to find out the minimum settings for your printer.

TRY THIS

To change the margins for part of a document, select the text, and then set the margins by entering the new values in the 'Page Setup' dialog box. In the 'Apply to box', click **Selected text**.

Word

▶ Word

TRY THIS

When you select text or images in Word, a hover toolbar appears. This contains the main formatting commands. If it doesn't show at first, move your mouse over the selection.

WORK WITH TEXT

Learn the basics of working with text in Word – from inserting and deleting text to cutting and pasting selected text.

Add text

The cursor, a blinking vertical line in the upper-left corner of the page, shows you where the words you type will appear on the page.

1 If you want to start typing further down the page, press the **Enter** key on your keyboard until the cursor is where you want to type

2 Alternatively, move your mouse to the location you wish text to appear in the document and click the mouse. The cursor will appear here

3 Start typing

Delete text

1 Move your cursor next to the text you wish to delete

NEXT STEP ▶

Learn more about keyboard shortcuts for Word on page 88.

2 Press the **Backspace** key on your keyboard to delete text to the left of the cursor

3 Press the **Delete** key on your keyboard to delete text to the right of the cursor

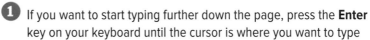

way to convert your newsletter to a Web publication. So, when you're finished writing your newsletter, convert it to a Web site and post it.

The purpose of a newsletter is to provide specialized information to a targeted audience. Newsletters can be a great way to communicate with family and friends on a regular basis.

You can tell stories about your life, your children's activities, your vacations or travel plans, new pets, or whatever you want to tell those closest to you! You can add pictures, too.

Capti...

Select text

1 Move your cursor next to the text you wish to select

2 Click and hold down the mouse button while dragging the cursor over the text to select it

3 Release the mouse button. A highlighted box will appear over the selected text

Copy and paste text

1 Select the text you wish to copy

2 Click the **Home** tab, then **Copy**

Copy (Ctrl+C)

3 Place your cursor where you wish the text to appear

4 Click the **Home** tab, then **Paste**. The text will appear

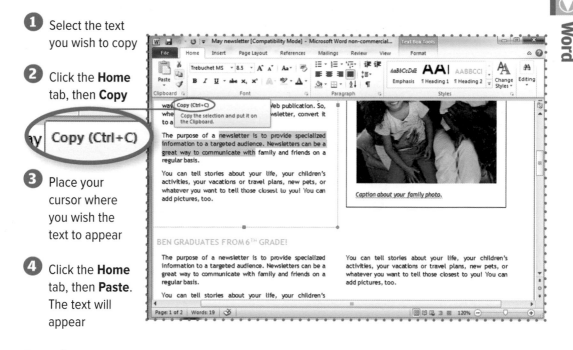

Cut and paste text

1 Select the text you wish to cut

2 Click the **Home** tab, then **Cut**. The text will be 'cut' from the document, and disappear

Cut (Ctrl+X)

3 Place your cursor where you wish the text to reappear

4 Click the **Home** tab, then **Paste** for the text to appear

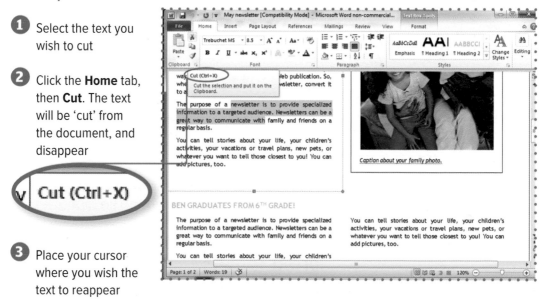

FORMAT TEXT

To create good-looking documents that capture your readers' attention, you can change the way your text looks from Word's default settings. Word's formatting tools let you customise everything from the style of font, size and colour of text to its alignment and placement.

Change the size of text

1 Select the text you wish to change. On the **Home** tab, in the 'Font' group, click the **Font Size** drop-down arrow

2 From the drop-down menu select a font size. When you move your cursor over each font size, a live preview of the sized text will appear in the document

TRY THIS

To remove text formatting, select the text that you want to clear the formats from (or press **Ctrl + A** to select everything in the document), then on the **Home** tab, in the 'Font' group, click **Clear Formatting**.

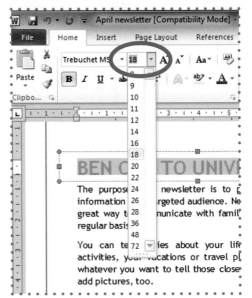

Change the font

1 Select the text you wish to change

2 On the **Home** tab, in the 'Font' group, click the drop-down arrow next to the Font box

3 From the 'Font' drop-down menu, select a font. As you move the cursor over a font in the list, the selected text in the document will change so you can preview each font

Change the colour of text

1 Select the text you want to change

2 On the **Home** tab, in the 'Font' group, click the **Font Color** drop-down arrow

3 From the 'Font Color' menu, select a new colour. As you move your cursor over a colour the selected text in the document will change so you can preview each colour

Use the Bold, Italic, and Underline commands

1 Select the text you wish to change

2 On the **Home** tab, in the 'Font' group, click the **Bold** (B), **Italic** (I), or **Underline** (U) command

Change the text case

1 Select the text you want to change

2 On the **Home** tab, in the 'Font' group, click **Change Case**

3 Select an option, such as UPPERCASE, from the list

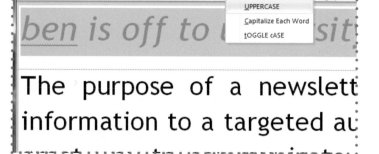

Word

FORMAT PARAGRAPHS

With the paragraph section of the Home tab you can alter the layout of your text in paragraphs.

Change text alignment

By default, Word aligns text to the left-hand side of the page, but you can change this to align text to the right page margin, centre your text or justify text so that a paragraph lines up equally to the right and left margins.

1 Select the text you wish to modify

2 Click the **Home** tab

3 Select one of the four alignment options from the 'Paragraph' group:

▶ **Align Text Left:** Aligns all the selected text to the left margin

▶ **Center:** Aligns text an equal distance from the left and right margins

▶ **Align Text Right:** Aligns all the selected text to the right margin

▶ **Justify:** Justified text is equal on both sides and lines up equally to the right and left margins

TIP

If you don't see the horizontal ruler, click **Ruler** on the **View** tab.

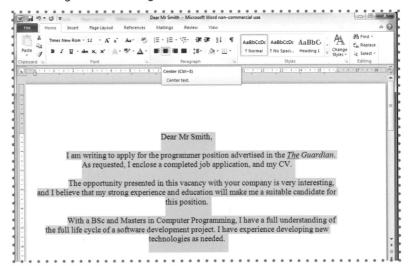

Work with tabs

Tabs are a great way to accurately position text in your document. Every time you press the tab key on your keyboard, your cursor moves half an inch to the right by default. By adding different tab stops to the ruler you can change the position and alignment of tabs.

The types of tab stops available include:
- ▶ **Left Tab:** left-aligns the text at the tab stop
- ▶ **Center Tab:** centres the text around the tab stop
- ▶ **Right Tab:** right-aligns the text at the tab stop
- ▶ **Decimal Tab:** aligns decimal numbers using the decimal point

You can choose which tab stop to use by clicking on the tab selector, which is found to the left of the horizontal ruler.

Add tab stops

1 Select the paragraph or paragraphs that you want to add tab stops to. If you don't, the tabs will apply only to the current paragraph and any paragraphs you subsequently type beneath it

2 Click the **tab selector** until the tab stop you wish to use appears. In this case the decimal tab is shown

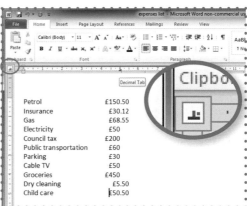

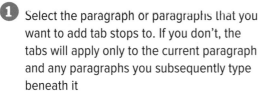

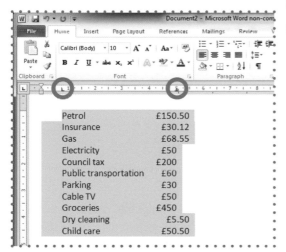

3 On the horizontal ruler, click where you want your tab stop to appear. You can add as many tab stops as you want. In this case there is a left-aligned tab at 0.75cm and a decimal tab at 5cm

TRY THIS

When working with tabbed text, it often helps to see the tab key markings. On the **Home** tab, click **Show/Hide ¶** in the 'Paragraph' group to show page layout characters such as the spacebar, paragraph (¶), and tab key markings. These hidden characters are known as nonprinting characters as they don't appear when you print your document.

4 Now, in your paragraph, place your cursor before the text you wish to tab and press the **Tab** key. The text will jump to the next tab stop

5 To get rid of a tab stop, simply drag it off the Ruler

Indent text

Indenting the first line of every paragraph is a good way to visually separate paragraphs. You can also choose to indent every line of a paragraph or every line except the first line – known as a hanging indent. There are several ways to indent text in Word including using the horizontal ruler and the Indent commands on the 'Home' tab.

1 To create a first line indent or hanging indent, select the paragraph you want to indent. On the horizontal ruler, drag the First Line Indent marker ⟵ to the position where you want the text to start

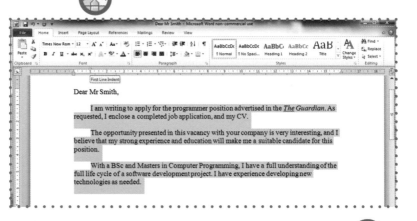

2 To create a hanging indent, drag the Hanging Indent marker ⟵ to the position at which you want the indent to start

Indent all of the lines in a paragraph

1 Select the text you wish to indent

2 Click the **Home** tab

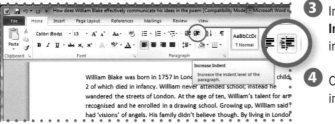

3 In the 'Paragraph' group, click **Increase Indent** to increase the indent by increments of 1/2 inch

4 Click **Decrease Indent** to reduce the indent by increments of 1/2 inch

Make a bulleted or numbered list

1 Type your list into the document, remembering to press **Enter** on your keyboard after each item so that they are all on separate lines

2 Select all the text in your list

3 On the **Home** tab, in the 'Paragraph' group, click the **down arrow** on the bullet point button

4 In the drop-down menu, preview the different bullet styles by holding your cursor over them

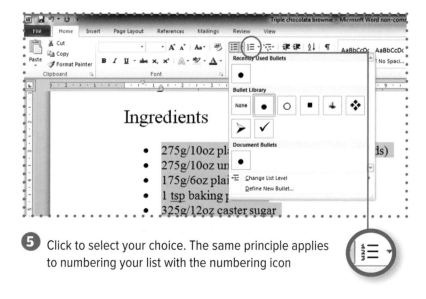

5 Click to select your choice. The same principle applies to numbering your list with the numbering icon

BE CAREFUL

Reducing line spacing will fit more lines of text on the page but as each line will sit more tightly on top of the next, it makes the text much harder to read.

LINE AND PARAGRAPH SPACING

Line and paragraph spacing is a vital part of good page layout, ensuring your text is legible and comfortable to read. Line spacing refers to the amount of vertical space between the lines of text in a paragraph. Paragraph spacing determines the amount of space above or below a paragraph.

Line spacing – also known as leading – can either be measured in lines or points. So, for example, when text is double-spaced, the spacing is two lines high. Or you might have 10-point size text with a 12-point spacing.

Change line spacing

1 Select the text for which you want to change the line spacing

2 Click the **Home** tab and, in the 'Paragraph' group, click **Line Spacing**

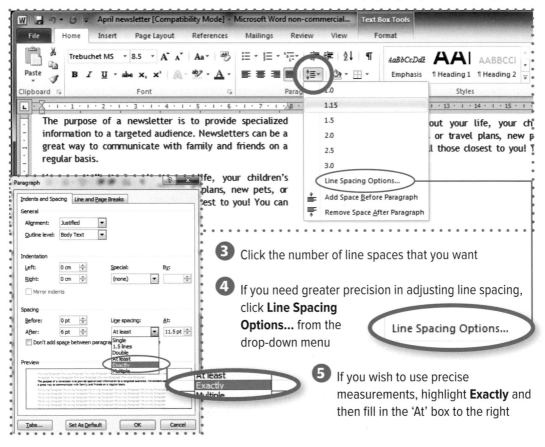

3 Click the number of line spaces that you want

4 If you need greater precision in adjusting line spacing, click **Line Spacing Options...** from the drop-down menu

5 If you wish to use precise measurements, highlight **Exactly** and then fill in the 'At' box to the right

Change paragraph spacing for selected paragraphs

By default, paragraphs are separated by a blank line. As with line spacing, you can also adjust the spacing between each paragraph.

1 Select the text for which you want to change the line spacing

2 On the **Home** tab, click **Line and Paragraph Spacing**

3 Select **Add Space Before Paragraph** or **Remove Space After Paragraph** from the drop-down menu

TRY THIS

In print, the general rule is to set the line spacing of text blocks at about 2 points above the size of the type: for example, 12-point text with 14 points of line spacing. If a document is to be read online, a more generous line spacing will compensate for the lower resolution of the computer screen.

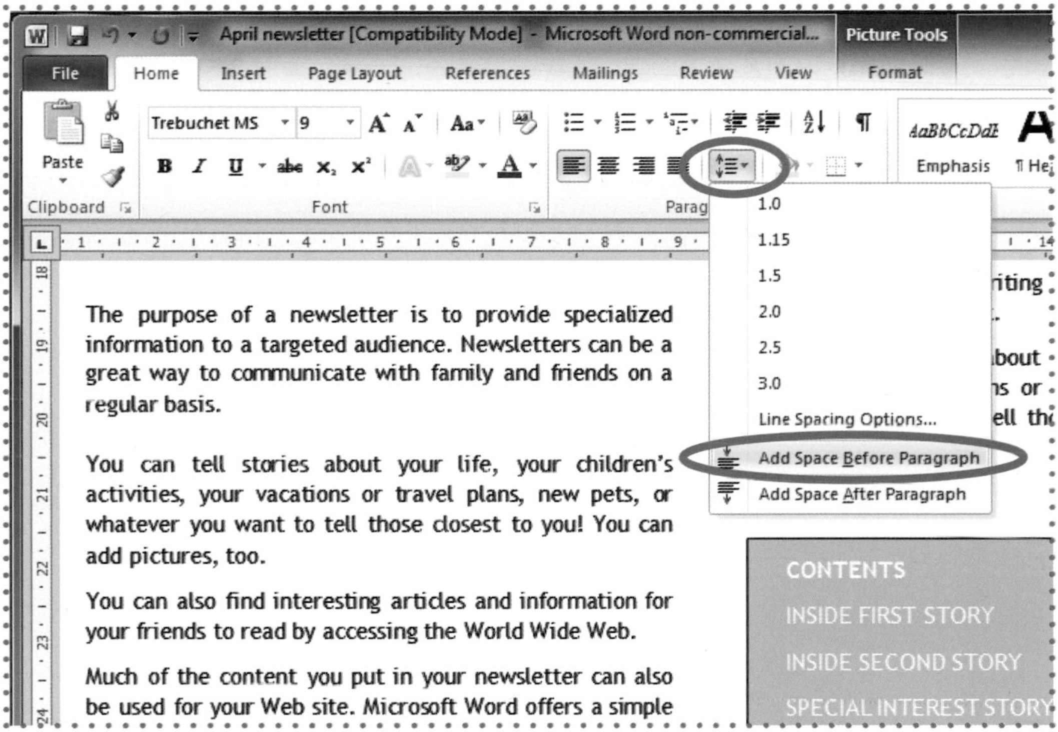

Word

4 You can also select **Line Spacing Options...** on this menu to open the 'Paragraph' dialog box. Here, you can control exactly how much space there is before and after the paragraph

5 If you've applied a style set (see page 54) for line spacing, you can customise paragraph spacing using the paragraph spacing options. On the **Home** tab, in the 'Styles' group, click **Change Styles**. Point to 'Paragraph Spacing', and then click the option that you want

▶ Word

WORK WITH COLUMNS

By default, the text you enter into a Word document appears as one column across the entire page. Using more than one column can make your document more interesting and, with shorter line lengths, your text will be easier to read.

Add columns to a document

1 Select the text you want to format

2 Click the **Page Layout** tab

3 In the 'Page Setup' group, click **Columns**

4 From the drop-down menu, select the number of columns you would like to insert

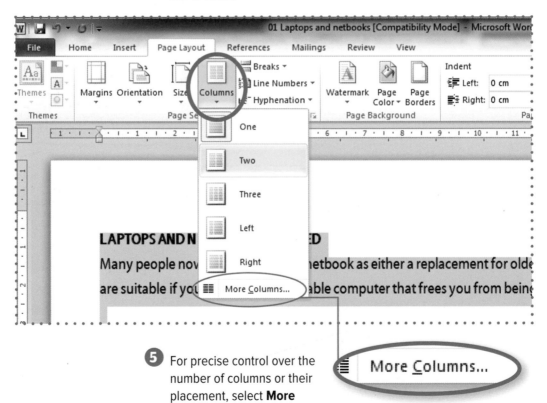

5 For precise control over the number of columns or their placement, select **More Columns...** from the drop-down menu. In the dialog box that appears adjust the settings to design your document

Add column breaks

Once you've created columns in your document, the text will automatically flow from one column to the next. You may, however, want to control exactly where your text appears in a column. For example if you're creating a newsletter, you may need each column to start with a story heading. To do this, you can create column breaks.

1 Place the cursor where you want to add the break. In this case, in front of the words 'LAPTOPS TOUR'

2 Click **Page Layout**

3 In the 'Page Setup' group click **Breaks**

4 From the list of break types select **Column**

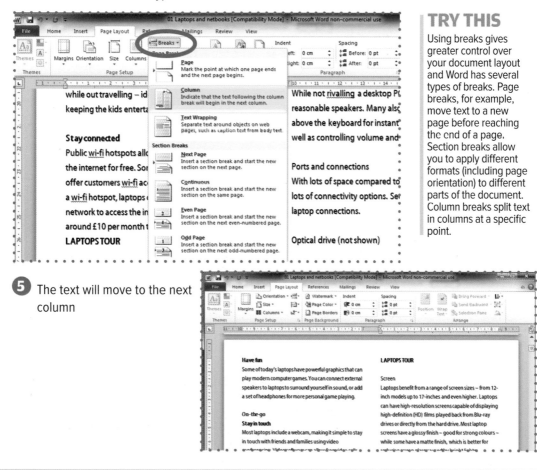

TRY THIS

Using breaks gives greater control over your document layout and Word has several types of breaks. Page breaks, for example, move text to a new page before reaching the end of a page. Section breaks allow you to apply different formats (including page orientation) to different parts of the document. Column breaks split text in columns at a specific point.

5 The text will move to the next column

Word

USE HEADERS AND FOOTERS

Using headers and footers can make your Word document look more professional. A header is an area that appears at the top of every page, while a footer appears in the bottom margin of every page. They are generally used to show information such as page number, the document name and date.

Add a header or footer

1 Click the **Insert** tab

2 In the 'Header & Footer' group, click either **Header** or **Footer**

3 From the drop-down menu, select **Blank** to insert a blank header or footer, or choose one of the other preformatted options

4 The 'Design' tab will appear on the Ribbon, and the header or footer will appear in the document

5 Type in the text you wish to appear into the header or footer. If placeholder text exists, click on it and type the replacement text

6 Click **Close Header and Footer** in the 'Design' tab

TIP

To edit a footer or header, click the **Insert** tab and, in the 'Header & Footer' group, choose **Header>Edit Header**.

Add the date or time into a header or footer

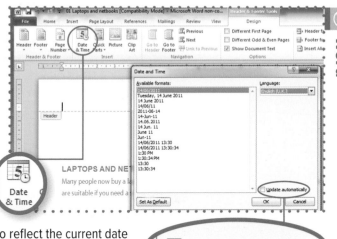

1 Double click anywhere on the header or footer to unlock it. The 'Design' tab will appear

2 From the **Design** tab and in the 'Insert' group, click **Date & Time**. Select a data and/or time format in the dialog box

3 Tick the **Update automatically** box if you want it to reflect the current date and time. Otherwise it will not update to show the correct information when the document is opened at a later stage

4 Click **OK**. The date/time now appears in the document

Add page numbers

When creating a large document with several pages, you may want to add page numbers to keep them in order. You can use headers and footers to automatically add page numbers to your document.

1 Click the **Insert** tab and, in the 'Header & Footer' area, click **Page Number**

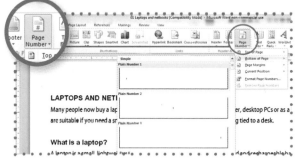

2 A drop-down menu appears. From here you can choose where you want the page numbers to appear in the document and what format they will take. First choose a location for your page numbers such as 'Top of Page', 'Bottom of Page' and 'Page Margins' (side of the page)

3 Next, choose a page-numbering style. There are lots of numbering styles to choose from so scroll fully through the list before you choose. Click on the **Design** tab and then **Close Header and Footer** (under 'Header & Footer Tools')

WORK WITH STYLES AND THEMES

Styles and themes are useful features that can help you quickly create professional Word documents. Applied to selected text, a style is a combination of text formats that includes font style, colour and size of text. A theme is a set of colours, fonts and effects that can be applied to the entire document to give it a consistent look.

Apply a style

1 Select the text that you want to format

2 On the **Home** tab, in the 'Styles' group move your cursor over each style to see a live preview

3 Click the **More** drop-down arrow to see additional styles

4 Click a style and your selected text will be formatted in that style

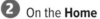

Apply a style set

Style sets include a mix of title, heading and paragraph styles. They provide a fast way to format your document in one go rather than formatting individual lines of text and paragraphs.

1 On the **Home** tab and in the 'Styles' group, click **Change Styles**

2 From the drop-down menu, select **Style Set**

3 Click a Style Set – in this case, 'Formal' – and your document will change accordingly

Choose a theme

Word comes with several built-in themes including the default Office theme. You can also download more themes from Microsoft Office Online as well as create and save your own themes. You choose a theme from the themes gallery found on the 'Page Layout' tab in the 'Themes' group.

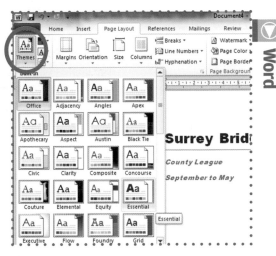

 On the **Page Layout** tab, click **Themes**

 Move your cursor over a theme to see a live preview of it

 Click on a theme to apply it

Modify a theme

You may find a theme in which you like the fonts and effects but you'd prefer to use different colours. Word lets you tweak a theme's colours, fonts and effects to create your own custom themes.

 To change the theme colours, on the **Page Layout** tab click **Theme Colors**

 On the drop-down menu, move your cursor over the colour sets to see a live preview

 Click a set of **Theme Colors**, or select **Create New Theme Colors...** to adjust each colour separately

 To change the theme fonts, on the **Page Layout** tab click **Theme Fonts**. On the drop-down menu, move your cursor over the font sets to see a live preview

 Click a set of **Theme Fonts**, or select **Create New Theme Fonts** to choose each font separately

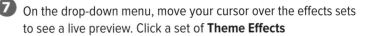 To change the theme effects, on the **Page Layout** tab click **Theme Effects**

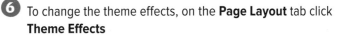 On the drop-down menu, move your cursor over the effects sets to see a live preview. Click a set of **Theme Effects**

TRY THIS

You can choose to save a customised theme so you can use it in other documents. On the **Page Layout** tab, click **Themes** and select **Select Save Current Theme**. Give your theme a name and click **Save**.

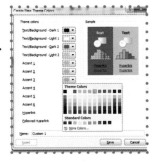

Word

▶ Word

Jargon buster ▶

Clip art
Ready-made artwork that is included with your Office software or can be downloaded from the web for use in your documents and presentations. Clip art includes both subject-related illustrations and elements such as horizontal lines, symbols, bullets and backgrounds.

ADD IMAGES

Add interest to your documents with a picture: useful for creating family or club newsletters, for example. You can add a picture from a file – such as a photo you've taken – or copy one from a web page or use one of Word's many clip art images. You can change how a picture or clip art is positioned in relation to text within a document by using the 'Position' and 'Wrap Text' commands.

Add clip art

1 Place your cursor in the document where you wish to insert the clip art

2 On the **Insert** tab, in the 'Illustrations' group, click **Clip Art**

3 In the clip art task pane, enter keywords in the Search for box. Use words or a phrase that describes the clip art that you want, or type in all or some of the file name of the clip art

4 To limit the search results to a specific media type, click the arrow in the **Results should be** box and deselect the check boxes next to 'Illustrations', 'Photographs', 'Videos' or 'Audio' as required

5 To expand your search to include clip art on the web, click the **Include Office.com** content checkbox. Otherwise the search will be limited to only your computer hard drive

BE CAREFUL

While it's easy to copy and paste pictures and even video from websites, be sure to check the copyright of these items before you do. Check the website for copyright notices. Copyright is owned by the person who created the picture or video. It's illegal to copy and use anything protected by copyright without permission of the copyright owner.

6 Click **Go**

7 In the list of results, click the clip art to insert it. It will appear in your document

Insert a picture from a file

1 Place your cursor in the document where you wish to the image to be

2 On the **Insert** tab, click **Picture** from the 'Illustrations' group. The 'Insert Picture' dialog box appears

3 Choose the picture file you want and click **Insert** to place it in your document

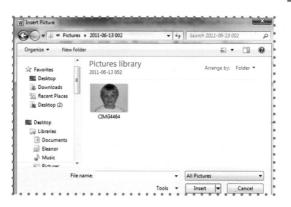

Insert a picture from a web page
You can drag a picture from a web page into your open Word document. However, avoid dragging a picture that has a link to another web page. If you do, it will be appear in your document as a link (a line of text giving the address of the linked web page) rather than the image itself.

Resize clip art or a picture

1 Select the clip art or picture you've placed in the document

2 Drag a sizing handle away from or toward the centre of the image. To keep the image's proportions, press and hold **Shift** while you drag the sizing handle

Jargon buster

Sizing handles
When you click an object, such as a shape, image or clip art, in Word, a border with little white squares and circles will appear around it. These squares and circles are the sizing handles. You click on the squares to change the height or width, while the circles are used to make the whole object smaller or bigger.

Positioning images

By default, Word inserts images as inline pictures. This means they keep their position relative to the text where they were inserted. This can make it difficult to move an image exactly where you want. You can solve this problem with the text wrapping setting.

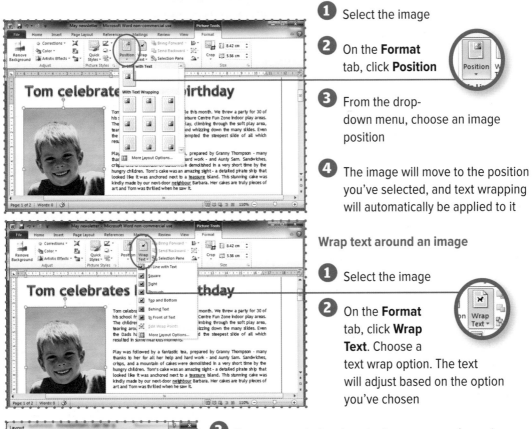

1 Select the image

2 On the **Format** tab, click **Position**

3 From the drop-down menu, choose an image position

4 The image will move to the position you've selected, and text wrapping will automatically be applied to it

Wrap text around an image

1 Select the image

2 On the **Format** tab, click **Wrap Text**. Choose a text wrap option. The text will adjust based on the option you've chosen

3 For more control on how text wraps around your image, click **More Layout Options...** from the menu. In the 'Advanced Layout' dialog box that appears, you can make more precise adjustments such as specifying the exact size of the text wrap around an image – with measurements for both top and bottom as well as left and right

Work with irregular shapes

Word's default text wrap settings are great for working with square or rectangular shaped images. But when you place an irregularly shaped image in your document, text may wrap haphazardly around the image. So, use Word's 'Edit Wrap Points' tool to fine-tune the text wrap. Wrap points are small black square handles, similar to the resize handles. Moving or removing or adding wrap points affects the shape of the flow of text around your image.

Edit wrap points

1 Select the picture

2 On the **Format** tab, click **Wrap Text** in the 'Arrange' group. Select **Edit Wrap Points** from the drop-down list

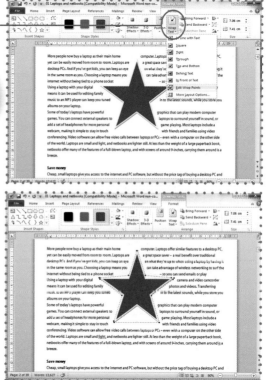

3 A dashed red line will appear around your picture. Click and drag on the handles to adjust the edge of the text wrap. The text will adjust accordingly around your image

4 To fine tune the text wrap you can create your own wrap points. Simply click anywhere on the red outline where you want the new wrap point. You can then drag the new point to a new position

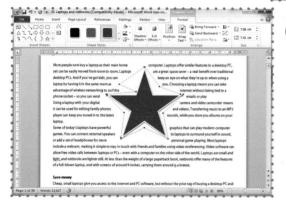

5 To delete a wrap point, hold down **Ctrl** and click the wrap point you want to remove

 **Word**

EDIT IMAGES

Once you've positioned pictures in your document, you can make changes to them using Word's picture tools. There are lots of ways to adjust your images including changing their shape, cropping or compressing pictures, and adding borders and artistic effects.

Crop an image

1 Select the image you want to crop

2 On the **Format** tab, in the 'Size' group, click **Crop**

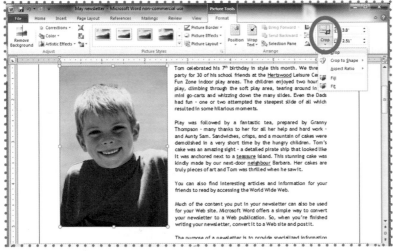

3 Black cropping handles appear around your picture – similar to those used to resize an image. Click and drag a handle to crop an image. Clicking on the corner handles simultaneously crops the image horizontally and vertically

4 When you've finished, click **Crop** to deselect the crop tool

Crop an image to a shape

Word's crop tool not only removes unwanted areas of an image but can also be used to crop to a shape. Much like cookie cutters, you can choose a shape to stamp out of your image.

1 Select the image you want to work with

2 On the **Format** tab, click on the down arrow below 'Crop' and select **Crop to Shape**

3 From the drop-down menu, choose a shape. The image will take the shape that you have selected

Remove an image background

1 Click on the image

2 On the **Format** tab, click **Remove Background**

3 Word makes a guess which part of the image is the background. It colours this area pink and draws a box with selection handles around the part of the image that will remain

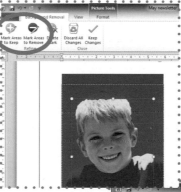

4 Make sure all of the image you wish to keep is within the box by adjusting the selection handles

5 To change the areas selected as background use the 'Mark Areas to Keep' and 'Mark Areas to Remove' commands:

▶ To show which parts of the image that you want to keep, click **Mark Areas to Keep**. The cursor changes into a pencil. Click and drag to draw a line in that region of the image

▶ If you want to remove part of the background but it hasn't been automatically been selected, click **Mark Areas to Remove**. The cursor changes into a pencil. Click and drag to draw a line in that region of the image

6 When you've made your adjustments, Word will readjust the image automatically

7 Click **Keep Changes**. All of the pink areas will be removed from the image

TRY THIS

When removing a picture background, if you change your mind about an area you've marked with a line, either to keep or to remove it, click **Delete Mark** and then click the line to change it.

Rotate an image

1 Click the picture that you want to rotate

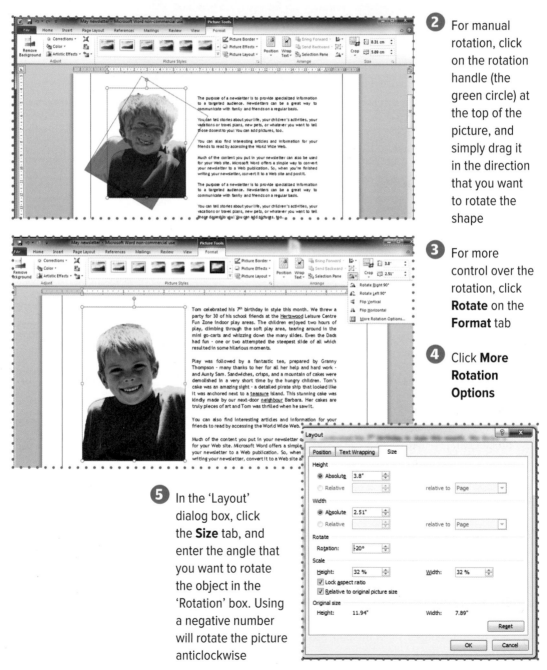

2 For manual rotation, click on the rotation handle (the green circle) at the top of the picture, and simply drag it in the direction that you want to rotate the shape

3 For more control over the rotation, click **Rotate** on the **Format** tab

4 Click **More Rotation Options**

5 In the 'Layout' dialog box, click the **Size** tab, and enter the angle that you want to rotate the object in the 'Rotation' box. Using a negative number will rotate the picture anticlockwise

Add a border to an image

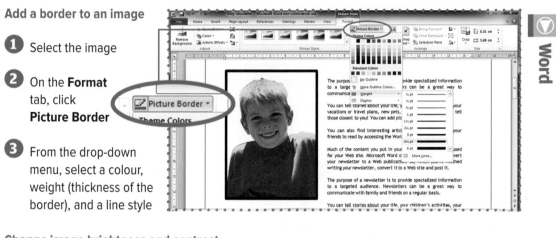

1 Select the image

2 On the **Format** tab, click **Picture Border**

3 From the drop-down menu, select a colour, weight (thickness of the border), and a line style

Change image brightness and contrast

1 Select the image. The 'Format' tab will appear

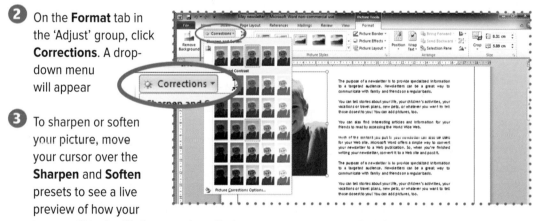

2 On the **Format** tab in the 'Adjust' group, click **Corrections**. A drop-down menu will appear

3 To sharpen or soften your picture, move your cursor over the **Sharpen** and **Soften** presets to see a live preview of how your image will look with the preset applied

4 Click on a preset to apply it

5 To adjust the brightness, move your cursor over the **Brightness** and **Contrast** presets to see a live preview of how your image will look with the preset applied

6 Click on a preset to apply it

TRY THIS

For greater control over sharpness, brightness and contrast, click **Picture Corrections Options** from the 'Corrections' drop-down menu to refine the settings.

▶ Word

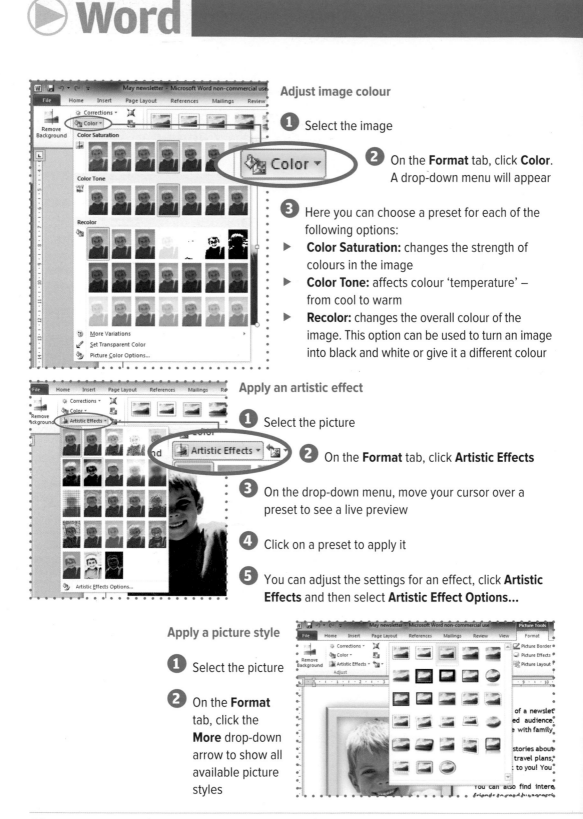

Adjust image colour

1. Select the image

2. On the **Format** tab, click **Color**. A drop-down menu will appear

3. Here you can choose a preset for each of the following options:
   ▶ **Color Saturation:** changes the strength of colours in the image
   ▶ **Color Tone:** affects colour 'temperature' – from cool to warm
   ▶ **Recolor:** changes the overall colour of the image. This option can be used to turn an image into black and white or give it a different colour

Apply an artistic effect

1. Select the picture

2. On the **Format** tab, click **Artistic Effects**

3. On the drop-down menu, move your cursor over a preset to see a live preview

4. Click on a preset to apply it

5. You can adjust the settings for an effect, click **Artistic Effects** and then select **Artistic Effect Options...**

Apply a picture style

1. Select the picture

2. On the **Format** tab, click the **More** drop-down arrow to show all available picture styles

Move your cursor over a picture style to see a live preview of the style in your document

 Click on the style to apply it

5 To fine-tune your chosen picture style, click **Picture Effects** to see the 'Effects' drop-down menu

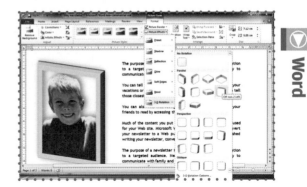

Compress pictures

Using lots of large, high-resolution pictures can have a big impact on the file size of your Word document, which may make it difficult to share with others via email. Fortunately, you can reduce the file size of your document by lowering image resolution, applying compression and deleting unwanted areas such as cropped parts of an image.

1 Select the picture

2 On the **Format** tab, in the 'Adjust' group, click **Compress Pictures**

3 In the dialog box that appears, choose a 'Target output'. If you're emailing your document, you may want to select **Email**, which produces the smallest file size

4 Tick the box next to **Delete cropped areas of pictures**

5 You can choose whether to apply these settings to this picture only or to all pictures in the document. Tick the **Apply only to this picture** box to apply these settings to just the image selected

6 Click **OK**

▶ Word

WORK WITH SHAPES

Using shapes such as arrows, lines, squares, stars, flowchart shapes and banners not only adds visual appeal to your document, they can help make your text more legible and bring a message to life.

Add a shape

1 On the **Insert** tab, in the 'Illustrations' group, click **Shapes**

2 Click on the shape that you want

3 Click anywhere in your document, and then drag to place the shape at the size you want

4 Release the mouse button

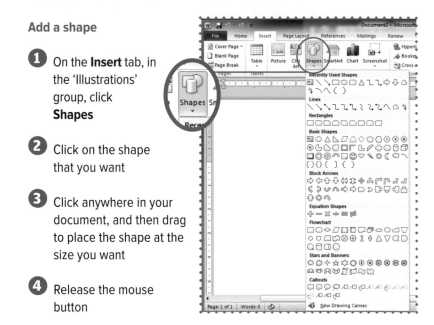

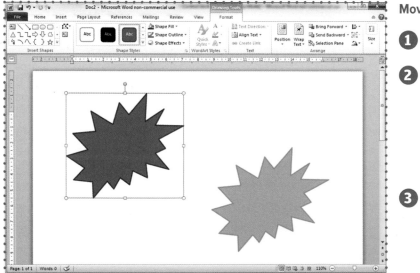

Move a shape

1 Click on the shape

2 Hover the cursor over one of the box's edges until it changes into a cross with arrows on each end

3 Click and drag the shape to the desired location on the page

Resize or rotate a shape

 1 Click on the shape to select it

2 Click and drag one of the sizing handles on the corners and sides of the text box until it is the desired size

3 Drag the green circle to rotate the shape (see also page 68)

Change shape style

1 Select the shape

2 On the **Format** tab, click the **More** drop-down arrow in the 'Shape Styles' group to show more style options

3 Move your cursor over a style to see a live preview in your document

4 Select a style

Fill with colour

 1 Select the shape

2 On the **Format** tab, click **Shape Fill**

3 From the drop-down list, select either a colour, 'No Fill' or 'More Fill Colors…' for custom colour. You can also add a picture, gradient or texture to the shape

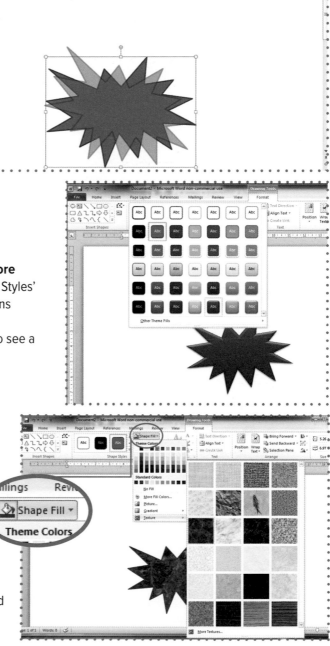

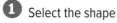

 **Word**

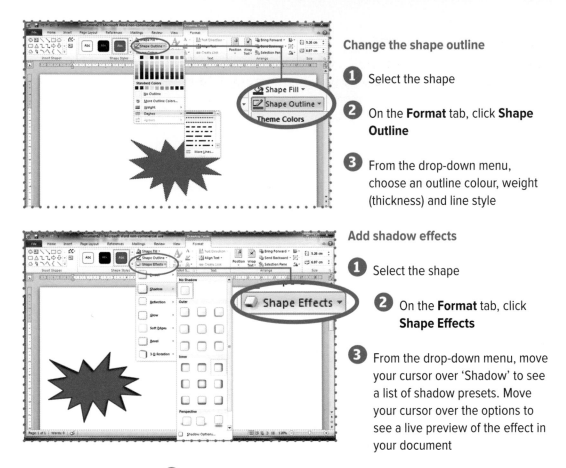

Change the shape outline

1 Select the shape

2 On the **Format** tab, click **Shape Outline**

3 From the drop-down menu, choose an outline colour, weight (thickness) and line style

Add shadow effects

1 Select the shape

2 On the **Format** tab, click **Shape Effects**

3 From the drop-down menu, move your cursor over 'Shadow' to see a list of shadow presets. Move your cursor over the options to see a live preview of the effect in your document

4 Click a shadow effect to apply it to your shape

Rotate a shape in 3D

1 Select the shape

2 On the **Format** tab, click **Shape Effects** from the 'Shape Styles' group

3 Move your cursor over '3-D Rotation'. A drop-down menu will appear

4 Choose a rotation preset. For more precise control, click **3-D Rotation Options...** to type in custom values

CREATE A TEXT BOX

Text boxes are a great way to draw your reader's attention to a particular piece of text or link information to images such as with a caption. Using text boxes means, for example, you can easily move text around your document and, as with shapes, you can apply similar effects to text boxes.

Add a text box

1 On the **Insert** tab, in the 'Text' group, click **Text Box**

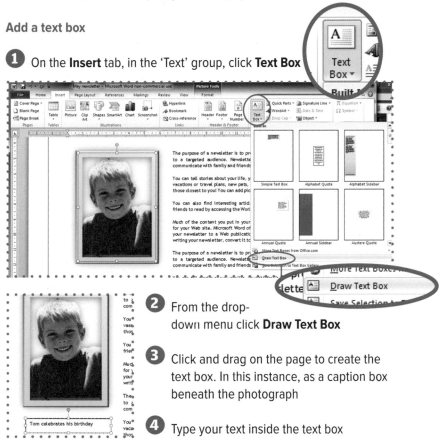

2 From the drop-down menu click **Draw Text Box**

3 Click and drag on the page to create the text box. In this instance, as a caption box beneath the photograph

4 Type your text inside the text box

Alternatively at step 2, select one of the built-in text boxes from the drop-down menu. These have a pre-defined size and position as well as colours and fonts. Once you select a built-in text box, it will appear automatically on the page.

Make changes to a text box

You can make changes to your text box – everything from size, position, border style, fill colour to 3D effects and rotation can be altered to suit. Simply treat your text box as a shape and follow the steps on pages 66–8 to make adjustments.

STYLE TEXT WITH WORDART

Add effects to the text inside a text box using WordArt – Word's text styling feature. You can change fill and line colour, add shadows or bevels or create special text effects such as curved, slanted or 3D text.

Add WordArt

1 On the **Insert** tab, in the 'Text' group, click **WordArt** and then click the WordArt style that you want

2 Type in your text

Add or modify text effects

1 Select the text box, or some text inside the text box

2 On the **Format** tab in the 'WordArt Styles' group, click **Text Effects**. A drop-down menu appears showing the different effect categories

3 Move your cursor over one of the effect categories to see a second drop-down menu of preset effects

4 Hover your cursor over a preset to see a live preview

5 Select an effect preset. The effect will be applied to your text. You can combine several different WordArt effects on one piece of text

ADD GRAPHICS WITH SMARTART

A feature of Microsoft Office, SmartArt graphics are predrawn diagrams and illustrations that can be inserted into your Office documents. You can edit the diagrams and change the style without having to fiddle with shape size and alignment, as SmartArt graphics automatically adjust to maintain their overall shape and design.

TIP
You can create SmartArt graphics in Excel and PowerPoint too.

Create a SmartArt graphic

1 Click on the page where you want the SmartArt graphic to be placed. On the **Insert** tab, in the 'Illustration' group, click **SmartArt**

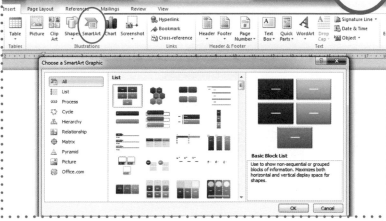

TRY THIS
SmartArt graphics work best when the number of shapes in the layout and the text they contain are limited to just key points. The 'Trapezoid List' is the best choice for larger amounts of text.

 2 Select a category in the left pane of the dialog box

3 In the centre pane, click on one of the layouts in this category to see a more detailed view in the right pane of the dialog box

4 Click a SmartArt graphic and click **OK**

Add text to a SmartArt graphic

 1 Select the graphic. Click the arrow on the left side of the graphic

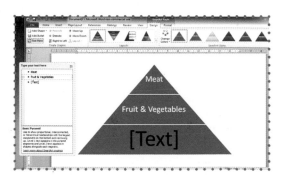

 2 Enter text next to each bullet in the task pane. It appears in the graphic, resizing automatically to fit inside the shape

Add or delete a shape

1 Select the SmartArt graphic

2 From the **Design** tab, click **Add Shape** in the 'Graphics' group

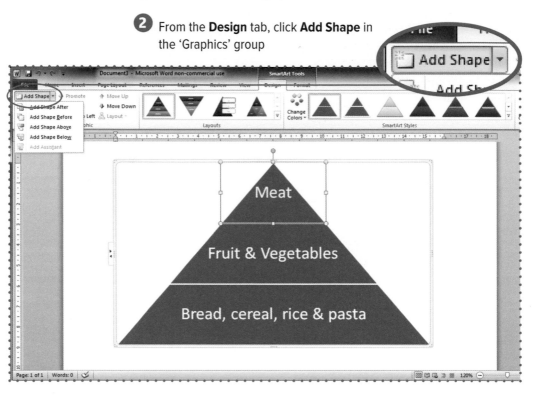

3 Click the shape that's positioned closest to where you want to add the new shape

4 Select **Add Shape Before** or **Add Shape After**

5 If you want to add a superior or a subordinate shape, select either the **Add Shape Above** or **Add Shape Below** options

6 To delete a shape, click the shape, and then press the **Delete** key on your keyboard. To delete the entire SmartArt graphic, click the border of the SmartArt graphic, and then press **Delete**

Change the SmartArt style

1 Select the graphic

2 On the **Design** tab in the 'SmartArt Styles' group, click the **More** drop-down arrow to view all of the styles

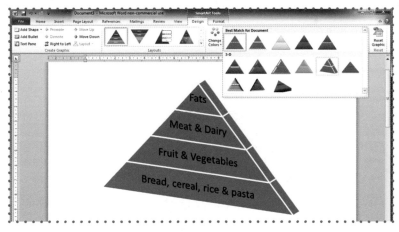

3 Move your cursor over a style to see a live preview

4 Click a style to apply it

Change the colour of a SmartArt graphic

Word offers a range of colour schemes to use with SmartArt graphics.

1 Click the SmartArt graphic

2 On the **Design** tab, click **Change Colors**

3 From the drop-down menu, choose a colour scheme

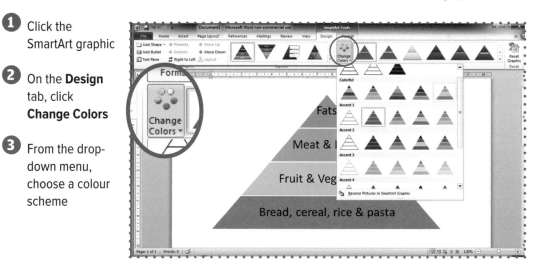

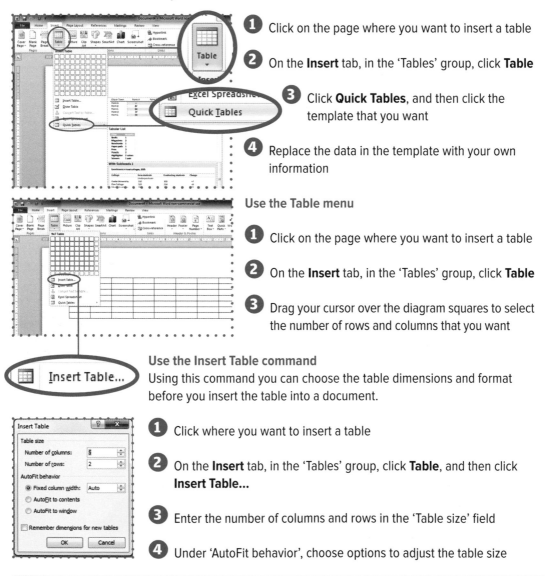

⊳ Word

GET STARTED WITH TABLES

There are a couple of ways to add a table to your Word document. You can later modify the table by adding, removing or resizing rows and columns.

Use a table template

You can choose from a gallery of pre-formatted table templates. These come with sample data so you can see how your table will look when you add your own data.

1 Click on the page where you want to insert a table

2 On the **Insert** tab, in the 'Tables' group, click **Table**

3 Click **Quick Tables**, and then click the template that you want

4 Replace the data in the template with your own information

Use the Table menu

1 Click on the page where you want to insert a table

2 On the **Insert** tab, in the 'Tables' group, click **Table**

3 Drag your cursor over the diagram squares to select the number of rows and columns that you want

Use the Insert Table command

Using this command you can choose the table dimensions and format before you insert the table into a document.

1 Click where you want to insert a table

2 On the **Insert** tab, in the 'Tables' group, click **Table**, and then click **Insert Table...**

3 Enter the number of columns and rows in the 'Table size' field

4 Under 'AutoFit behavior', choose options to adjust the table size

Add a column or a row

1 Right click in a cell to the left or to the right of where you want to add a column or above or below where you want to add a row

2 On the pop-up menu, click **Insert**, and then **Insert Columns to the Left** or **Insert Columns to the Right** or **Insert Rows Above** or **Insert Rows Below**

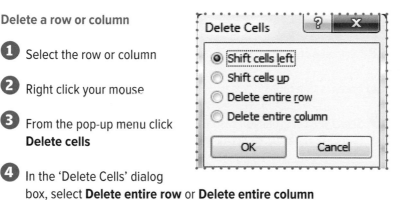

Delete a row or column

1 Select the row or column

2 Right click your mouse

3 From the pop-up menu click **Delete cells**

4 In the 'Delete Cells' dialog box, select **Delete entire row** or **Delete entire column**

5 Click **OK**

Change column width and row height

1 Hover your cursor over the right border of the column or on the bottom border of the row you want to change. The cursor will change into a resize pointer

2 Drag the border to increase or decrease the size

▶ Word

CHANGE THE LOOK OF A TABLE

Word provides lots of control over how your table looks. You can make changes to text and table formatting, add borders, make colour fills and adjust individual settings for cells, columns and row. But if you're in a hurry, Word can help with a pre-defined style for your table.

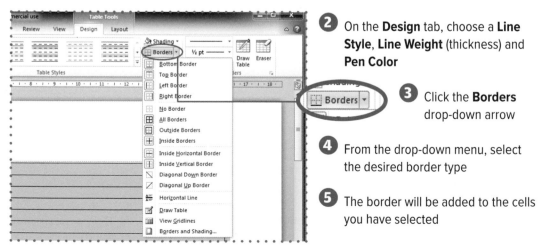

Apply a table style

1 Click anywhere on the table

2 On the **Design** tab, click the **More** drop-down arrow in 'Table Styles'

3 This will show all the available table styles. Move your cursor over a style to see a live preview

4 Click on a style to apply it your table

Add borders to a table

1 Select the cells that you wish to add a border to. If you want to add a border to the table select all the cells

2 On the **Design** tab, choose a **Line Style**, **Line Weight** (thickness) and **Pen Color**

3 Click the **Borders** drop-down arrow

4 From the drop-down menu, select the desired border type

5 The border will be added to the cells you have selected

FURTHER TABLE MODIFICATIONS

When you select a table in Word, two tabs appear under 'Table Tools' on the ribbon – the 'Design' and the 'Layout' tabs. Using commands on the 'Layout' tab, you can make a variety of changes to the table. Here are two of the text adjustments you can make.

Align text in cells

Just as with paragraphs, text in a cell can be aligned left, centre or right. It can also be aligned vertically: top, middle or bottom.

1 Select the cell whose text alignment you wish to change

2 On the **Layout** tab, click one of the buttons in the 'Alignment' group to apply

Fit text in cells

Microsoft Word usually wraps text in a table cell automatically. However, if your rows are set to an exact height, the cells won't expand as you add text to them. To overcome this, you can set the row height to change to allow for all the text that you add. Here's how:

1 Move your cursor over the table. A small square will appear at the top left of the table. Click this to select the table

2 Right click the table, click **Table Properties...**, and then click the **Row** tab

3 Tick the **Specify height** box

4 Click the arrow next to **Row height is**, and then click **At least**. Click **OK**

5 To show all the text, right click the selected table and then click **Distribute Rows Evenly**

Table Properties

| Table | Row | Column | Cell | Alt Text |

Rows 1-13:

Size

☑ Specify height: | 0 cm | ⬍ | Row height is: | At least ▼

Options

☑ Allow row to break across pages

☐ Repeat as header row at the top of each page

▲ Previous Row   ▼ Next Row

OK   Cancel

Word

⏵ Word

USE MAIL MERGE

Word's Mail Merge is a handy feature that lets you create a single document for multiple recipients using information stored in a list or spreadsheet. It's a great timesaver when creating letters, name tags and labels that contain the same basic information but also require personal details, such as name and address, of the respective recipient.

Open the Mail Merge Wizard

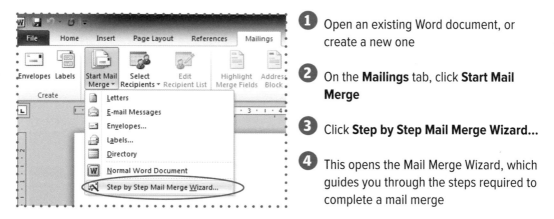

1 Open an existing Word document, or create a new one

2 On the **Mailings** tab, click **Start Mail Merge**

3 Click **Step by Step Mail Merge Wizard...**

4 This opens the Mail Merge Wizard, which guides you through the steps required to complete a mail merge

Create a Mail Merge

In this example we've used a letter that, when printed, will consist of the same basic message, but have different personal information (such as the name and address) for each recipient.

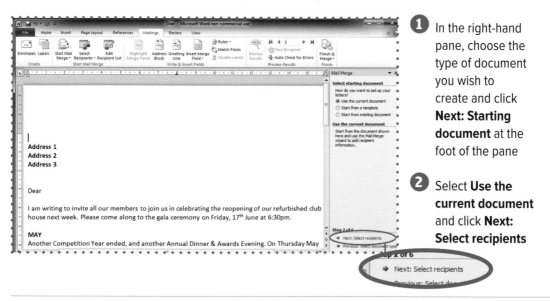

1 In the right-hand pane, choose the type of document you wish to create and click **Next: Starting document** at the foot of the pane

2 Select **Use the current document** and click **Next: Select recipients**

3 Now select a list to use with the Mail Merge. You can choose an existing file, such as an Excel spreadsheet, or type a new list from within the Mail Merge Wizard. In this example, click **Type a new list**

4 Enter the recipient information that you want to use

5 When finished click **OK**. A 'Save As' dialog box will pop up, allowing you to save the recipient list

6 In the 'Mail Merge Recipients' dialog box, you can tick or untick those recipients to be used in the mail merge. Click **OK** and then **Next: Write your letter**

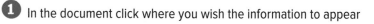
Add recipient information

Now in your letter, you need to add placeholders for the recipient data, so that mail merge knows exactly where to add the data.

1 In the document click where you wish the information to appear

2 Select 'Address block', Greeting line', 'Electronic postage' or 'More items' from the task pane

3 Depending on what you've chosen, a dialog box may appear. Select the options you want and click **OK**

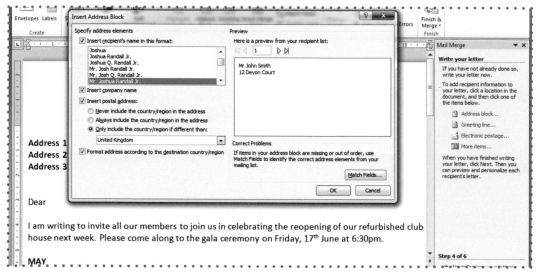

4 A placeholder appears in your document. For example: «AddressBlock»

5 Repeat these steps for each piece of recipient data in the letter. Then click **Next: Preview your letters**

6 Preview the letter to make sure the information from the recipient list appears correctly. Click **Next: Complete the merge**

7 Click **Print**. In the 'Merge to Printer' dialog box, click **All**, and then click **OK**. In the 'Print' dialog box, adjust the print settings if needed, and then click **OK**

CHECK YOUR SPELLING AND GRAMMAR

Word has several tools to pick up poor grammar and spelling errors, including the 'Spelling and Grammar' tool, which can help you produce perfect documents.

Run a spelling and grammar check

1 On the **Review** tab, click **Spelling & Grammar**

2 In the 'Spelling and Grammar' dialog box, Word offers one or more suggested replacements for the error. Click on a suggestion and then click **Change** to use it in your document as a replacement for the original word

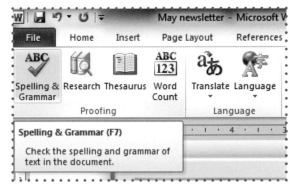

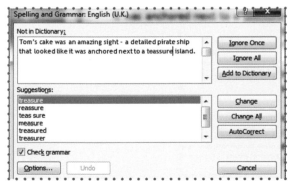

3 If no suggestions are given, or the correct replacement is not shown, you can type in the correct spelling

How to ignore errors

Word's spelling and grammar checker is not always accurate. Word may flag many words – such as people's names or place names – as potential spelling mistakes even if they're not. In this case, you can opt to leave it as it was originally written by choosing one of the following:

▶ **Ignore Once:** skips this instance of the word without changing it

▶ **Ignore All:** skips the word without changing it, and additionally it skips all subsequent instances of this word that appear in the document

▶ **Add to Dictionary:** click this to add the word to the dictionary so that it will never be flagged as a spelling error in future documents

For potential grammar errors flagged by Word, you can choose from the following:

- ▶ **Ignore Once:** skips the potential error without changing it
- ▶ **Ignore Rule:** skips the potential error along with all other instances that relate to this grammar rule
- ▶ **Next Sentence:** skips the sentence without changing it, but leaves it marked as an error. This means it will be flagged again on subsequent spelling and grammar checks

If you're not sure if something Word has flagged is actually a grammar error, click **Explain...** to see why Word thinks it's wrong. This will help you decide if it needs to be rewritten.

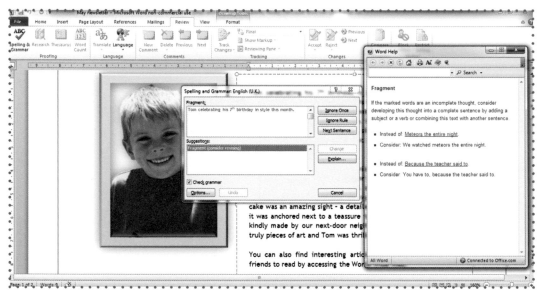

Check spelling and grammar automatically

You may not need to run a separate spelling and grammar check as Word can automatically check your document for both spelling and grammar errors as you type. Potential mistakes are underlined by wavy, coloured lines with a red line indicating a misspelled word, green a grammar mistake and blue a contextual spelling error.

A contextual spelling error is when a correctly spelled word is used in the wrong context. For example, if the text reads 'weather that is true or not', weather is a contextual spelling error because it should read 'whether'. Weather is accurately spelled, but used incorrectly in this instance.

Use the spell checker to fix automatically flagged errors

 Right click the underlined word

2 From the pop-up menu that appears, click on the correct spelling of the word from the listed suggestions

 The word will be corrected in your document

You can also choose to Ignore an underlined word, add it to the dictionary, or go to the 'Spelling' dialog box for more options.

Use the grammar checker

 Right click the underlined word or phrase

2 From the pop-up menu, click on the correct phrase from the listed suggestions

 The phrase will be corrected in your document

You can also choose to ignore an underlined phrase, go to the 'Grammar' dialog box, or click **About This Sentence** for information about the grammar rule.

Change automatic spelling and grammar check settings

If you prefer Word not to flag spelling and grammar problems as you type, you can turn off the automatic spelling and grammar checker or adjust the settings to make it more useful and relevant to your text.

1 Click the **File** tab to go to the Backstage view

2 Click on **Options**, then select **Proofing**

3 In this dialog box choose from the following options:
- ▶ To stop Word automatically checking spelling, untick **Check spelling as you type**
- ▶ To stop grammar errors from being marked, untick **Mark grammar errors as you type**
- ▶ To check for contextual spelling errors, tick **Use contextual spelling**
- ▶ If you want to stop Word from automatically checking just this document then tick the **Hide spelling errors in this document only** and **Hide grammar errors in this document only** boxes

4 Click **OK**

Change the spell check language

By default Word will spell check your text using a US English dictionary, but you can change the language used for spell checking.

1 Select the text you want to check

2 On the **Review** tab, in the 'Language' group, click **Language**

3 Click **Set Proofing Language...**

4 In the 'Language' dialog box, select the language you want to use for spell checking – for example, 'UK English'

5 Click **OK**. When you run a spell check, it will check in the language you have selected

USE FIND AND REPLACE

Once you've created a Word document, you may decide to replace a certain word or phrase used in the text. Searching for every instance of that word throughout a long document is not only tedious, there's a risk you may overlook one. Word's 'Find and Replace' feature can do the hard work for you. Here's how:

1 On the **Home** tab, in the 'Editing' group, click **Replace**

2 The 'Find and Replace' dialog box appears. Select the **Replace** tab

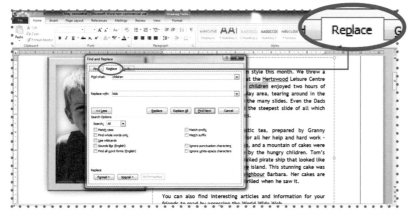

TRY THIS

As Word starts its search based on where your cursor is positioned in the document, place it at the beginning of your text to ensure a thorough search.

3 In the 'Find what' box, type the text you want to find

4 In the 'Replace with' box, type the text you want to replace it with

5 In the 'Search' drop-down menu in the 'Search Options' in the lower half of the pane, select **All**, **Up**, or **Down** so Word knows which part of the document to use for the search and replace text

6 If you want to manually replace each word or phrase, click **Find Next** and when the text is found, click **Replace**. Word replaces the found text, highlighted onscreen, with the text typed in the 'Replace with' box. It then immediately searches for the next instance of the text. Repeat this step until the entire document has been searched

7 Alternatively, to get Word to automatically search for and replace each instance of the word or phrase, click **Replace All** after Step 5

Use 'Find and Replace' to replace text formatting

'Find and Replace' can also be used to change styles – text formatting – that you have applied to text. You might, for example, want to replace all instances of a particular font with a new font.

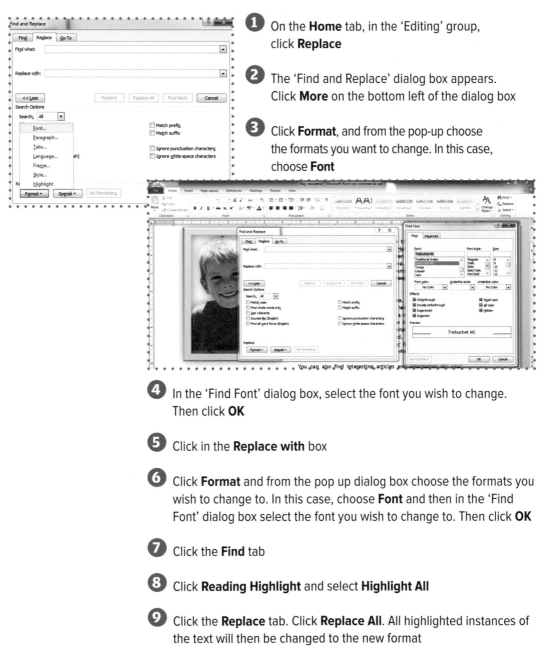

1 On the **Home** tab, in the 'Editing' group, click **Replace**

2 The 'Find and Replace' dialog box appears. Click **More** on the bottom left of the dialog box

3 Click **Format**, and from the pop-up choose the formats you want to change. In this case, choose **Font**

4 In the 'Find Font' dialog box, select the font you wish to change. Then click **OK**

5 Click in the **Replace with** box

6 Click **Format** and from the pop up dialog box choose the formats you wish to change to. In this case, choose **Font** and then in the 'Find Font' dialog box select the font you wish to change to. Then click **OK**

7 Click the **Find** tab

8 Click **Reading Highlight** and select **Highlight All**

9 Click the **Replace** tab. Click **Replace All**. All highlighted instances of the text will then be changed to the new format

PRINT A DOCUMENT

Open your document (see page 31), then follow these steps to print out your work with the default settings:

1 Click **File**

2 Click **Print**. You'll see a preview of what you are about to print on the right-hand side

3 Under 'Settings', click on the individual settings to change them from the default. For example, if you wish to print only certain pages of your document, type the range. Otherwise, select **Print All Pages**

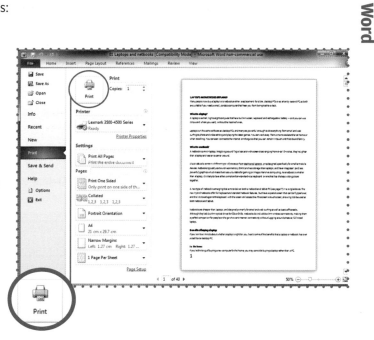

4 Click the **Print** button

To pick a different printer or printer style

1 To select a different printer, click the down arrow next to the current printer, and click instead on the one you want to use

2 To make changes to your printer's settings, click **Printer Properties**

3 Click **Advanced** for more options

4 Depending on your printer model, you may be able to select which printer tray the paper should come from, change the size of the paper you print on or opt for double-sided printing

5 Click **OK** when you're happy with the changes you've made

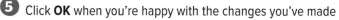

TIP
When you've saved your work, close your document by clicking **File** and then **Close**.

Word

87

Word

KEYBOARD SHORTCUTS

Press these keys	To do this
Ctrl + N	Create a new document
Ctrl + O	Open a document
Ctrl + W	Close a document
Ctrl + S	Save a document
Esc	Cancel an action
Ctrl + Home	Move to the beginning of a document
Ctrl + End	Move to the end of a document
Backspace	Delete one character to the left
Ctrl + Backspace	Delete one word to the left
Delete	Delete one character to the right
Ctrl + Delete	Delete one word to the right
Ctrl + C	Copy the selected text or object
Ctrl + X	Cut the selected text or object
Ctrl + V	Paste text or an object
Ctrl + Alt + V	Opens the 'Paste Special' dialog box, which allows you choose how text or images are added to the document
Ctrl + F	Find text
Ctrl + Z	Undo an action
Ctrl + Y	Redo or repeat an action
Ctrl + Shift + spacebar	Inserts a non-breaking space
Ctrl + Shift + Enter	Creates a column break
Ctrl + Shift + L	Applies bullets
Ctrl + Shift + A	Converts selected text to capital letters or vice versa
Ctrl + Shift + F	Displays the 'Font' dialog box
Ctrl + Shift + P	Font size select
Ctrl +]	Increase font size one point
Ctrl + B	Bold text
Ctrl + I	Italicise text
Ctrl + U	Underline text
Ctrl + Spacebar	Remove paragraph or character formatting
Ctrl + J	Justifies paragraph
Ctrl + L	Left align a paragraph
Ctrl + E	Centre a paragraph
Ctrl + R	Right align a paragraph

EXCEL

By reading this chapter you'll learn how to:

- ▷ **Create spreadsheets**

- ▷ **Use formulas and functions to perform calculations**

- ▷ **Create tables from data**

▶ Excel

EXCEL EXPLAINED

Part of Microsoft's Office suite, Excel 2010 is a spreadsheet program that uses a grid of columns and rows so you can store, organise, and analyse information. It can perform a wide range of calculations on numeric data – making it ideal for managing home finances. It can also be used to create a wide range of graphs and charts, or even act as a simple database program to store, search and retrieve information such as names and addresses. Here is the Excel interface showing a typical spreadsheet used for a household budget

QUICK ACCESS TOOLBAR
This provides quick access to common commands such as Save, Undo and Repeat, no matter which Ribbon tab you're in. You can add your own commands. See pages 26–7 for how to do this.

RIBBON
On the Ribbon's multiple tabs, you'll find the commands you need to complete everyday tasks. You can add your own tabs that contain your favourite commands. Some groups of commands have an arrow in the bottom right corner, which you can click on to see more options. You can customise the Ribbon to suit your own needs. See pages 28–9 for how to do this.

ROW
A row is a group of cells that runs across the worksheet from left to right.

WORKSHEET
By default, an Excel workbook contains three worksheets (also known as spreadsheets). Clicking on the tab will bring that worksheet to view. You can also use the scroll buttons on the left to move between worksheets. You can add, delete, reorder and rename worksheets.

Household budget - M

| File | Home | Insert | Page Layout | Formulas | Data | Review | View |

PivotTable | Table | Picture | Clip Art | Shapes ▾ | SmartArt | Screenshot ▾ | Column | Line | Pie | Bar | Area | Scatte

Tables | Illustrations | Charts

Q13 | fx

	A	B	C	D	E	F	G
1	**Monthly Household budget**						
2		Jan	Feb	March	April	May	June
3	**HOUSE**						
4	Mortgage	920	920	920	920	920	9
5	Gas	38	38	38	38	38	
6	Electricity	58	58	58	58	58	
7	Water	40	40	40	40	40	
8	Council Tax	150	150	150	150	150	1
9	TV licence	11.6	11.6	11.6	11.6	11.6	1
10	BT phone& broadband	40	40	40	40	40	
11	Home Insurance	25	25	25	25	25	
12	**House totals**	1282.6	1282.6	1282.6	1282.6	1282.6	128
13							
14	**TRANSPORT**						
15	Petrol	110	125	100	132	140	1
16	Car Insurance	30	30	30	30	30	
17	Road Tax	25	25	25	25	25	
18	Parking	32	48	24	10	18	
19	Public transport	45	30	35	60	48	
20	**Transport totals**	242	258	214	257	261	2
21							
22	**LIVING**						
23	Groceries	250	240	300	278	255	3
24	Child care						

⏮ ◀ ▶ ⏭ | 2011 / Sheet2 / Sheet3

Ready

FORMULA BAR
The formula bar allows you to make mathematical calculations using the data you've entered in the cells of your spreadsheet.

COLUMN
A column is a group of cells that run vertically from the top to the bottom of the worksheet.

CELL
On the worksheet grid each rectangle at the intersection of a row and a column is called a cell. A cell's location is given by the letter of the column followed by the number of the intersecting row, for example the intersection of column L and row 5 is cell L5.

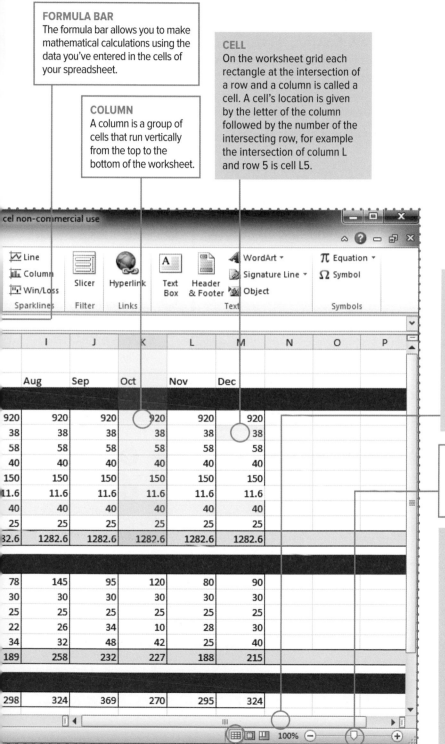

	I	J	K	L	M	N	O	P
	Aug	Sep	Oct	Nov	Dec			
920	920	920	920	920	920			
38	38	38	38	38	38			
58	58	58	58	58	58			
40	40	40	40	40	40			
150	150	150	150	150	150			
11.6	11.6	11.6	11.6	11.6	11.6			
40	40	40	40	40	40			
25	25	25	25	25	25			
32.6	1282.6	1282.6	1282.6	1282.6	1282.6			
78	145	95	120	80	90			
30	30	30	30	30	30			
25	25	25	25	25	25			
22	26	34	10	28	30			
34	32	48	42	25	40			
189	258	232	227	188	215			
298	324	369	270	295	324			

100%

HORIZONTAL SCROLL BAR
If you have more data in a worksheet than you can view on screen, click and drag the horizontal scroll bar to the left or right to see a particular part of the worksheet.

ZOOM
Click and drag on the slider to zoom in and out of a worksheet.

PAGE VIEWS
You have three ways to view your worksheets:

▶ **Normal** shows an unlimited number of cells and columns. This is selected by default

▶ **Page Layout** separates the worksheet into pages

▶ **Page Break** shows an overview of the worksheet – useful for adding page breaks

OPEN AN EXCEL WORKBOOK

An Excel file is called a workbook and each one contains several worksheets (spreadsheets).

Create a new, blank workbook

1 Click the **File** tab to see the Backstage view

2 Click **New**

3 Select **Blank** workbook under 'Available Templates'

4 Click **Create**. A new, blank workbook appears in the Excel window

Open an existing workbook

1 Click the **File** tab to see the Backstage view

2 Click **Open**

3 Select a workbook and click **Open**

4 If you've opened an Excel workbook recently, you can access it from the Recent list. Click on the **File** tab and select **Recent**

USE A TEMPLATE

Excel comes with many templates that can save you time and effort. These pre-designed spreadsheets come with ready made formatting and pre-defined formulas – so you don't need to worry about performing calculations and writing your own formulas.

Create a new workbook using a template

 Click the **File** tab to go to Backstage view

 Select **New**. The 'Available Templates' pane appears

3 Click **Sample templates** to choose a built-in template or select an 'Office.com Templates' category to choose a template from Microsoft's website

4 Thumbnail images of the templates can be seen in the centre. Click on one of these to see a larger preview on the right.

5 Click a template and then click **Create**. If using an Office.com template, 'Create' will be replaced by **Download**

6 A new workbook will appear using your selected template

SAVE AN EXCEL WORKBOOK

As with Word, Excel has two commands that let you save your workbook – which one you use depends on whether you're saving for the first time or saving a file you have previously saved.

Use Save As command

This lets you choose a name for your workbook and a location where it should be saved to. Use this when saving a workbook for the first time (even if you select 'Save', the 'Save As' dialog box will appear) or if you want to save a different version of a workbook but keep the original.

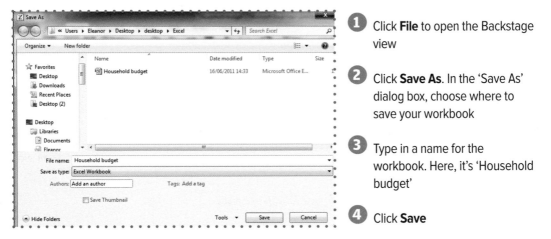

1 Click **File** to open the Backstage view

2 Click **Save As**. In the 'Save As' dialog box, choose where to save your workbook

3 Type in a name for the workbook. Here, it's 'Household budget'

4 Click **Save**

Use the Save Command

To save your workbook with same name and location, use the 'Save' command. Do this regularly as you work to ensure your data is safe should something unexpected like a computer crash happen.

1 Click **Save** on the Quick Access Toolbar

2 Your workbook is saved

Save as an older format

Excel 2010 workbooks are saved in the .xlsx file format, which means you can share them with anyone using Excel 2010 or 2007. Earlier versions of Excel, however, use a different file format, so to open your spreadsheet in these versions, you must save it as an Excel 97-2003 workbook.

1 Click **File** to open the Backstage view

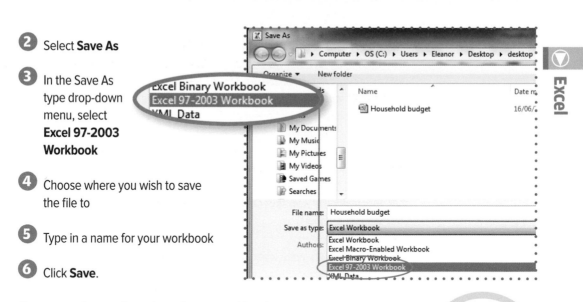

2 Select **Save As**

3 In the Save As type drop-down menu, select **Excel 97-2003 Workbook**

4 Choose where you wish to save the file to

5 Type in a name for your workbook

6 Click **Save**.

Open an autosaved version of your workbook

If you accidently close a file without saving or Excel crashes, you may not face the loss of all your work. Excel automatically saves your workbook to a temporary folder while you're working on it and you can recover this autosaved file.

TIP

Excel autosaves every 10 minutes by default. If you're working for less than this, Excel will not autosave.

1 Open a workbook that was previously closed without saving

2 Click **File** to get to the Backstage view

3 In Backstage view, click **Info**

4 If there are autosaved versions of your workbook, they will appear under 'Versions'. Click on the file to open it

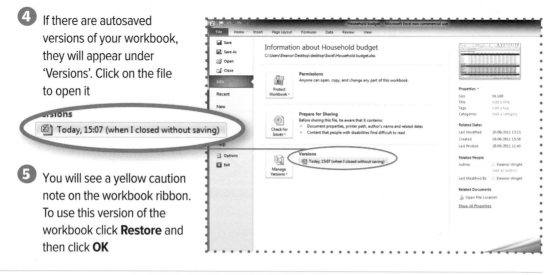

5 You will see a yellow caution note on the workbook ribbon. To use this version of the workbook click **Restore** and then click **OK**

Excel

GET STARTED WITH WORKSHEETS

When you open an Excel workbook, you'll see it consists of three worksheets with the default names of Sheet1, Sheet2 and Sheet3. You can rename worksheets, and add, move, copy or delete worksheets. You may, for example, wish to create a household finance workbook that consists of 12 worksheets – one for each month – or a worksheet for each year.

Rename a worksheet

1 Right click the worksheet tab you want to rename

2 On the pop-up menu, click **Rename**

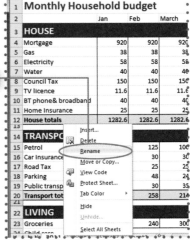

3 The text on the worksheet tab will now be highlighted in black. Type a name for your worksheet

4 Click anywhere outside of the tab to apply the new name

Add a new worksheet

1 Click on the **Insert Worksheet** icon that can be found to the right of the worksheet tabs

19	Public transport	45	30	35	60	48
20	**Transport totals**	242	258	214	257	261
21						
22	**LIVING**					
23	Groceries	250	240	300	278	255

2011 / Sheet2 / Sheet3

Ready

2 A new worksheet will appear

Move or copy a worksheet

1 Right click the tab of the worksheet you want to move or copy

2 From the worksheet menu click **Move or Copy...**

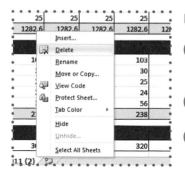

3 In the 'Move or Copy' dialog box, tick the **Create a copy** box if you want to copy the worksheet or leave blank if you just want to move the selected sheet

4 Select a location for the worksheet

5 Click **OK**. Your worksheet will appear in the new location. If you selected 'Create a copy' (see Step 3), your worksheet will be copied with the same name as the original worksheet, but the title shows a version number, such as 2011 (2)

Delete a worksheet

1 Right click the tab of the worksheet you want to delete

2 On the pop-up menu, click **Delete**

3 The worksheet will be deleted from your workbook

TRY THIS

You can also move a worksheet using drag and drop. Simply click the tab of the worksheet you want to move. The mouse will change to show a small worksheet icon. Drag the worksheet tab to its new location and release your mouse.

Colour worksheet tabs

Changing the colour of individual worksheet tabs can help you organise your workbook.

1 Right click the worksheet tab you want to colour

2 On the pop-up menu, click **Tab Color**

3 From the menu, select a colour

4 Click anywhere outside the tab to see the new tab colour applied

Excel

Excel

WORK WITH CELLS

Cells are the core building blocks of an Excel worksheet and you need to know how to work with cells and cell content before you can perform calculations or data analysis – each cell in a workbook can contain its own text, formatting, formulas and functions.

TRY THIS

You can navigate through your worksheet cell by cell, either vertically or horizontally, by using your keyboard's arrow keys. You can also press **Tab** on your keyboard to move forward to the next cell or **Enter** to move vertically.

Select a cell

1 Click on a cell to select it

2 When a cell is selected its border appears bold, and the row and column headings are highlighted

3 The cell will stay selected until you click on another cell in the worksheet

4 To select more than one cell, click and drag your mouse across adjoining cells to highlight them. Release your mouse. The cells will remain selected until you click on another cell in the worksheet

Add content to a cell

1 Select a cell

2 Type content directly into the selected cell. It will appear in the cell and the formula bar

3 You also can enter or edit cell content using the formula bar

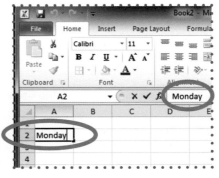

Delete content from a cell

1 Select the cell whose content you wish to delete

2 On the ribbon, click **Clear**

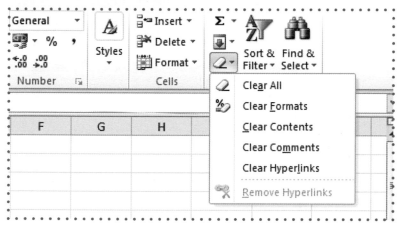

3 From the drop-down menu, click **Clear Contents**

4 Alternatively, use the keyboard's Backspace key to delete content from a single cell

Paste content into a cell

You can use Excel's paste command to copy – or cut – content from one cell to another.

1 Select the cell or cells you wish to copy

2 On the ribbon, click either **Copy** or **Cut**. You'll see the border of the selected cells change in appearance to a dotted line

3 Select the cell or cells where you want to paste the content. On the ribbon, click **Paste**. The content will then appear in the highlighted cells

Excel

TRY THIS

Excel has further Paste options that are useful when working with cells that contain formulas or formatting. To access these options, click the drop-down arrow under 'Paste' on the Ribbon.

Move cells by dragging and dropping

1 Select the cells you wish to move

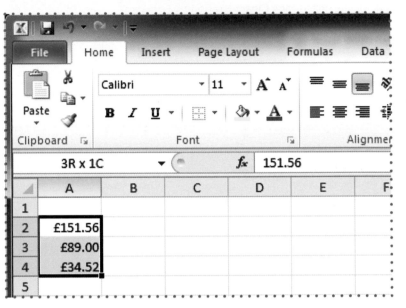

2 Position your mouse on one of the outside edges of the selected cells. The mouse changes from a white cross to a black cross with four arrows

3 Click and drag the cells to the new location

4 Release your mouse key and the cells will be dropped there

MODIFY CELLS, COLUMNS AND ROWS

When you first open an Excel workbook, you'll see that all the cells are the same default size and it's unlikely that they'll be big enough to display all the text you've entered into them. Fortunately, you can modify cells and adjust column widths and row heights to ensure your content is viewable.

Change column width

1 Move your cursor over the column line in the column heading. The white cross will become a double arrow

2 Click and drag the column to the right to increase the column width or to the left to decrease the column width

3 Release the mouse. The column width will change

Change row height

1 Move your cursor over the row line in the row heading. The white cross will become a double arrow

2 Click and drag the row downwards to increase the row height or upwards to decrease the row height

3 Release the mouse. The row height will change

Excel

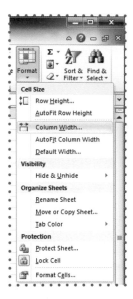

Set row height or column width with a specific measurement

1 Select the rows or columns you want to modify

2 On the **Home** tab, click **Format**

3 From the drop-down menu, select either **Row Height** or **Column Width**

4 In the respective dialog box that appears, enter a specific measurement for row height or column width

5 Click **OK**

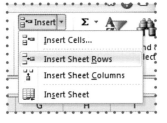

Add rows

1 Select the row below where you want the new row to appear

2 On the **Home** tab, click **Insert** and a new row will appear

Add columns

1 Select the column to the right of where you want the new column to appear. For example, if you want to insert a column between A and B, select column B

2 On the **Home** tab, click **Insert** and a new column will appear

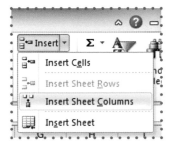

Delete rows and columns

1 Select the rows or columns you want to delete

2 On the **Home** tab, click **Delete** and the rows or columns will be deleted

MAKE TEXT FIT

Often a cell will contain more text than it can display but you don't want to extend the entire column width. You can solve this by either wrapping text within the cells so that it appears on several lines or merging the cell with an empty adjoining cell.

Wrap text

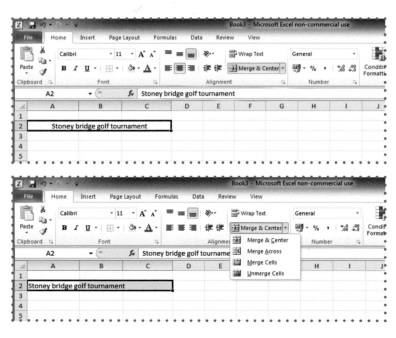

 Select the cells with text you want to wrap

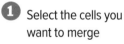 On the **Home** tab, click **Wrap Text**

❸ The text in the selected cells will be wrapped within the cell, and appear on more than one line

Merge cells

❶ Select the cells you want to merge

❷ On the **Home** tab, click **Merge & Center**. The selected cells will be merged and the text will be centred

❸ If you don't want the text to be centred, click the arrow next to 'Merge & Center'. From the drop-down menu click **Merge Cells**

Excel

FORMAT CELLS

Changing the colour, size and alignment of your text and applying other formatting to cells and numbers will help make your text and data more readable and easier to understand. Once you've entered text or data into the cells of an Excel worksheet and adjusted columns and row widths, you can then format the cell content.

Change the font

1 Select the cells you want to change

2 On the **Home** tab, in the 'Font' group, click the drop-down arrow at the right of the current font box

3 On the drop-down menu that appears, move your cursor over a font to see a live preview on your worksheet

4 Click a font to apply it to the selected cells

Change font size

1 Select the cells you want to change

2 On the **Home** tab, in the 'Font' group, click the drop-down arrow at the right of the current font size box

3 On the drop-down menu that appears, move your cursor over a font size to see a live preview on your worksheet

4 Click a font size to apply it to the selected cells

Use the Bold, Italic, and Underline commands

 Select the cells you want to change

2 On the **Home** tab, in the 'Font' group, click **Bold** (B), **Italic** (I), or **Underline** (U)

Change font colour

 Select the cells you wish to change

 On the **Home** tab, in the 'Font' group, click the drop-down arrow next to the 'Font colour' command

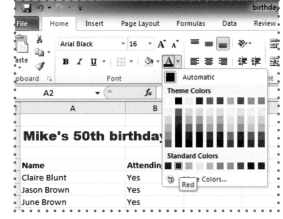

TRY THIS

When changing the colour of a font or a cell fill, you're not limited to the colours that appear on the drop down menu. Click **More Colors...** at the bottom of the menu to see more colour options.

5 On the drop-down menu, move your cursor over a colour to see a live preview

6 Click a font colour to apply it to the selected cells

Add a border to a cell or cells

 Select the cell or cells you want to add a border to

2 On the **Home** tab, in the 'Font' group, click the drop-down arrow next to the 'Borders' command

3 From the drop-down menu, select a border style to apply to the selected cells

105

Add a background fill colour

1 Select the cell or cells you want to add a fill colour to

2 On the **Home** tab, in the 'Font' group, click the drop-down arrow next to the 'Fill Color' command

3 On the drop-down menu, move your cursor over a colour to see a live preview

4 Click a fill colour to apply it to the selected cells

Change horizontal text alignment

1 Select the cell or cells you want to change

2 On the **Home** tab, in the 'Alignment' group, select one of the following horizontal alignment options:
- ▶ **Align Text Left:** aligns text to the left of a cell
- ▶ **Center:** centres text within a cell
- ▶ **Align Text Right:** aligns text to the right of a cell

Change vertical text alignment

By default, Excel aligns content to the bottom of a cell, but you can change the vertical alignment to suit your needs.

1 Select the cell or cells you want to change

2 On the **Home** tab, in the 'Alignment' group, select one of the following vertical alignment options:
- ▶ **Top Align:** aligns text to the top of the cell
- ▶ **Middle Align:** aligns text to the middle of the cell
- ▶ **Bottom Align:** aligns text to the bottom of the cell

FORMAT NUMBERS AND DATES

Along with adjusting font size and colour, Excel lets you choose how numbers in a cell are displayed as a value. For example, you may have created a worksheet to manage your household budget and therefore need to add a £ sign to some of the figures (see the example below). Or you may wish to display your dates in a certain way such as 08/08/2012 rather than 8 August 2012.

To add a monetary value to a number

1 Select the cell or cells you wish to change

2 On the **Home** tab, in the 'Numbers' group, click the arrow to the right of the 'Number Format' box (this will say 'General' by default)

3 From the drop-down menu, click **Currency**

4 Click **OK**

5 For more options or to customise a format (such as change the currency symbol from £ to $), click **More Number Formats...** at the bottom of this menu

TRY THIS

Use 'Currency' on the 'Number Format' command for general money figures, and to align decimal points in a column, select 'Accounting'.

	Jan	Feb	March	April	May	June	July	Aug	Sep	Oct	Nov	Dec
Monthly Household budget												
HOUSE												
Mortgage	£920.00	£920.00	£920.00	£920.00	£920.00	£920.00	£920.00	£920.00	£920.00	£920.00	£920.00	£920.00
Gas	£38.00	£38.00	£38.00	£38.00	£38.00	£38.00	£38.00	£38.00	£38.00	£38.00	£38.00	£38.00
Electricity	£58.00	£58.00	£58.00	£58.00	£58.00	£58.00	£58.00	£58.00	£58.00	£58.00	£58.00	£58.00
Water	£40.00	£40.00	£40.00	£40.00	£40.00	£40.00	£40.00	£40.00	£40.00	£40.00	£40.00	£40.00
Council Tax	£150.00	£150.00	£150.00	£150.00	£150.00	£150.00	£150.00	£150.00	£150.00	£150.00	£150.00	£150.00
TV licence	£11.60	£11.60	£11.60	£11.60	£11.60	£11.60	£11.60	£11.60	£11.60	£11.60	£11.60	£11.60
BT phone	£40.00	£40.00	£40.00	£40.00	£40.00	£40.00	£40.00	£40.00	£40.00	£40.00	£40.00	£40.00
Home Insurance	£25.00	£25.00	£25.00	£25.00	£25.00	£25.00	£25.00	£25.00	£25.00	£25.00	£25.00	£25.00
House totals	£1,282.60	£1,282.60	£1,282.60	£1,282.60	£1,282.60	£1,282.60	£1,282.60	£1,282.60	£1,282.60	£1,282.60	£1,282.60	£1,282.60
TRANSPORT												
Petrol	110	125	100	132	140	103	78	145	95	120	80	90
Car Insurance	30	30	30	30	30	30	30	30	30	30	30	30
Road Tax	25	25	25	25	25	25	25	25	25	25	25	25
Parking	32	48	24	10	18	24	22	26	34	10	28	30
Public transport	45	30	35	60	48	56	34	32	48	42	25	40
Transport totals	242	258	214	257	261	238	189	258	232	227	188	215
LIVING												

Excel

FREEZE ROWS AND COLUMNS

Excel lets you freeze or lock panes so that top rows or left-hand columns remain visible even when you scroll to another area of the spreadsheet. This is really useful when working on a large spreadsheet, as you can see column headers or row labels at all times when scrolling through.

Freeze a row

1 Select the column to the right of the columns you want to freeze. For example, if you want column A and B to always appear on the left of the worksheet as you scroll, then select column C

2 On the **View** tab, in the Window group, click **Freeze Panes**

3 From the drop-down menu, click **Freeze Panes**

4 A solid black line under row 2 shows that the rows are frozen, keeping column labels in place as you scroll downwards

Freeze a column

1 Select the column to the right of the columns you want frozen. For example, if you want column A and B to always appear to the left of the worksheet even as you scroll, then select column C

2 On the **View** tab, in the Window group, click **Freeze Panes**

3 From the drop-down menu, click **Freeze Panes**

4 A solid black line appears to the right of the frozen area. Scroll across the worksheet to see the columns to the right of the frozen columns

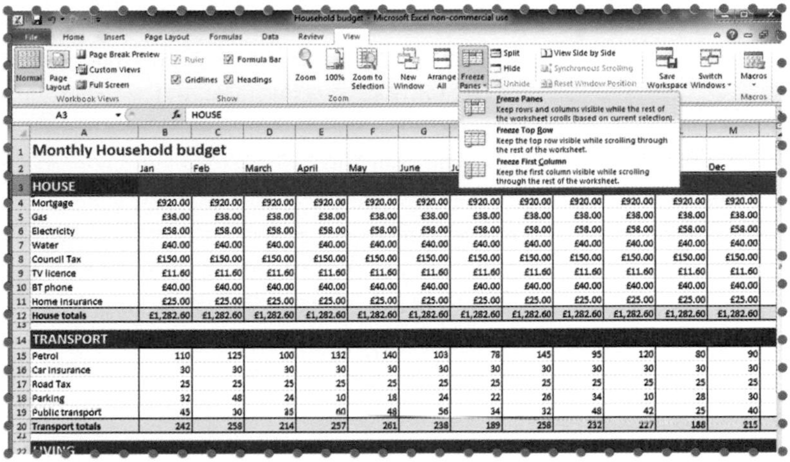

Freeze both rows and columns

You can freeze both rows and columns at the same time.

1 To lock both rows and columns, click the cell below and to the right of the rows and columns that you want to keep visible when you scroll

2 Click the **View** tab

3 In the 'Window' group, click **Freeze Panes**

4 From the drop-down menu, click **Freeze Panes**

5 A solid black line appears under and to the right of the frozen area

Unfreeze panes

1 Click the **View** tab

2 In the 'Window 'group, click **Freeze Panes**

3 From the drop-down menu click **Unfreeze Panes**. The panes will be unfrozen and the black lines will disappear

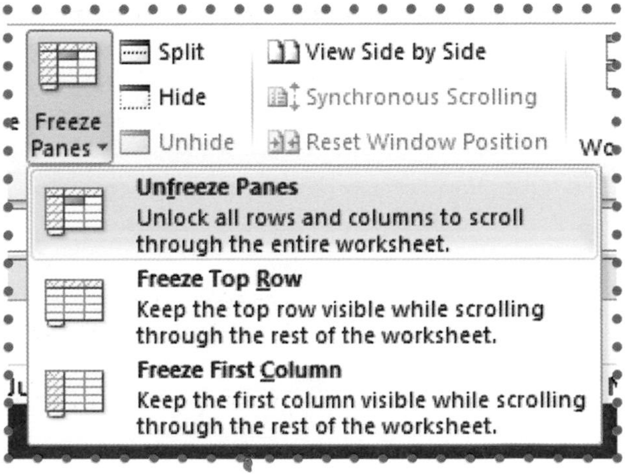

Excel

CREATE FORMULAS

Excel isn't just for storing and displaying your information. Like a calculator, it can perform calculations on numerical data that add, subtract, multiply, and divide. So, for example, when working on a household budget, if you want to find out how much money you have left over each month, Excel can help.

Excel performs these calculations using formulas. A formula is a mathematical equation that is used to perform a calculation, for example x+x=z is used to represent the calculation 2+2 =4. An Excel formula always starts with an equal sign (=). This is because the cell contains, or is equal to, the formula and its value.

Excel uses standard mathematical operators in its equation. The most-used ones are:

- ▶ **A plus sign** for addition (+)
- ▶ **A minus sign** for subtraction (-)
- ▶ **An asterisk** for multiplication (*)
- ▶ **A forward slash** for division (/)

Create a simple formula

1 Select the cell where the answer will appear (B6, for example)

2 Type the equal sign (=)

3 Type in the values and the mathematical operator that you want Excel to calculate. For example, '450/40'

4 Press **Enter**. Excel will perform the calculation and the value will be displayed in the cell you selected

File	Home	Insert	Page Layout	Formulas	Data	Review

SUM ▾ × ✓ *fx* =450/40

◢	A	B	C	D	E
1					
2	**Tiling costs per square feet**				
3	Total tile cost	£450.00			
4	Square feet	40			
5					
6	Total	=450/40			

Create a simple formula using cell references

Excel uses cell references to identify data included in the calculation. So a typical formula using cell references might be =D6+F4

Creating a formula with cell references is usually easier because you can subsequently change the data in your worksheet and it will recalculate automatically without the need to rewrite the values in the formula.

1 Click the cell where you want the answer to appear. In this case, B3

2 Type the equal sign (=)

3 Type the cell address that contains the first number in the equation. In this case, B1

4 Type the operator required for the formula. In this case, the addition sign (+)

5 Type the cell address that contains the second number in the equation. In this case, it's B2

6 Press **Enter**. The formula will be calculated and the value displayed in the cell

Edit a formula

1 Click on the cell you want to edit

2 Click on the formula bar and edit the formula. Alternatively, double click the cell to edit the formula directly in the cell

3 When finished, press **Enter**

4 The new value will be displayed in the cell

COMPLEX FORMULAS

A complex formula is one that has more than one mathematical operation, for example w+x-y = z. Excel follows the standard order of mathematical operations, as taught at school, to know which operation to calculate first. So, the calculation 2+4-3 will be rewritten by Excel as =(2+4)-3 or, more commonly, using cell references such as =(D6+F4)-G8

Order of operations

Excel calculates formulas based on the following standard order of operations:

1 Parentheses

2 Exponents (to the power of)

3 Multiplication and division, whichever comes first

4 Addition and subtraction, whichever comes first

Create a complex formula

As an example, follow these steps for creating a formula using cell references to work out the amount of VAT payable on the items for sale in a club shop: 20%.

1 Click the cell where you want the formula result to appear. In this case, the cell is D3

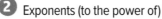

	ITEM NUMBER	PRICE	VAT	QUANTITY	TOTAL
Herts Lawn Bowls Club Shop					
3 Gents White Bowling Trousers	AWT123	£30.99	=(C3/100)*20	2	£61.98
4 Gents Grey Bowling Trousers	AGT234	£28.99		1	£28.99
5 Ladies Blazer	BLZ765	£40.99		3	£122.97
6 Gents Blazer	BLZ236	£40.99		1	£40.99
7 Ladies White Bowling Trousers	LWT987	£30.99		3	£92.95

2 Type the equal sign (=)

3 Type an open parenthesis, then click on the cell that contains the first value you want in the formula (in this example, C3)

4 Type the first mathematical operator (for example, the division sign) and value in the formula – in this case, 100 – and then type a closed parenthesis

5 Type the next mathematical operator (for example, the multiplication sign)

6 Type the next value in the formula

7 Click **Enter** to calculate your formula

Copy formulas

1 Select the cell you want to copy (for example, D3) and, on the **Home** tab, click on **Copy**

2 Select the cells where you want to paste the formula and, on the **Home** tab, click on **Paste**. Alternatively, select the cell whose formula you want to copy. Drag the selected cell's border over the cells where you want to paste the formula

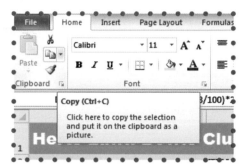

3 The formula is copied to these cells as a relative reference and values for each cell are then calculated

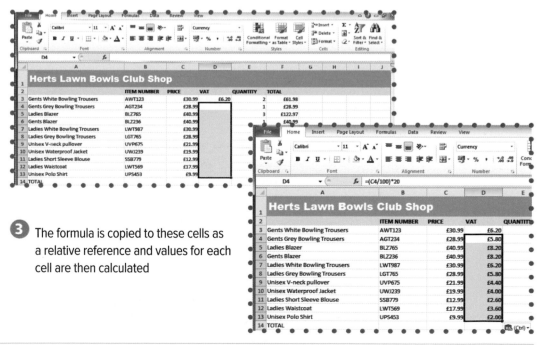

USE FUNCTIONS

Writing formulas can be tedious and tricky so, if possible, consider using a function. A function is a predefined formula that performs a calculation using specific values in a particular order. Excel comes with a hundreds of different functions ready to use, which can save you time and effort.

Excel's functions can be accessed in the 'Function Library' on the 'Formulas' tab. Here you can search for functions based on categories such as 'Financial', 'Text', 'Date & Time' and more.

Common functions such as SUM (adds all the numbers in a range of cells) and AVG (calculates the average of the values of cells) can be found on the **Home** tab under the **AutoSum** button.

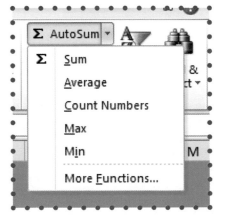

Use a function to add up a column of numbers

1 Highlight the column of numbers you want to add up by clicking on the first cell, holding down the mouse button and dragging it, letting go when you reach the last cell

2 On the **Home** tab, in the 'Editing' group, click the **AutoSum** button

3 The total sum of all the values in your selection will be displayed in the cell directly underneath the value for your final, highlighted cell

	A	B	C	D	E	F	G	H
1	**Herts Lawn Bowls Club Shop**							
2		ITEM NUMBER	PRICE	VAT	QUANTITY	TOTAL		
3	Gents White Bowling Trousers	AWT123	£30.99	£6.20	2	£61.98		
4	Gents Grey Bowling Trousers	AGT234	£28.99	£5.80	1	£28.99		
5	Ladies Blazer	BLZ765	£40.99	£8.20	3	£122.97		
6	Gents Blazer	BLZ236	£40.99	£8.20	1	£40.99		
7	Ladies White Bowling Trousers	LWT987	£30.99	£6.20	3	£92.97		
8	Ladies Grey Bowling Trousers	LGT765	£28.99	£5.80	2	£57.98		
9	Unisex V-neck pullover	UVP675	£21.99	£4.40	0	£0.00		
10	Unisex Waterproof Jacket	UWJ239	£19.99	£4.00	2	£39.98		
11	Ladies Short Sleeve Blouse	SSB779	£12.99	£2.60	4	£51.96		
12	Ladies Waistcoat	LWT569	£17.99	£3.60	1	£17.99		
13	Unisex Polo Shirt	UPS453	£9.99	£2.00	5	£49.95		
14	TOTAL					£565.76		

Excel

TRY THIS

Excel's 'Sort' command changes to display either 'Sort A to Z'/'Sort Smallest to Largest' options depending on the type of data selected in your spreadsheet. If the data has a value, i.e. it is a number, Excel offers the option to sort it from smallest to largest or vice versa, while if you have text selected, it will offer the option to sort alphabetically instead.

SORT DATA

By using Excel's Sort commands, you can make more sense of the spreadsheet data by changing the order in which it appears. For example, if you're creating a guest list for a birthday or anniversary party, you can sort the guests by name alphabetically.

Sort data alphabetically

1 Select a cell in the column you want to sort by

2 On the **Data** tab, in the 'Sort & Filter' group, click the ascending command sort **Sort A to Z**. If you want to see them in the opposite order click the descending command sort **Sort Z to A**

3 Your data will now be organised alphabetically

Sort data numerically

1 Select a cell in the column you want to sort by

2 On the **Data** tab, in the 'Sort & Filter' group, click either the ascending command sort **Sort Smallest to Largest**, or the descending command sort **Sort Largest to Smallest**

3 Your data will now be organised numerically

Customise your sorting

You can create your own sorting order using a Custom List. So, for example, in a wedding or party list, you could sort guests by their dietary requirements.

1 Select the data you wish to sort

2 From the **Data** tab, click **Sort** to open the 'Sort' dialog box

3 Select the column you want to Sort by clicking the drop-down arrow in the 'Column' field. In this example, Dietary

4 Make sure 'Values' is selected in the 'Sort On' field

5 Click the drop-down arrow in the 'Order' field, and choose **Custom List...**

6 In the 'Custom Lists' dialog box select **NEW LIST**, and enter how you want your data sorted in the List entries box. Here, the guests' dietary requirements are described as Chicken, Fish, Vegetarian

7 Click **Add** to save the list, then click **OK**

8 Click **OK** to close the 'Sort' dialog box and sort your data

9 The spreadsheet will be sorted in order of Chicken, Fish, Vegetarian options

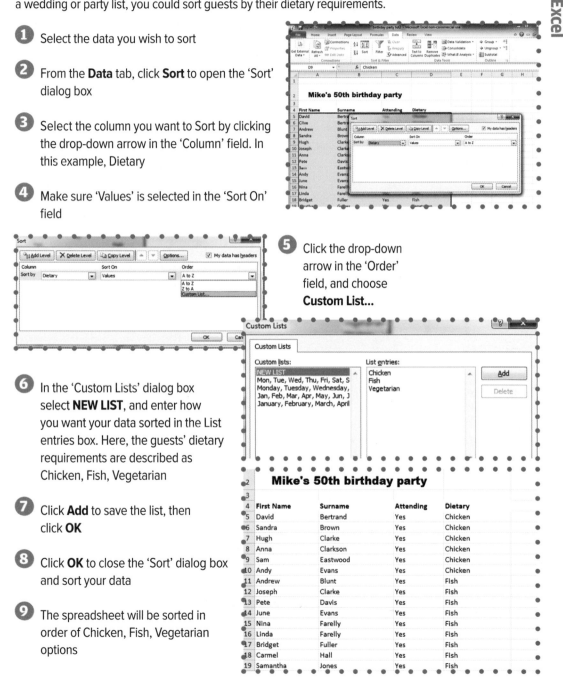

117

 **Excel**

Jargon buster

Filtering in Excel
Excel allows you to filter – select specific – information in your spreadsheet columns so you can find values quickly. It's a quick and easy way to work with a subset of information in a range of cells or table. You can filter information by choosing a category of data or you can create custom filters to focus on specific data.

TIP
Tables include filtering by default. You can filter your data using the drop-down arrows in the header.

FORMAT YOUR DATA AS A TABLE

To make working with your spreadsheet data as simple as possible, you can format it as a table.

Format data as a table

1 Select the cells you want in the table

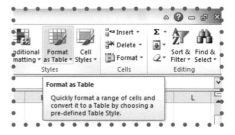

2 On the **Home** tab, in the Styles group, click **Format as Table**

3 Select a table style from the list of predefined table styles

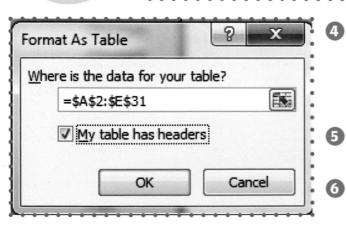

4 A dialog box will appear, confirming the range of cells you've selected. You can change the range here by selecting a new range of cells directly on your spreadsheet

5 If your table has headers, check the box next to **My table has headers**

6 Click **OK**. The data will be formatted as a table in the style that you chose

Add rows or columns to a table

1 Select any cell in your table

2 On the **Design** tab, in the 'Properties' group, click **Resize Table**

3 On your worksheet, select the new range of cells that you want to include – be sure to include the original table cells as well

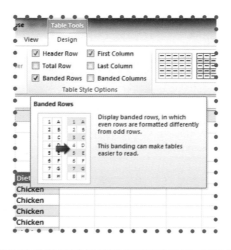

4 Click **OK**. The new rows and/or columns will be added to your table

Change the table style

1 Select any cell in your table

2 On the **Design** tab, in the 'Table Styles' group, click the **More** drop-down arrow to see all of the table styles

3 Move the cursor over a style to see a live preview

4 Select a style. Your table will change accordingly

Change the Table Style Options

On the **Design** tab, there are six 'Table Style Options' that you can turn on or off to change a table's appearance: Header Row, Total Row, Banded Rows, First Column, Last Column, and Banded Columns. Depending on the table style you are using, these options can have different effects, so you may need to experiment to achieve the look you're after.

TRY THIS

To convert a table back into ordinary cells, in the 'Tools' group, click the **Convert to Range** command in the Tools group. The filters and the 'Design' tab will then disappear, but the cells will retain their data and formatting.

WORK WITH CHARTS

Displaying data graphically as a chart can make it easier to understand and analyse. Excel comes with many different types of charts, including columns, line and pie charts, so you can choose one that displays your data to best effect. You can even create a combination chart by using more than one chart type at a time.

Create a chart

1 Select the cells that you want to chart, including the column titles and the row labels. The content of these cells will provide the source data for the chart

2 On the **Insert** tab, in the 'Charts' group, click a chart category such as 'Column'

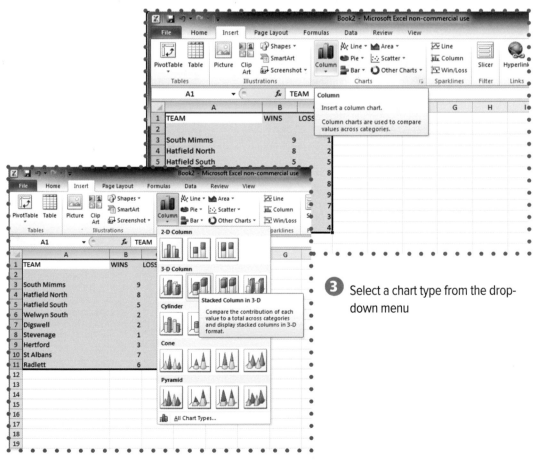

3 Select a chart type from the drop-down menu

4 The chart will appear in the worksheet

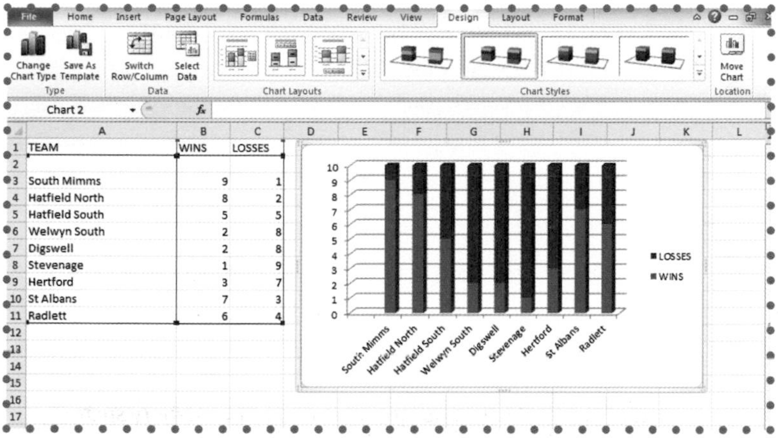

Change the chart type

1 From the **Design** tab, in the 'Type' group, click **Change Chart Type**. A dialog box appears

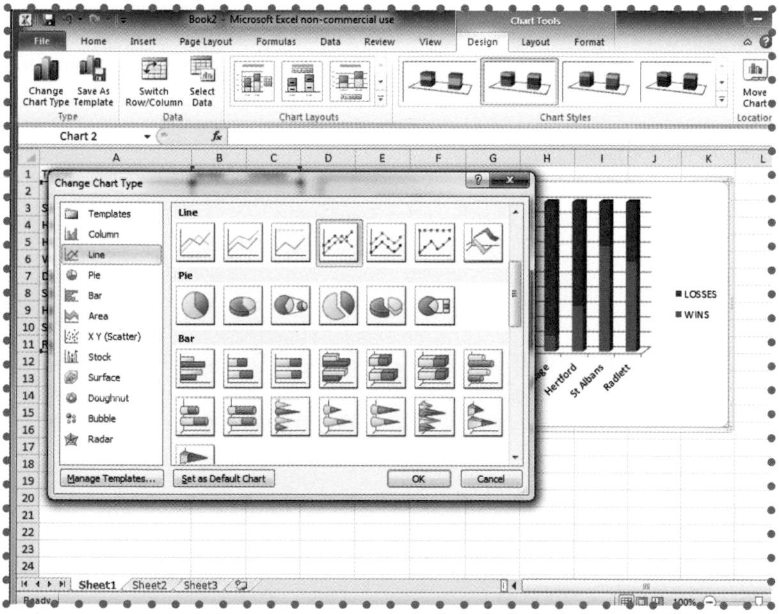

2 Click a chart type

3 Click **OK**

Excel

Change the chart layout

1 On the **Design** tab, in the 'Chart Layouts' group, click the **More** drop-down arrow next to see all of the chart layouts

2 Select a layout

3 The chart will update to reflect the new layout

Change the chart style

1 On the **Design** tab, in the 'Chart Styles' group, click the arrow next to **More** to see all available styles

2 Click a style

3 The chart will update to reflect the new style

GET STARTED WITH SPARKLINE GRAPHICS

Sparklines are miniature charts that fit into a single cell. Unlike a chart, sparklines are usually adjacent to the data, so can help bring immediate meaning and context to numbers and are particularly good for showing trends and patterns.

There are three types of sparklines: 'Line', 'Column' and 'Win/Loss' and you find them in the 'Insert' tab.

'Line' and 'Column' are similar to line and column charts, while 'Win/Loss' shows whether each value is positive or negative, rather than how high or low it is. All three can display markers at key points, such as the highest and lowest points, which makes them easier to read.

Create sparklines

In this example, sparklines are created to illustrate the wins and losses of a team in a local competition. As with formulas, create a single sparkline first and then use the fill handle to automatically create the sparklines for the remaining rows.

1 Select an empty cell or group of empty cells where you want to show your sparkline

2 On the **Insert** tab, in the 'Sparklines' group, click the type of sparkline that you want to create: **Line**, **Column**, or **Win/Loss**. In this case, 'Line'

3 In the 'Create Sparklines' dialog box that opens, type the range of the cells that contain the data on which you want to base the sparklines in the 'Data Range' box. Alternatively, click and drag on the worksheet with your cursor to select the data range. This will automatically fill the data range

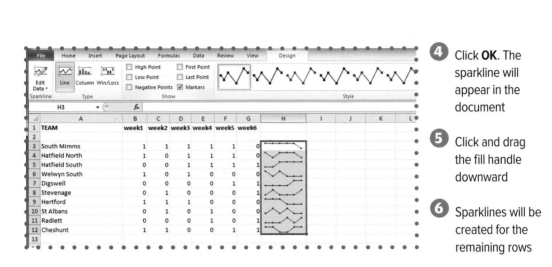

4 Click **OK**. The sparkline will appear in the document

5 Click and drag the fill handle downward

6 Sparklines will be created for the remaining rows

Change the sparkline style

1 Select the sparklines that you want to change

2 On the **Design** tab, in the 'Style' group, click the **More** drop-down arrow to show all of the available styles

3 Click a style

4 The sparklines will update to show the selected style

Show points on the sparkline

You can emphasise certain points on the sparkline with markers or dots – helping to add meaning to the chart.

1 Select the sparklines that you want to change

2 On the **Design** tab, in the 'Show' group, tick the checkbox of the points you want to illustrate

3 To change the dots colour, on the **Design** tab, click on **Marker Color** and select a colour for each type of marker you're using

PRINT AN EXCEL DOCUMENT

In Excel you can preview and print selected worksheets from the Print pane. To open this, click the 'File' tab to see the Backstage view, then click **Print**. The 'Print' pane appears, with the print settings on the left and a preview of your worksheets on the right.

Print a worksheet

1 Select the worksheet you wish to print. To print more than one worksheet, click on the first worksheet tab, then while holding down the Ctrl key, click on the other worksheet tabs

2 Click the **File** tab to go to the Backstage view

3 Click **Print** to access the 'Print' pane

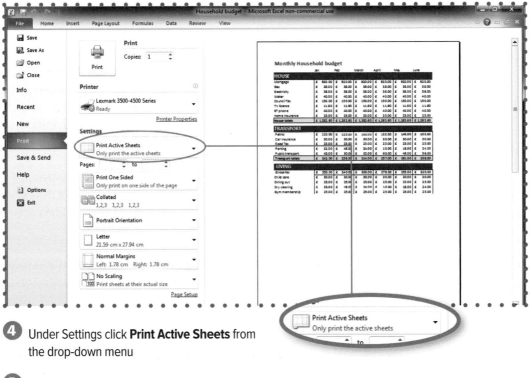

4 Under Settings click **Print Active Sheets** from the drop-down menu

5 Click **Print**

▶ Excel

Print a selection

You can choose to print just part of a worksheet – specific rows or columns. Here's how:

1 Select the cells that you want to print

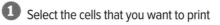

2 Click the **File** tab to go to the Backstage view

3 Click **Print** to access the 'Print' pane

4 Under 'Settings', click the down arrow to see all the options

5 Click **Print Selection**

6 Click **Print**

Change page orientation

Depending on the structure of your Excel spreadsheet – how many rows and columns it has – you may want to change the page orientation to fit more on the page when printed. Selecting 'Portrait' will orient the page vertically and 'Landscape' will orient the page horizontally.

1 Click the **File** tab to see the Backstage view

2 Click **Print** to access the 'Print' pane

3 Under **Settings**, click either **Portrait Orientation** or **Landscape Orientation** from the orientation drop-down menu. The page orientation will change and you can see this in the preview pane

Fit a worksheet on one page

1 Click the **File** tab to see the Backstage view

2 Click **Print** to access the 'Print' pane

3 Under 'Settings', click **Fit Sheet on One Page** from the scaling drop-down menu

4 The worksheet will be reduced in size until it fits on one page

Print row and column headers on every page

If you do need to print your worksheet on several pages, you can make it easier to read if you use Excel's 'Print Titles' feature to print row and column headers on every page.

1 Click the worksheet that you want to print with row and column headings

2 Click the **Page Layout** tab

3 In the 'Page Setup' group, click **Print Titles**

4 The 'Page Setup' dialog box appears. Click the icon at the end of the 'Rows to repeat at top' field

5 Your cursor becomes the small selection arrow. Click on the rows you want to appear on each printed page. The 'Rows to repeat at top' dialog box will record your selection

6 Click the icon at the end of the 'Rows to repeat at top' field to record your selection. Repeat for 'Columns to repeat at left', if necessary

7 Click **OK**. Click the **Print Preview** button to open the 'Print' pane to see a preview of how each page will look when printed

BE CAREFUL

Resizing a worksheet so that it can fit on one page may seem a good idea, but if it's scaled too small it could be difficult to read.

Excel

KEYBOARD SHORTCUTS

Press these keys	To do this
Ctrl + N	Create a new workbook
Ctrl + O	Open a workbook
Ctrl + S	Save the active workbook with its current file name and location
Ctrl + P	Print a workbook
Ctrl + W	Closes the selected workbook window
Ctrl + A	Selects the entire worksheet
Ctrl + Z	Undo the last action
Ctrl + C	Copy the selected cells
Ctrl + X	Cut the selected cells
Ctrl + V	Paste copied cells
Ctrl + L	Displays the 'Create Table' dialog box
Ctrl + B	Applies or removes bold formatting
Ctrl + I	Applies or removes italic formatting
Ctrl + H	Displays the 'Find and Replace' dialog box
Shift + F11	Insert a new worksheet in the current workbook
Ctrl + page down	Move to the next worksheet in the current workbook
Ctrl + page up	Move to the previous worksheet in the current workbook
Tab	Move left to right, cell by cell
Shift + Tab	Move right to left, cell by cell
Enter	Move down, cell by cell
Shift + Enter	Move up, cell by cell
Ctrl + Shift + Down Arrow or Up Arrow	Move down or up to the last empty or non-empty cell
Ctrl + Shift + Right Arrow or Left Arrow	Move to the last empty or non-empty cell to the right or left
Backspace	Delete data in the current cell
Alt + Enter	Insert a return within a cell
Ctrl + Page Down	Go to the next workstation
Ctrl + Page Up	Go to the previous worksheet
Ctrl + ;	Enters the current date
Ctrl + 1	Displays the 'Format Cells' dialog box
Alt + F1	Creates a chart of the selected data

POWERPOINT

By reading this chapter you will get to grips with:

 Working with slides to build a presentation

 Adding animation, video and audio to slides

 Presenting a successful slideshow to an audience

▶ PowerPoint

GET STARTED WITH POWERPOINT

Part of Microsoft Office, PowerPoint 2010 is a presentation software package that uses slides to create a presentation. You can add text, bulleted lists, images, video and animation as well as graphs and charts to the slides. You can have as many slides as you like in a presentation, and you can preview the presentation at any time by clicking on one of the 'Slide Show' play options.

QUICK ACCESS TOOLBAR
This provides quick access to common commands such as 'Save', 'Undo' and 'Repeat', no matter which Ribbon tab you're in.

OUTLINE
This shows the text content of each slide in a simple-to-edit way.

RIBBON
On the Ribbon's multiple tabs, you'll find the commands that you need to complete common tasks. Some tabs may appear only when you're creating certain elements – such as the 'Drawing Tools' tab when you're working with images.

SLIDES
The 'Slides' tab lets you see and work with the slides in your presentation. You can add, delete, move and duplicate slides here.

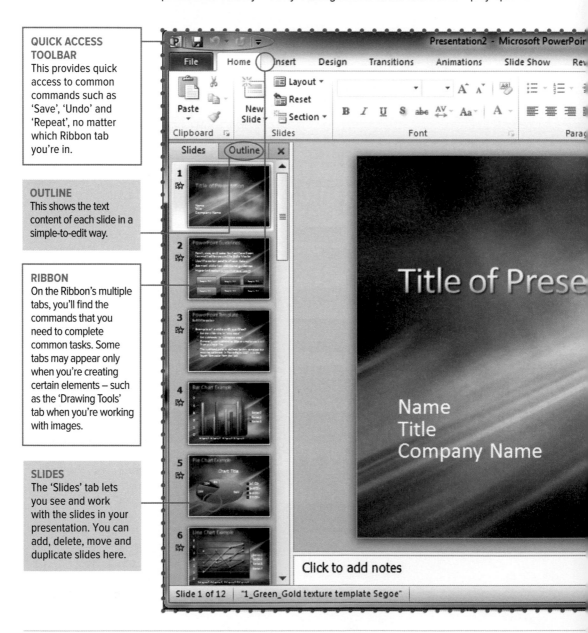

As with Word and Excel, PowerPoint's interface includes the Ribbon, the Quick Access Toolbar and a Backstage view. As in Word and Excel, you can customise the Ribbon in PowerPoint (see pages 28–9) and add commands to the Quick Access Toolbar (see pages 26–7). Here is the PowerPoint interface showing a typical presentation layout.

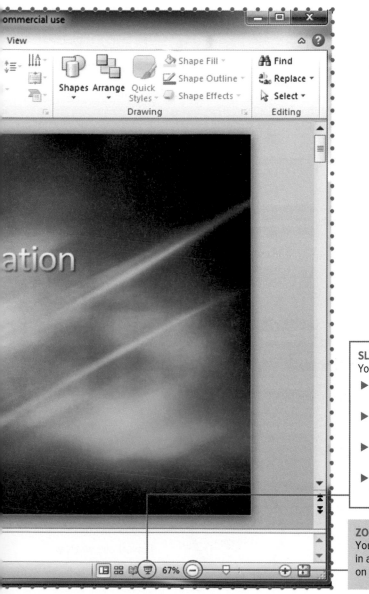

SLIDE VIEWS
You have several ways to view your slides:

▶ **Normal** shows the current slide as well as the 'Slide' and 'Outline' tabs

▶ **Slide Sorter** shows small versions of all the slides in your presentation

▶ **Reading** shows only the slides with buttons at the bottom of the screen for navigation

▶ **Slide Show** plays the slides as a presentation

ZOOM
You can click and drag on the slide to zoom in and out of a current slide or you can click on the **Fit slide to current window button**.

PowerPoint

CREATE AND OPEN A PRESENTATION

Create a new, blank presentation by following these steps:

1 Click

2 Click **All Programs** and then click **Microsoft PowerPoint**. A new blank presentation will open automatically

3 If you already have the software open and want to create a new presentation, click the **File** tab. This shows you the Backstage view

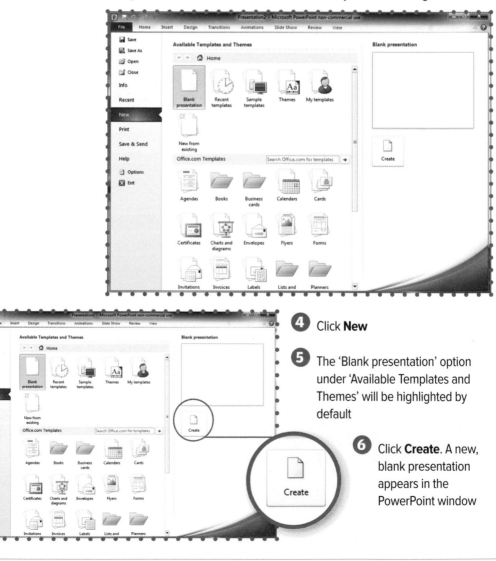

4 Click **New**

5 The 'Blank presentation' option under 'Available Templates and Themes' will be highlighted by default

6 Click **Create**. A new, blank presentation appears in the PowerPoint window

Open an existing presentation

1 Click **File** to go to the Backstage view

2 Click **Open**. The 'Open' dialog box will appear showing folders and files on your computer hard drive

3 Select a presentation and then click **Open**

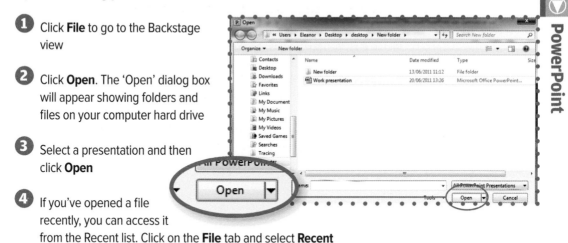

4 If you've opened a file recently, you can access it from the Recent list. Click on the **File** tab and select **Recent**

Recover autosaved files

PowerPoint automatically saves an open presentation to a temporary folder so, if you forget to click 'Save', or if your computer crashes, you can recover the autosaved file.

1 Open the presentation that was closed without saving

2 Click the **File** tab to go to the Backstage view

3 Click **Info**

4 Autosaved versions of the file will appear under 'Versions'. Click on the file to open it

5 To save changes, click **Restore** and then click **OK**

▶ PowerPoint

USE A TEMPLATE

A PowerPoint template is a blueprint of a slide or group of slides that usually share a common theme. It may contain layouts, theme colours, theme fonts, theme effects, background styles and even content. These pre-designed slides let you quickly create a presentation without worrying about text or image placement and formatting.

PowerPoint comes with a range of sample templates and there are lots more to choose from on Microsoft's website www.office.com. You can also create and save your own templates, which you can share with others.

Open a template

1 Open PowerPoint and click the **File** tab to go to the Backstage view

2 Select **New** to open the 'New Presentation' pane

3 Under 'Available Templates and Themes', click **Sample** templates to choose a built-in template, or select an 'Office.com Templates' category to select and download a template from Microsoft's website

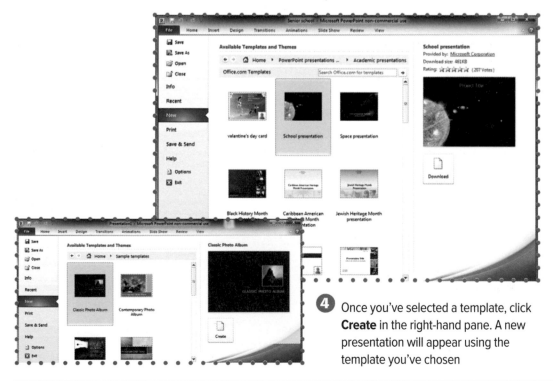

4 Once you've selected a template, click **Create** in the right-hand pane. A new presentation will appear using the template you've chosen

SAVE AND PRINT A PRESENTATION

 Click the **File** tab, and then click **Save As**. This lets you choose a name and location for your presentation

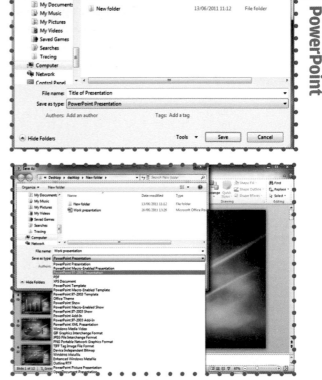

2 In the **File name** box, type a name for your presentation

3 Click **Save**

Save as an older format

By default, PowerPoint 2010 saves files in the .pptx file format. To save your presentation in a format that can be opened in earlier versions of PowerPoint, click the **Save As** type list, and then select **PowerPoint 97-2003**, which will save it as a .ppt file.

Print a presentation

In the 'Print' pane, the properties and settings for your printer appear in the left-hand section, and a preview of your presentation can be seen in the right-hand pane.

 Click the **File** tab, and then click **Print**

2 Under 'Settings', click on the individual settings to change them from the default. For example, if you wish to print only certain slides of your presentation, type the range of slide numbers. Otherwise, select **Print All Slides**

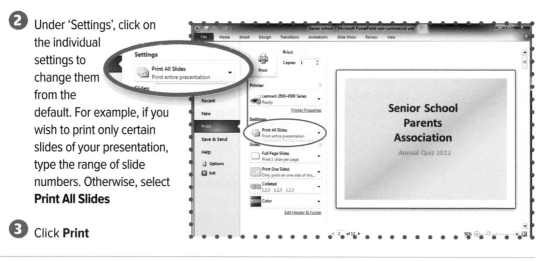

3 Click **Print**

PowerPoint

GET STARTED WITH SLIDES

When you create a new PowerPoint presentation, you'll start with a single slide that appears automatically. This slide has two text 'placeholders' – areas on the slide that are enclosed by dotted borders – in this case one pre-formatted for a title and the other for a subtitle for your presentation.

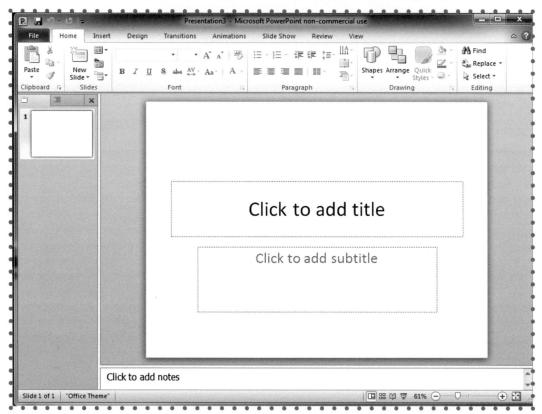

Placeholders can also contain other elements such as pictures, charts and SmartArt graphics. Some text placeholders show text that you can replace. They also have thumbnail-sized icons that show specific commands such as 'Insert Picture' and 'Insert Clip Art'. To see the type of content you can insert in a placeholder, move your cursor over the icons.

Slide layout

The arrangement of placeholders on a slide is called a layout. PowerPoint comes with nine different slide layouts. When you add a new slide to your presentation, you need to choose a layout for that slide – otherwise it will adopt the same layout as the slide on the screen. You can also apply layouts to existing slides in your presentation.

Add a slide with the same layout as the previous slide

 On the **Home** tab, in the 'Slides' group, click **New Slide**

 A new slide appears on the screen and in the 'Slides' tab

Add a slide with a different layout

❶ On the **Home** tab, in the 'Slides' group, click the arrow next to **New Slide**

❷ A gallery appears that shows thumbnails of the various slide layouts available. The name will show the type of content that each layout is designed for, for example, Title Slide is designed to be the opening slide of a presentation. Placeholders icons also show the type of content that can be placed

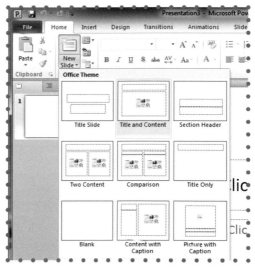

❸ Click the layout that you want for the new slide

❹ If you prefer to design your own slide layout, choose a blank slide – a slide without placeholders. You can then customise the slide by adding your own text boxes, pictures, charts and so on (as explained throughout this chapter)

❺ A new slide will be added your presentation

Change the layout of an existing slide

❶ On the **Slides** tab in the left pane, click on the slide you wish to change

❷ On the **Home** tab, in the 'Slides' group, click **Layout**

❸ Choose a layout from the menu

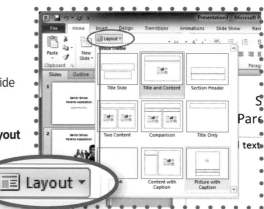

 The slide's existing layout will change

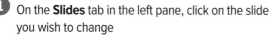
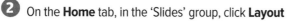

COPY, DELETE AND MOVE SLIDES

If your presentation has two or more slides that will share similar content and layout, you can save time by creating and formatting one slide, and then either duplicating or copying the slide before tweaking each slide individually. By duplicating, PowerPoint copies the selected slide and pastes it directly after the current slide, while copy and paste lets you place the copied slide anywhere in the presentation.

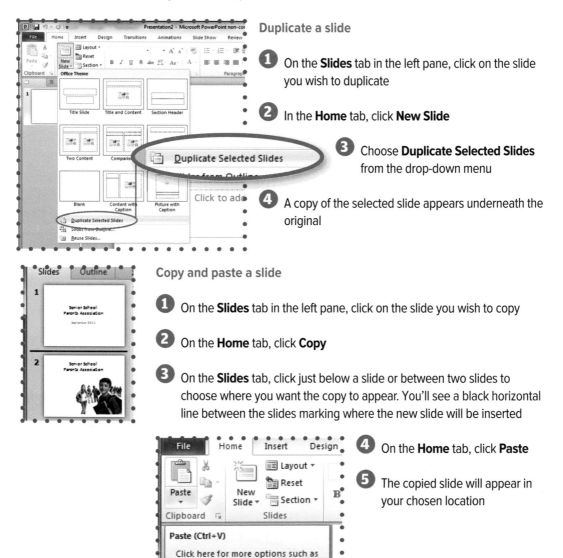

Duplicate a slide

1 On the **Slides** tab in the left pane, click on the slide you wish to duplicate

2 In the **Home** tab, click **New Slide**

3 Choose **Duplicate Selected Slides** from the drop-down menu

4 A copy of the selected slide appears underneath the original

Copy and paste a slide

1 On the **Slides** tab in the left pane, click on the slide you wish to copy

2 On the **Home** tab, click **Copy**

3 On the **Slides** tab, click just below a slide or between two slides to choose where you want the copy to appear. You'll see a black horizontal line between the slides marking where the new slide will be inserted

4 On the **Home** tab, click **Paste**

5 The copied slide will appear in your chosen location

Delete a slide

 On the **Slides** tab in the left pane, right click the slide you want to delete

2 From the pop-up menu, click **Delete Slide**

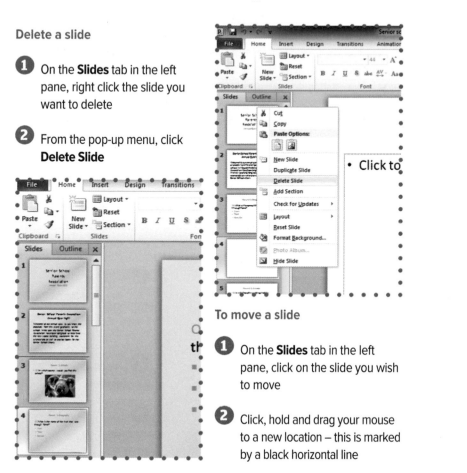

To move a slide

1 On the **Slides** tab in the left pane, click on the slide you wish to move

2 Click, hold and drag your mouse to a new location – this is marked by a black horizontal line

3 Release the mouse button. The slide will appear in the new location

Delete a placeholder

You can change a slide's layout by deleting unwanted placeholders

1 Move your cursor over the dotted border of a placeholder until it changes to a cross-with-arrows-shaped cursor

2 Click the border to select it

3 Press **Backspace** or **Delete** on your keyboard. The placeholder will be removed from the slide

▶ PowerPoint

ADD TEXT TO A TEXT PLACEHOLDER

The easiest way to add text to your slide is to use the content placeholders that appear by default as part of the slide layout. If you want to add extra text outside the existing text placeholders, you can position a text box anywhere you want on the slide. For example, you may want to add a caption to a picture, so you can add a text box and position it underneath.

The main difference between a text placeholder and a text box is that only placeholder text content can be viewed and edited in the presentation's Outline view.

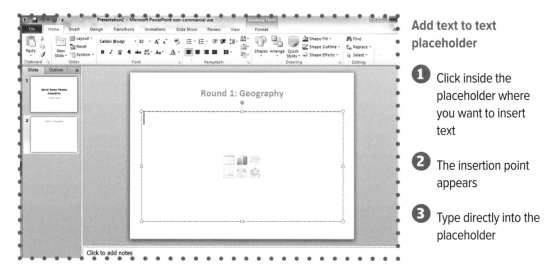

Add text to text placeholder

1 Click inside the placeholder where you want to insert text

2 The insertion point appears

3 Type directly into the placeholder

Add text to a text box

1 On the **Insert** tab, in the 'Text' group, click **Text Box**

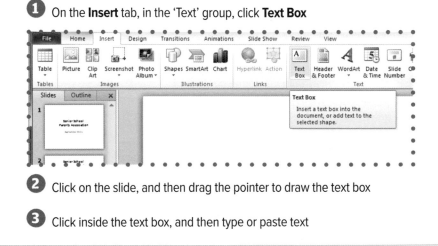

2 Click on the slide, and then drag the pointer to draw the text box

3 Click inside the text box, and then type or paste text

Move a placeholder or text box

 1 Click the box you want to move

2 Move your cursor over the border of the box so it changes to a cross with arrows

3 Click and hold the mouse button as you drag the box to the desired location

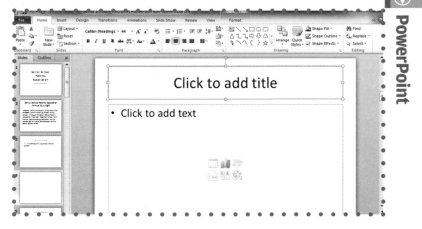

4 Release the mouse button. The box will be moved to the new location

Resize a placeholder or text box

1 Click the box you wish to resize

2 Move your cursor over one of the sizing handles on the corners and sides of the box. The cursor changes into a cursor that sports a pair of arrows. This is the resize cursor

3 Click and hold the cursor on a sizing handle, and drag your mouse until the text box is the size you want

4 Release the mouse button. The box will be resized

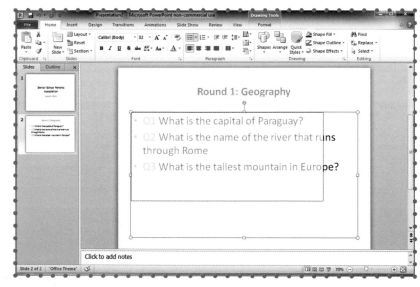

PowerPoint

MODIFY TEXT ON A SLIDE

Once you've positioned your text on a slide, you can alter the way it looks by changing the font, size, colour, style and spacing.

Text formatting options are available in the 'Font' group on the 'Home' tab. You'll also find a small button at the bottom right with an arrow pointing bottom right that, when clicked, opens the 'Font' dialog box for further formatting options as well as the 'Clear All Formatting' button for removing all formatting from selected text.

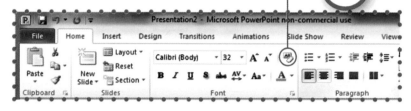

Formatting text in PowerPoint works the same way as formatting in Word. For more information on text formatting see pages 42–7.

Change horizontal text alignment

 Select the text you wish to change

2 On the **Home** tab, in the 'Paragraph' group, click one of the four alignment options
- ▶ **Align Text Left:** aligns all the selected text to the left margin
- ▶ **Centre:** aligns text an equal distance from the left and right margins
- ▶ **Align Text Right:** aligns all the selected text to the right margin
- ▶ **Justify:** justified text is equal on both sides and lines up equally to the right and left margins

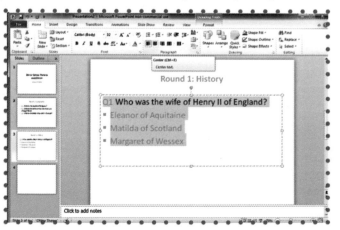

Change vertical text alignment

1 Select the text you wish to modify

2 On the **Home** tab, in the 'Paragraph' group, click **Align Text**

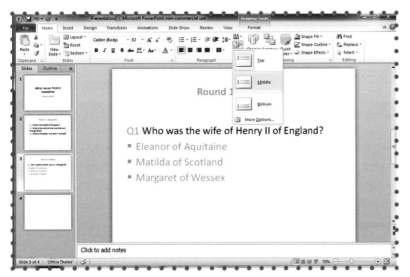

3 Select an option to align text at the 'Top', 'Middle' or 'Bottom' of the text box

Change text direction

1 Select the text you want to change

2 On the **Home** tab, in the 'Paragraph' group, click **Text Direction**

3 Select a text direction: 'Horizontal', 'Rotate' (with options for degree of rotation) or 'Stacked'

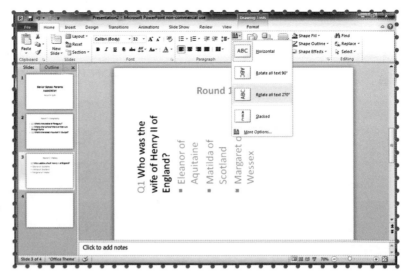

WORK WITH LISTS

Bulleted or numbered lists are a good way to present information that's easy for your audience to read.

Add a bulleted list

1 Select the text box – or specific text – that you want to format as a bulleted list

2 On the **Home** tab, in the 'Paragraph' group, click **Bullets**

3 A bulleted list will appear

You can change the style, colour, and size of the bullets in your list or switch to a numbered list. To change one bullet, place the cursor at the start of the line that you want to change. To change more than one bullet, select the text in all of the bullets that you want to change.

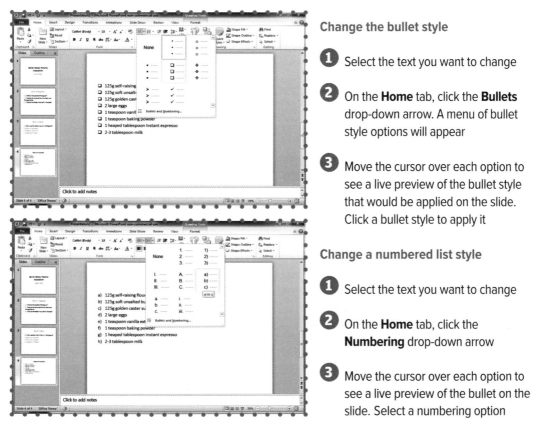

Change the bullet style

1 Select the text you want to change

2 On the **Home** tab, click the **Bullets** drop-down arrow. A menu of bullet style options will appear

3 Move the cursor over each option to see a live preview of the bullet style that would be applied on the slide. Click a bullet style to apply it

Change a numbered list style

1 Select the text you want to change

2 On the **Home** tab, click the **Numbering** drop-down arrow

3 Move the cursor over each option to see a live preview of the bullet on the slide. Select a numbering option

Change the starting number

By default, PowerPoint counts numbered lists from the number one, but you can change this to start counting from a different number.

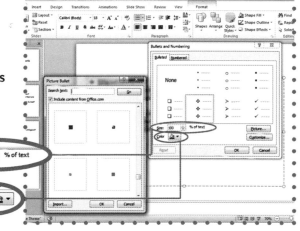

 Select the text you want to change. On the **Home** tab, click the **Bullets** drop-down arrow

 From the drop-down menu, select **Bullets and Numbering...**

③ In the dialog box that appears, click on the **Numbered** tab. Enter the number you wish the list to start from in the 'Start at' field. The list will update the numbering to begin with the new number

Change bullet size and colour

① Select an existing bulleted list. On the **Home** tab, click the **Bullets** drop-down arrow

② From the drop-down menu, select **Bullets and Numbering...**

③ On the **Bulleted** tab, set the bullet size using the 'Size' field. Click the down arrow next to 'Color' and choose a colour. Click **OK**. The list will update to show the new size and colour

Change bullet spacing

You can adjust the space between a bullet in a list and the text that applies to it by using PowerPoint's Ruler. The ruler is hidden by default. To show it, on the **View** tab, in the 'Show' group, tick the **Ruler** check box.

 Select the lines that you want to adjust

② On the Ruler, drag the 'First Line Indent' marker (see page 46) to the right or left. The bullet will move independently from the text

▶ PowerPoint

Use the 'Tab' key to create a quick indent. Place your cursor at the start of the paragraph and press the 'Tab' key. The first line will be indented. If the paragraph is part of a bulleted or numbered list, the entire paragraph will be indented.

INDENTS AND LINE SPACING

Adjusting line spacing and using indents can help make the text on your slides more readable. Also, by indenting some of the lines in a bulleted or numbered list, you can create a multi-level list.

Adjust indents

You can use PowerPoint's Indent commands on the 'Home' tab to quickly adjust indents. Alternatively, for more control over indents, you can manually adjust the indent markers and tab stops on the ruler. PowerPoint's indents work the same way as in Word – see page 46 for more on using indents.

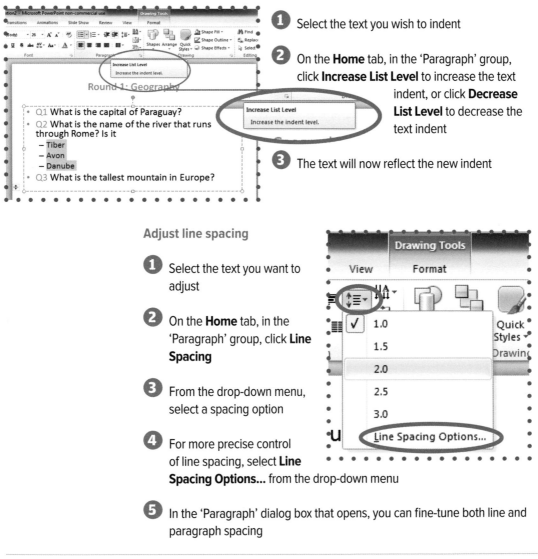

1 Select the text you wish to indent

2 On the **Home** tab, in the 'Paragraph' group, click **Increase List Level** to increase the text indent, or click **Decrease List Level** to decrease the text indent

3 The text will now reflect the new indent

Adjust line spacing

1 Select the text you want to adjust

2 On the **Home** tab, in the 'Paragraph' group, click **Line Spacing**

3 From the drop-down menu, select a spacing option

4 For more precise control of line spacing, select **Line Spacing Options...** from the drop-down menu

5 In the 'Paragraph' dialog box that opens, you can fine-tune both line and paragraph spacing

APPLY A THEME

PowerPoint comes with a range of built-in themes – pre-defined combinations of colours, fonts and effects that can be applied to your presentation. Using pre-designed themes makes it easy to create a consistent and professional-looking presentation or quickly change the overall look of your presentation at any time.

By default, PowerPoint uses the Office theme, which consists of a white background, the Calibri font and mostly black text, but it's easy to change the theme.

 On the **Design** tab, in the 'Themes' group, select a theme

 To access more themes, click the down arrow

 Move your cursor over a theme to see a live preview of it in the presentation

4 Click a theme to apply it to all the slides

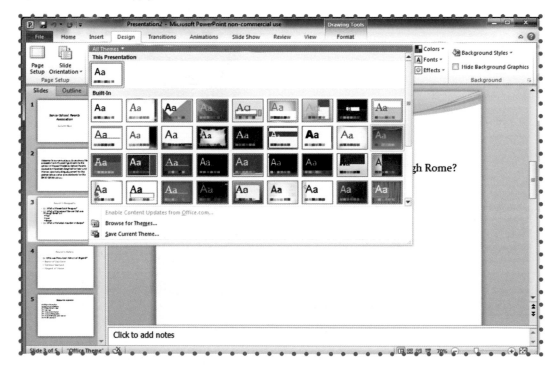

⏵ PowerPoint

TRY THIS

Once you've added pictures to your slides, you can edit them using picture tools. You can change their shape, crop and remove backgrounds as well as add borders and artistic effects. PowerPoint's pictures tools are found on the 'Home' tab and work exactly as Word's picture tools. See pages 60–5.

ADD IMAGES

Using photographs or clip art in your presentation helps communicate your ideas and engage the audience. You may even want to use PowerPoint to present a photo slideshow – for example, of a recent holiday or family event. You can add an image from a file, copy one from a web page or use a clip art image.

Add an image from a file

1 On the **Insert** tab, in the 'Images' group, click **Picture**

2 Find the picture that you want to insert, and click **Insert**

BE CAREFUL

While it's easy to copy and paste pictures and even video from websites, be sure to check the copyright of these items before you do. Check the website for copyright notices. Copyright is owned by the person who created the picture or video. It's illegal to copy and use anything protected by copyright without permission of the copyright owner.

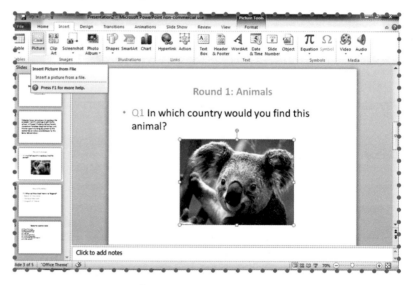

3 The picture will appear in your slide

Add an image from a web page

1 On the web page right click the picture you want, and then click **Copy**

2 In PowerPoint, right click on the slide where you want to place the picture and click **Paste**

Add clip art

 1 Place your cursor on the slide where you wish to insert the clip art

2 On the **Insert** tab, in the 'Images' group, click **Clip Art**

3 In the 'Clip Art' task pane, enter keywords in the **Search for** box. Use words or a phrase that describes the clip art that you want, or type in all or some of the file name of the clip art

TIP

You can also select the 'Insert Picture' from 'File' or the 'Insert Clip Art' from 'File' command in a placeholder to insert the relevant image type.

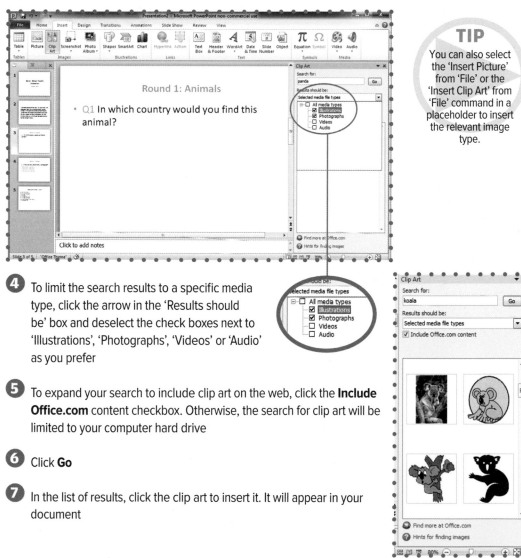

4 To limit the search results to a specific media type, click the arrow in the 'Results should be' box and deselect the check boxes next to 'Illustrations', 'Photographs', 'Videos' or 'Audio' as you prefer

5 To expand your search to include clip art on the web, click the **Include Office.com** content checkbox. Otherwise, the search for clip art will be limited to your computer hard drive

6 Click **Go**

7 In the list of results, click the clip art to insert it. It will appear in your document

Use a picture or clip as a slide background

You can use an image as a background to one or more slides in your presentation. Here's how:

1 In the **Slides** tab, click the slide that you want to add a background picture to. To select multiple slides, click the first slide, and then press and hold **Ctrl** while you click the other slides

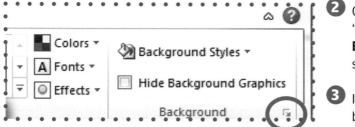

2 On the **Design** tab, in the 'Background' group, click the **Dialog Box Launcher** button, which is the small button at the bottom right

3 In the 'Format Background' dialog box that appears, click **Fill**, and then click **Picture or texture** fill

4 Under Insert from, choose one of the following:

▶ To insert a picture from a file, click **File...**, locate the picture that you want to insert, and then double click it

▶ To paste a picture that you have copied, click **Clipboard**

▶ To use clip art, click **Clip Art...**, and then in the 'Search text' box, type a keyword that describes the clip that you want, click **Go**, and then click the clip to insert it. To include clip art from Office.com in your search, remember to tick the **Include content from Office.com** box

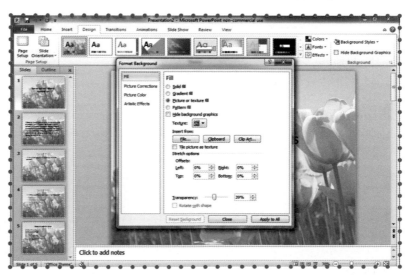

Resize an image

 Click on the image in the slide

 Move your cursor over any one of the corner sizing handles. The cursor will become a pair of directional arrows

3 Click and hold the cursor on the resizing handle, and drag your mouse until the image is the desired size

4 Release the mouse. The image will be resized

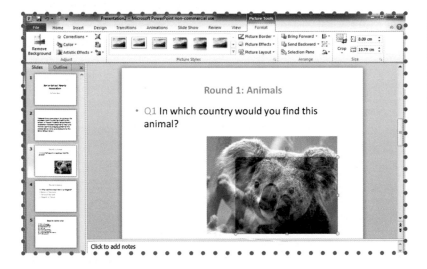

TRY THIS

When resizing an image, use the corner handles to keep its existing proportions. To rotate the image, click and drag on the green circle located at the top of the image.

Move an image

1 Click on the image. The cursor will turn into a cross with arrows

2 Hold down the mouse button and drag the image to the new location

 Release the mouse button. The box will be moved

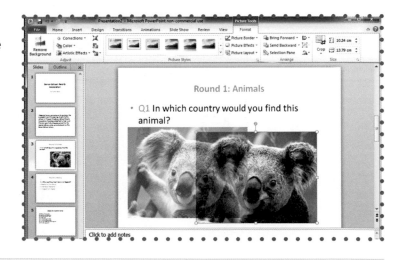

PowerPoint

WORK WITH SHAPES AND WORDART

Make your slides more visually exciting by using PowerPoint's shape and WordArt features.

You can add a wide range of shapes including rectangles, circles, lines, arrows, stars, suns and moons. PowerPoint's Shapes tools work in exactly the same way as in Word. See pages 66–8 for how to add, move, and modify a shape.

As with Word, PowerPoint's WordArt feature lets you create stylised text with effects such as shadows, outlines and textures. You can also transform the text to give it a wavy, slanted, or distorted look. WordArt effects can be applied to any text on a slide.

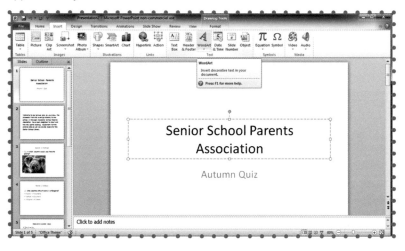

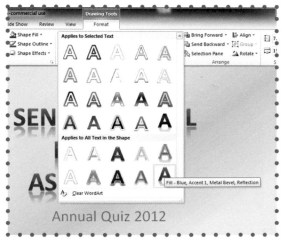

Apply a WordArt style to text

A WordArt Style automatically applies several effects to your text at once. You can then fine-tune text with individual effects.

1 Select the text box or some of the text inside a text box

2 On the **Format** tab, in the 'WordArt Styles' group, click the **More** drop-down arrow to see all available styles. Select the desired style preset to apply the style to your text

Modify WordArt effects

1 Select the text box, or some of the text inside a text box

2 On the **Format** tab, in the 'WordArt Styles' group, click **Text Effects**. A drop-down menu appears showing the effect categories

3 Move your cursor over an effect category to see a drop-down menu with a range of presets. Moving your cursor over a preset shows a live preview of that effect

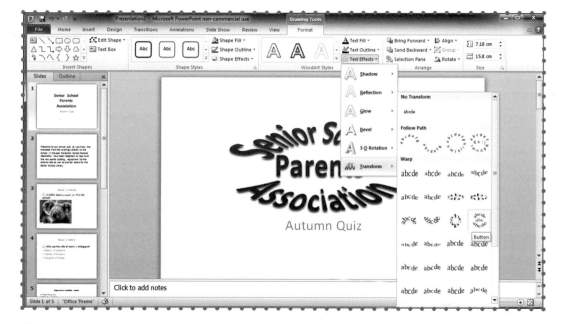

4 Click an effect preset to apply it to your text. You can combine several different effects to achieve the look you want

5 Use the 'Text Fill' and 'Text Outline' drop-down boxes in the 'WordArt Styles' group to modify the fill and outline colour if required

▶ PowerPoint

ARRANGE SHAPES AND OBJECTS

Any one of PowerPoint's presentation slides may contain several elements such as placeholders, text boxes, pictures and shapes. It can be fiddly and time-consuming trying to arrange items individually, but PowerPoint has several tools that solve the problem. You can select and then arrange several items at once – and by grouping objects you can rotate, flip, move or resize all items at the same time as if they were a single object.

Align two or more objects

1 Click and drag your mouse to draw a selection box around the objects to be aligned

2 On the **Format** tab, click **Align** and select **Align Selected Objects**

3 Click **Align** again and choose one of the six alignment options. The objects will align to each other based on the option you select

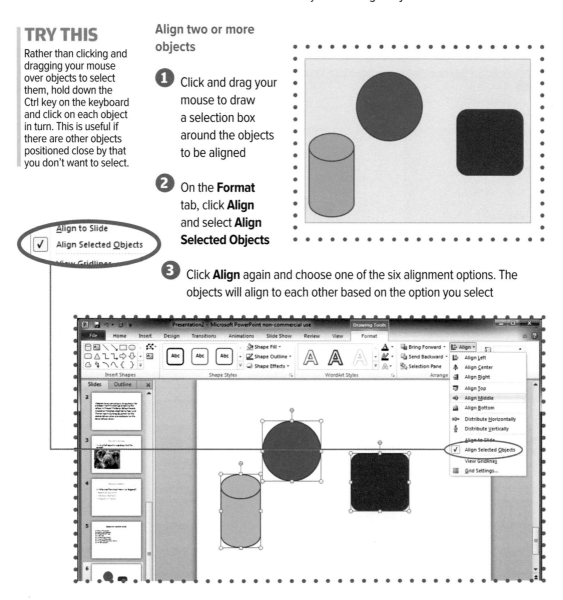

Distribute objects evenly

To make a slide with several objects in a row or column look neater, you can position them at an equal distance from one another. This can be done either horizontally or vertically.

1 Click and drag your mouse to form a selection box around the objects you want to align

2 On the **Format** tab, click **Align**

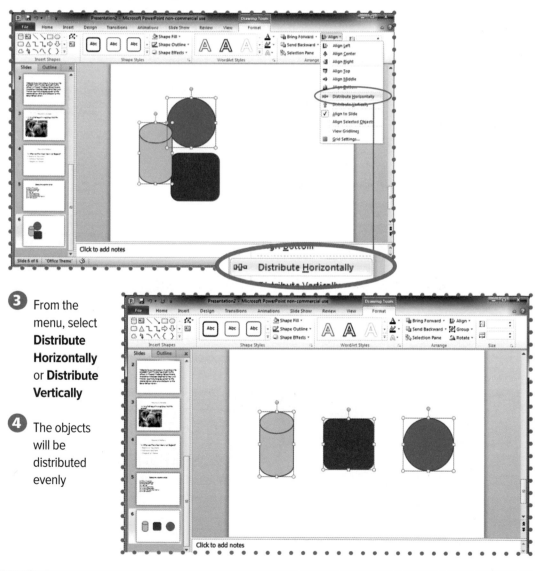

3 From the menu, select **Distribute Horizontally** or **Distribute Vertically**

4 The objects will be distributed evenly

Align objects to the slide

You can align one or more objects to a specific location on a slide, such as the top or bottom by selecting the 'Align to Slide' option before aligning the objects themselves.

1 Click and drag your mouse to create a selection box around the objects you want to align

2 On the **Format** tab, click **Align** and then click **Align to Slide**

3 Click **Align** again and select one of the six alignment options

4 The objects will align to the slide based on your selection

Stack objects

You can stack objects so that one appears in front of another or even change the order in which each appears on a slide.

1 Right click the object (or set of grouped objects) that you want to bring to the front or send to the back

2 From the pop-up menu select a stacking order. The object will move according to your selection

> **TIP**
> To ungroup objects, select the group and on the **Format** tab, click **Group** and then select **Ungroup**.

Group objects

Rather than selecting multiple objects each time you want to move or change them, you can group them into one object.

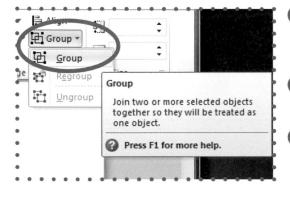

1 Click and drag your mouse to create a selection box around the objects you want to group

2 On the **Format** tab, in the 'Arrange' group, click the **Group** button, and then click **Group**

3 The selected objects will be grouped and shown surrounded by a single selection box with sizing handles

USE SMARTART, TABLES AND CHARTS

PowerPoint 2010 offers lots of ways to present information. You can use SmartArt graphics to visually show information rather than simply using lines and paragraphs of text. PowerPoint's SmartArt tools and commands are the same as those in Word 2010. See pages 71–3 to learn how to add and modify SmartArt graphics in your presentation.

Tables are another popular way to display information and numerical data on a slide. You can insert a table on your slide, apply table styles and format tables using various commands. PowerPoint and Word share the same commands and tools for working with tables – see pages 74–7 for step-by-step guidance on creating and modifying tables.

Charts are also a good way to communicate information graphically and PowerPoint includes a wide range of charts and graphs. You can choose from line graphs, column charts, pie charts, bar charts, area graphs, scatter graphs and stock charts to name a few – so it's easy to find one that's perfect for your data.

PowerPoint 2010 uses an Excel worksheet as a placeholder for entering chart data. When you insert or edit a chart in PowerPoint, an Excel 2010 window will automatically open.

Add a chart

1 On the **Insert** tab, in the Illustrations group, click **Chart**

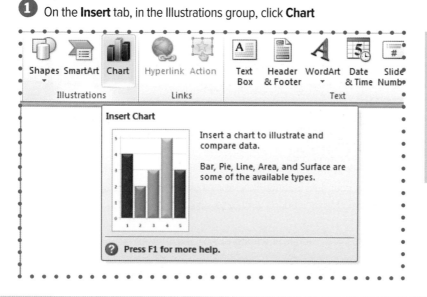

TRY THIS

Once you've added a chart to a slide, a set of 'Chart Tools' will appear on the Ribbon when the chart is selected. You can use the three tabs under 'Chart Tools' to modify your chart – from chart type, layout and style to switching row and column data.

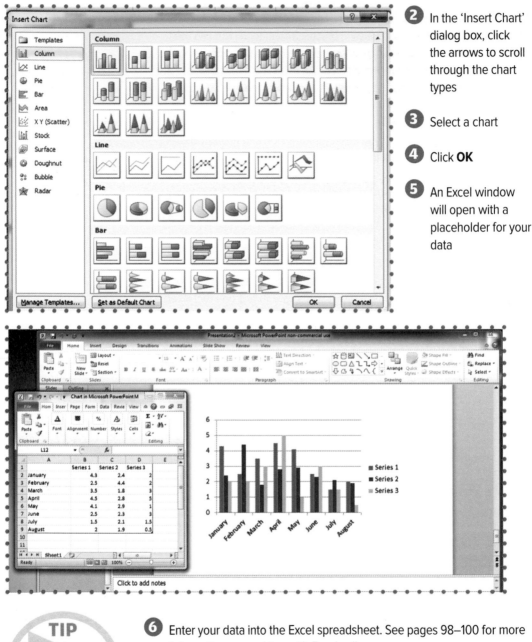

2 In the 'Insert Chart' dialog box, click the arrows to scroll through the chart types

3 Select a chart

4 Click **OK**

5 An Excel window will open with a placeholder for your data

TIP

Edit chart data at any time by selecting your chart and clicking **Edit Data** in the Data group on the **Chart Tools Design** tab.

6 Enter your data into the Excel spreadsheet. See pages 98–100 for more information on working with Excel cells

7 Close Excel – there's no need to save the spreadsheet

8 The PowerPoint chart will update to reflect the new source data

Add a linked Excel spreadsheet

You can import and link an existing Excel spreadsheet to your PowerPoint 2010 presentation. The advantage of doing this is that if you make any updates to the original Excel spreadsheet, it will automatically update in your PowerPoint presentation, as long as the files remain linked.

1 On the **Insert** tab, in the Text group, click **Object**

2 In the dialog box, select **Create from file**

TRY THIS

In the Excel spreadsheet, you can choose the data you want to include in the chart by clicking and dragging the lower-right corner of the blue line to increase or decrease the data range for rows and columns. Only the data inside the blue lines will appear in the chart.

3 Click **Browse...**

4 Select an Excel chart, then click **OK**

TIP

To edit an imported chart, double click it to open the Excel placeholder. When you've finished, save the chart in Excel.

5 Click the **Link checkbox** to link the data to the Excel chart. This mean the PowerPoint chart will update itself when changes are made to the Excel chart

6 Click **OK**. The chart will now appear in your PowerPoint presentation

PowerPoint

ANIMATE OBJECTS AND TEXT

In PowerPoint 2010 you can animate text, pictures, shapes, SmartArt graphics and other objects to give your presentation more impact and draw your audience's attention to important content.

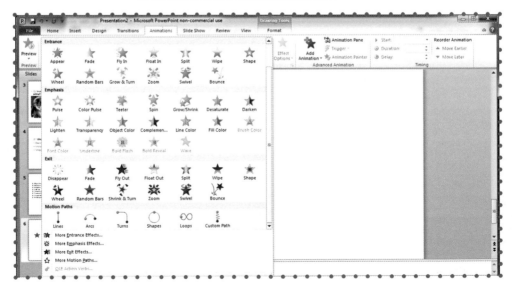

There are four types of animation effects in PowerPoint:

▶ **Entrance** affects how an object enters a slide, for example you can make an object fly onto the slide from the left edge

▶ **Emphasis** effects apply to the object while it's viewable on the slide; for example, an object could grow in size or change colour

▶ **Exit** affects how an object leaves a slide. These effects include making an object fly off the slide, disappear from view or spiral off the slide

▶ **Motion Paths** can be used to make an object move, for example to follow a path across the slide or move in a circular pattern

Add an animation to an object

1 Select the object

2 On the **Animations** tab, in the 'Animation' group, click the **More** drop-down arrow to see available animations

3 Select an animation effect

4 The object will now have a small number next to it to show that it has an animation. In the 'Slide' pane, a star symbol will appear next to the slide with the animation

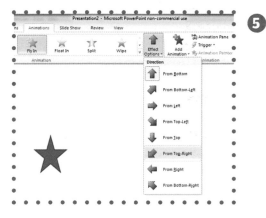

5 Some effects have options that you can change. For example, with the 'Fly In' effect, you can specify which direction the object enters the slide from. You can find these options in the **Effect Options** command in the 'Animation' group

Add multiple animation effects to a single object

Sometimes you may want to use more than one animation on an object, such as an 'Entrance' and an 'Exit' effect. To do this, use the 'Add Animation' command, which lets you add new animations while keeping existing ones.

1 Select the text or object to which you want to add multiple animations

2 On the **Animations** tab, in the 'Advanced Animation' group, click **Add Animation**

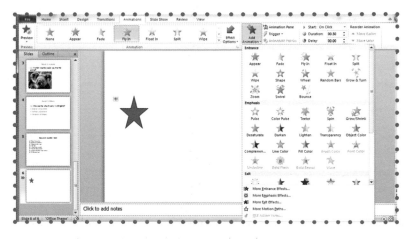

▶ PowerPoint

3 Select an animation effect

4 A different number will appear next to the object for each animation effect applied. The numbers indicate the order in which the effects take place

Change the order of the animations

1 Select the number of the effect that you want to change

2 On the **Animations** tab, click the **Move Earlier** or **Move Later** commands to change the ordering

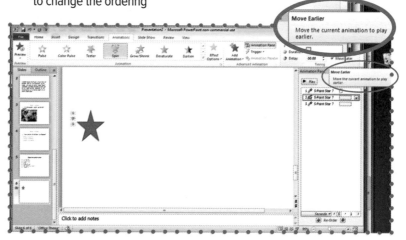

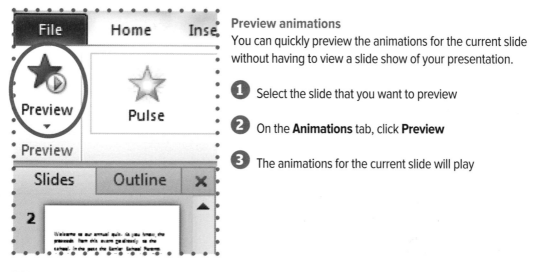

Preview animations

You can quickly preview the animations for the current slide without having to view a slide show of your presentation.

1 Select the slide that you want to preview

2 On the **Animations** tab, click **Preview**

3 The animations for the current slide will play

ADD VIDEO

PowerPoint lets you add video (see pages 200–10) to your presentation from a file on your computer or from a website such as YouTube. You can edit the video within PowerPoint and change its appearance with a 'Video Style'.

Insert a video from a file on your computer

1 On the **Insert** tab, click the **Video** drop-down arrow and select **Video from File**

2 Select a video file and click **Insert**

3 The video will be added to the slide

Insert a video from a website

PowerPoint lets you embed web videos in your slides. This only works with videos from websites such as YouTube that provide the embed code.

1 On the website that contains the video (YouTube, for example), locate and copy the embed code. On YouTube, for example, click the **Share** button under the video playback window and then click **Embed** to view the embed code

2 In PowerPoint, click the **Insert** tab

Jargon buster

Embed code
Program code that's provided by some websites such as YouTube that lets you place their video or audio content on your own webpage. You copy the embed code and paste it into your website where you want the content to play.

3 Click the **Video** drop-down arrow, and select **Video from Web Site**

4 In the space provided, right click and select **Paste**. The embed code will appear

5 Click **Insert**. The video will be added to the slide

Resize the video

1 Select the video. A box with resizing handles will appear around the video

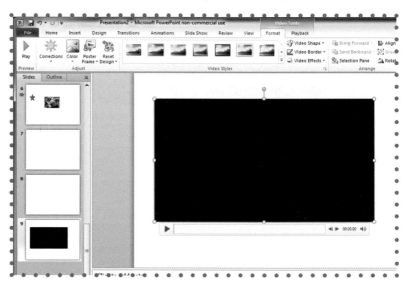

2 Click and drag any of the handles to resize the movie

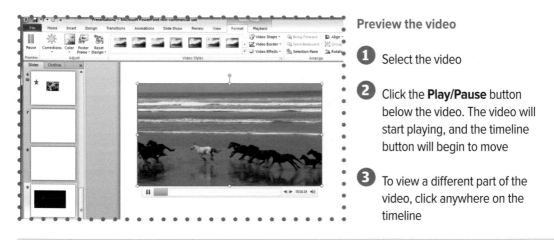

Preview the video

1 Select the video

2 Click the **Play/Pause** button below the video. The video will start playing, and the timeline button will begin to move

3 To view a different part of the video, click anywhere on the timeline

ADD AUDIO

You can add a sound to your presentation in a number of ways from adding background music and sound effects to a spoken commentary that accompanies the slides. PowerPoint comes with a collection of Clip Art audio or you can add an audio file stored on your computer.

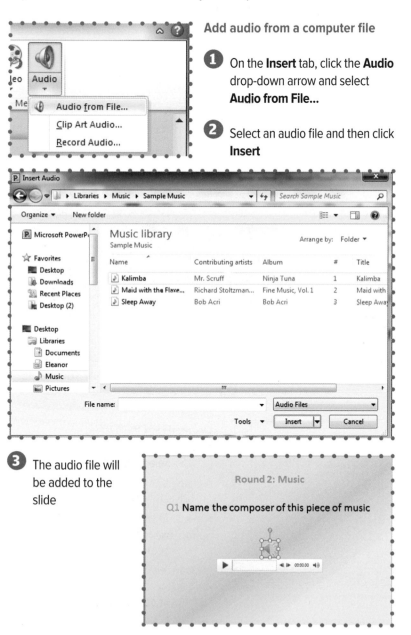

Add audio from a computer file

1 On the **Insert** tab, click the **Audio** drop-down arrow and select **Audio from File...**

2 Select an audio file and then click **Insert**

3 The audio file will be added to the slide

▶ PowerPoint

Add clip art audio

1 On the **Insert** tab, click the **Audio** drop-down arrow and select **Clip Art Audio**

2 In the 'Clip Art' pane on the right, type keywords in the 'Search for' field and click **Go**

3 The results will appear in the 'Clip Art' pane

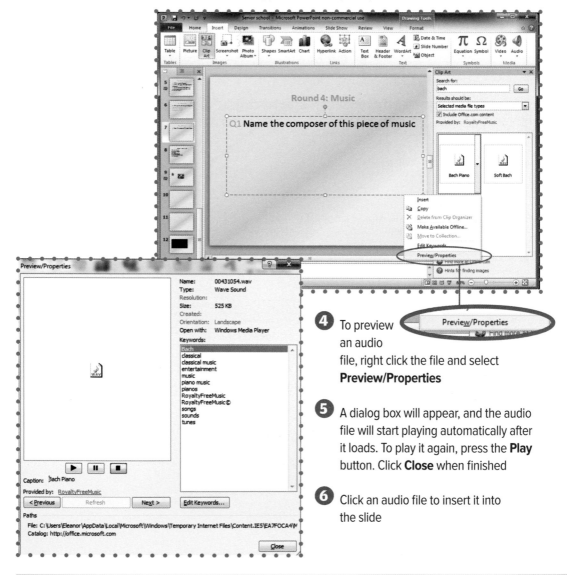

4 To preview an audio file, right click the file and select **Preview/Properties**

5 A dialog box will appear, and the audio file will start playing automatically after it loads. To play it again, press the **Play** button. Click **Close** when finished

6 Click an audio file to insert it into the slide

Record your own audio

If you want the presentation to include narration, PowerPoint lets you record your own audio using a microphone. Most computers have built-in microphones or you can buy one that plugs into the computer's microphone port.

1 On the **Insert** tab, click the **Audio** drop-down arrow and select **Record Audio**

2 Type a name for the audio recording

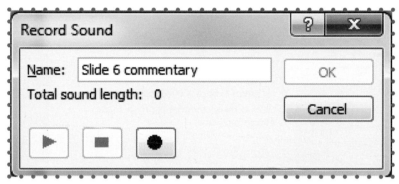

3 Click the red **Record** button to start recording

4 Click the blue **Stop** button to stop recording

5 To preview your recording, click the **Play** button

6 When you're done, click **OK**

7 The audio file will be added to the slide

PowerPoint

TRY THIS
To preview a transition,
click **Preview** on
the **Transitions** tab.
Alternatively, in the **Slides**
tab click on the **Play
Animations** icon on a
slide that includes
a transition.

APPLY TRANSITIONS

Make your presentation more engaging by using transitions. Transitions are motion effects that apply, in 'Slide Show View', when you move from one slide to another. There are lots of different styles of transitions to choose from and you can customise the speed of each and even add sound.

Add a transition

1 Select the slide you wish to apply a transition to

2 On the **Transitions** tab, in the 'Transition to This Slide' group, you'll see a list of transitions to choose from

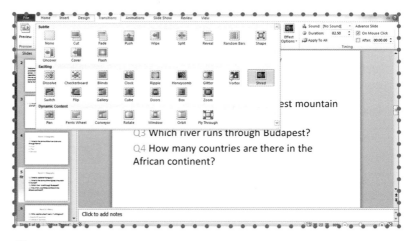

3 Click the **More** drop-down arrow to see all the transitions

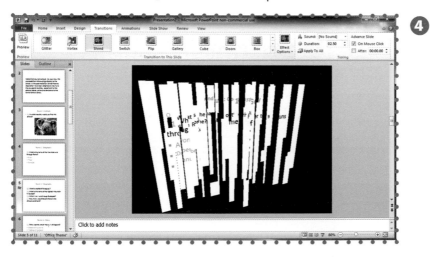

4 Click a transition to apply it to the selected slide. This will automatically preview the transition as well. In this case, 'Shred' makes the slide appear to be shredded into narrow strips as it moves to the next slide

Click the down arrow on the **Effect Options** button to fine-tune your chosen transition

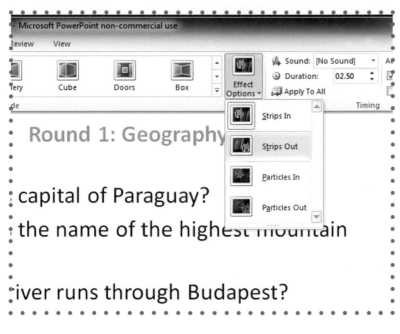

Change the duration of the transition

1 Select the slide that includes the transition you wish to modify

2 In the **Transitions** tab, in the 'Timing' group, enter the amount of time you want the transition to take in the 'Duration' field. In this example, the length is 3 seconds: 03.00

Add sound to a transition

1 Select the slide that includes the transition you wish to add sound to

2 On the **Transitions** tab, in the 'Timing' group, click the **Sound** drop-down menu

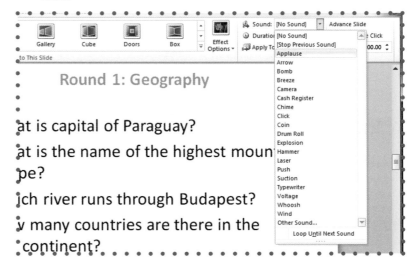

3 Hover over each sound to hear it and see a live preview of the transition

4 Click a sound to apply it to the selected slide transition

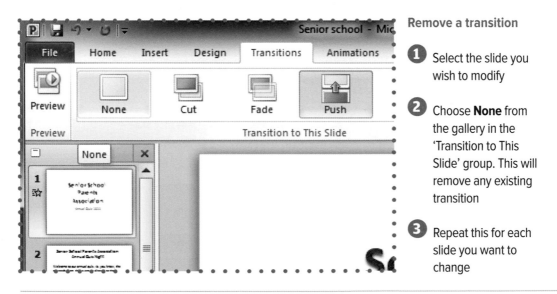

Remove a transition

1 Select the slide you wish to modify

2 Choose **None** from the gallery in the 'Transition to This Slide' group. This will remove any existing transition

3 Repeat this for each slide you want to change

Move through slides automatically

Usually when showing your presentation in 'Slide Show View', you move from one slide to another by clicking your mouse or pressing **Enter** on your keyboard. However, with the 'Advance Slide' settings in the 'Timing' group, you can set the presentation to progress through slides on its own – setting the amount of time each slide is displayed for.

1 Select the slide you wish to modify

2 On the **Transitions** tab, under 'Advance Slide' in the 'Timing' group, uncheck the box next to 'On Mouse Click'

3 In the 'After' field, enter the amount of time you want to display the slide

4 Select another slide and repeat the process until all the slides have the appropriate timing

▶ PowerPoint

TIP

Make the notes area bigger in Normal View by dragging the horizontal separator between slide and notes upwards.

CREATE NOTES

As you build your presentation, you can create notes for each slide. Notes can help you to focus on the important information when delivering the presentation. They're not viewable by your audience although, if you want to share them, they can be printed.

To add notes to slides you must be in 'Normal View', which is the default view when you first open PowerPoint. To switch to 'Normal View', if necessary, on the 'View' tab, in the 'Presentation Views' group, click **Normal**.

Add a note to a slide

1 In 'Normal View', you will see a narrow area below your slide that says Click to add notes

2 Click in the notes area and start typing

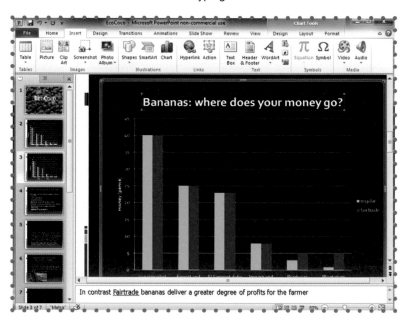

3 Although you can type lengthy notes here, you can view only a couple of lines at a time and will need to use the vertical scrollbar to scroll through text. To read a larger amount of text, click the **View** tab and in the 'Presentation Views' group click **Notes Page**. This shows a plan view of the page with the slide at the top, and a large area to type notes into at the bottom. Click in the box and start typing your notes

Print notes pages with slide thumbnails

1 Click the **File** tab

2 On the left-hand side of the 'Backstage view' dialog box, click **Print**

3 Under 'Settings', click the arrow next to **Full Page Slides**, and then under 'Print Layout', click **Notes Pages**

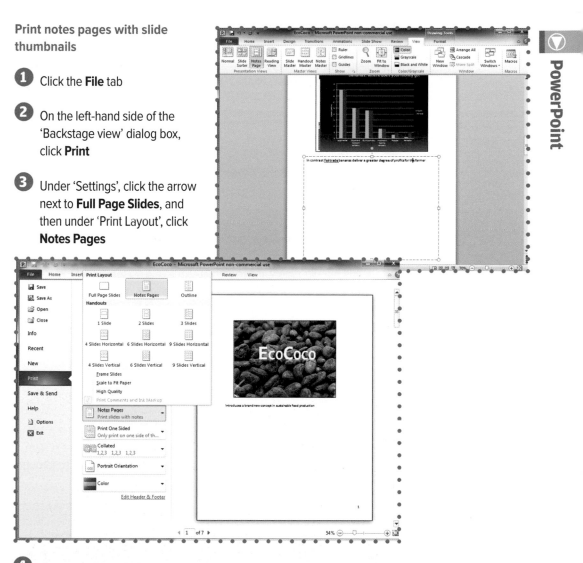

4 Specify the page orientation and the print options you want

5 Click **Print**

You can also print your notes without slide thumbnails. First open each slide in 'Notes Page' view and delete the slide thumbnail from each of the notes pages by clicking the thumbnail, and pressing **Delete** on your keyboard. Then follow the steps above to print your notes.

▶ PowerPoint

PRESENT YOUR SLIDE SHOW

Once you've created all the slides in your presentation, you can practise presenting them as a slide show to an audience. PowerPoint has several tools that help to make your presentation successful.

Start your slide show

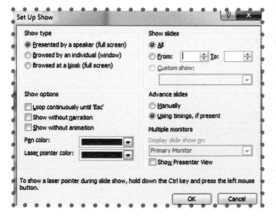

1 On the **Slide Show** tab, in the 'Start Slide Show' group, click **From Beginning** to start with the first slide

2 If you prefer to start with a different slide, select the slide and click on **From Current Slide** from the 'Start Slide Show' group

3 To end the slide show, move your cursor to the bottom left of the screen. A small icon that looks like a white box with lines of text will appear. Click this icon and from the pop-up menu click **End Show**. Alternatively, press the **Esc** key at the top left of your keyboard to end the slide show

Move forwards and backwards through the slides

1 Move your cursor over the bottom right of the screen. A menu will appear

2 Click on the right arrow to move onto the next slide or click on the left arrow to move backwards through the slides

Slide show set-up options

Use slide show set-up options to fine-tune your presentation, including setting timing for advancing through your slides and specifying which slides are shown. You can also create a self-running presentation with continuous looping. This is helpful if you're creating a slideshow for a shop window or small business, allowing it to run continually.

On the **Slide Show** tab, in the 'Set Up' group, click **Set Up Slide Show**. The 'Set Up Show' dialog box will appear. Choose from the options available. Click **OK** to apply the settings

TIPS FOR MAKING A GREAT PRESENTATION

Plan your presentation
Work out the structure of your presentation before you start creating slides. This not only saves time, it will help you to plan the right number and type of slides needed for a successful presentation.

Minimise the number of slides
To keep your audience's interest and communicate your key message, keep presentations short and to the point.

Use an audience-friendly font and font size
Remember that the audience has to view your slides from a distance, so choose a font that's easy to read and don't use it less than 24pt in size.

Use contrasting colours for text and background
A light background with dark coloured text or dark background with light coloured text work best. Aim for a consistent design and colour theme that doesn't detract from your message.

Keep text simple
If a slide has too much text, your audience will focus on reading it all rather than listening to your presentation. Use short sentences and bullets.

Use visuals
Photos, charts, graphs and SmartArt graphics can help communicate your information in a way that keeps your audience interested in the presentation. Make sure charts and graphs are understandable with clear short labels. However, try to avoid including too many visual aids on a slide.

Check the spelling and grammar
Poorly written slides full of spelling mistakes will ruin a presentation, so always check the spelling and grammar in your presentation. To check spelling in your presentation, click the **Review** tab and then click **Spelling**. This opens the 'Spelling' dialog box, which will offer one or more suggestions for each spelling mistake in your presentation. You can select a suggestion and then click **Change** to correct the error. PowerPoint's spelling command works the same way as the same command in Word 2010. See pages 81–4 for more information.

▶ PowerPoint

KEYBOARD SHORTCUTS

Press these keys	To do this
Ctrl + N	Create a new presentation
Ctrl + O	Open a presentation
Ctrl + S	Save the presentation with its current file name and location
Ctrl + P	Print a presentation
Ctrl + Z	Undo the last action
Ctrl + C	Copy selection
Ctrl + X	Cut selection
Ctrl + V	Paste copied selection
Ctrl + Shift + C	Copy formatting only
Ctrl + Shift + V	Paste formatting only
Ctrl + Alt + V	Open the 'Paste Special' dialog box
Ctrl + T	Open the 'Font' dialog box
Ctrl + Shift + >	Increase the font size of the selected text
Ctrl + Shift + <	Decrease the font size of the selected text
Shift + F3	Change the case of letters
Ctrl + B	Apply bold formatting
Ctrl + U	Apply an underline
Ctrl + I	Apply italic formatting
Ctrl + E	Centre a paragraph
Ctrl + J	Justify a paragraph
Ctrl + L	Left align a paragraph.
Ctrl + R	Right align a paragraph
End	Move to the end of a line
Home	Move to the beginning of a line
Ctrl + Up arrow	Move up one paragraph
Ctrl + Down arrow	Move down one paragraph
Ctrl + End	Move to the end of a text box
Ctrl + Home	Move to the beginning of a text box
Ctrl + Shift + Tab	Switch between 'Slides' and 'Outline' tabs in the 'Outline and Slide's pane in 'Normal' view
F5	Start a slideshow
N	Go to the next slide in slideshow
Enter or Page down or spacebar	Go to the next slide in slideshow
P or Page up	Go back to the previous slide
Esc	End a slide show

PDFs

By reading this chapter you will get to grips with:

 **Creating a PDF file**

Opening and printing a PDF file

Adding comments to shared PDF files

WHAT IS A PDF FILE?

Sometimes, you can spend lots of time and effort creating a document, spreadsheet or presentation only to find that the people you send it to can't open the file to read it. It may be they simply don't have the same software that was used to originally create the file, or have a different version that can't view your file. It may even be that you created your files on a Windows computer and they use an Apple Mac.

Whatever the reason, it can be frustrating. Fortunately, there's an easy solution – you can share your document as a special kind of file, known as a PDF file.

Created by Adobe, Portable Document Format or PDF is a file format that's independent of application software, hardware and operating systems. This means a PDF file can be opened on any type of computer or device using Adobe's free Adobe Reader software – no matter what software was originally used to create the file.

Furthermore, a PDF file faithfully preserves the look and feel of the original document complete with fonts, colours, images and layout.

You may have seen PDF documents already, as it's the most popular file format for sharing digital information. It is commonly used for online documents, manuals, government publications, leaflets, forms and downloadable menus from websites – and many ebooks and digital magazines are available as PDF files.

Advantages of PDF files

There are several key advantages of the format that makes PDF the most popular choice for sharing files digitally.

Free to read PDF files can be opened and viewed with a piece of free software called Adobe Reader. You can quickly and freely download the latest version from Adobe's website (www.adobe.com).

Compatibility PDF files can be viewed and printed on virtually any computer type including Windows, Apple Mac and Unix – as well as mobile devices such as ebook readers.

Accurate PDF documents look exactly as they do in the original application with text, photos, images and charts reproduced faithfully.

Small file size Although a PDF file keeps the exact layout and content of the original document, this information (particularly graphic elements such as photographs) is highly compressed, which results in smaller files. This means PDF is a popular choice for sending files by email or for downloading from a website.

Read-only format PDF files can be opened, but not altered. This makes a PDF file ideal for situations where the authenticity of a document is important, for example a legal contract or an invoice.

Searchable A PDF file can be searched, which makes finding the exact content you want easy. Long PDF documents can be organised with a table of contents linking all sections through an easy-to-use menu.

Interactive PDF files support interactive functions such as hyperlinks, music, video and file attachments. They can also include interactive forms, in which the reader can complete information, save the file and return it to the sender.

Security You can password protect a PDF file so that only those with your permission can open it.

Jargon buster

Hyperlink
A hyperlink can be either text or an image on a web page or in a PDF document that lets you jump straight to another web page when you click on it.

PDFs

BE CAREFUL

A smaller size PDF file will have poorer quality images, as they will have been highly compressed to create a small file. This won't matter if you are going to view the PDF file on screen but if you intend to print the PDF file, you won't be able to get a high-quality print. If you're unsure about which 'Optimise for setting' to choose, create a PDF file in each option, then compare the two for their image quality and file size.

CREATE A PDF FILE IN OFFICE 2010

Microsoft Office 2010 has a built-in PDF writer so you can create PDF files in Word, Excel and PowerPoint with a few clicks.

There are two ways to create PDF documents in the Office 2010 applications. You can use the 'Save As' function and select the PDF format or use the 'Share' menu and choose the option to create a PDF document. The example below uses Word 2010.

1 With the Word document open, click the **File** tab to go to the Backstage view

2 Click **Save As**

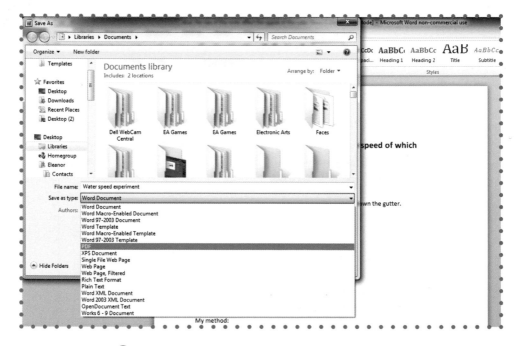

3 If necessary, enter a name for the file in the 'File name' box

4 In the 'Save as type' list, click **PDF**

5 When you choose the PDF file type, the options outlined on the next page become available:

Optimize for affects the file size and quality of the PDF that's created. If you want the smallest file size possible, perhaps for emailing the PDF to someone to read onscreen, choose **Minimum size (publishing online)**. If, at some point, you may want a high-quality print of the PDF choose **Standard (publishing online and printing)**

Open file after publishing: tick this box, if you want to view the document as a PDF after saving

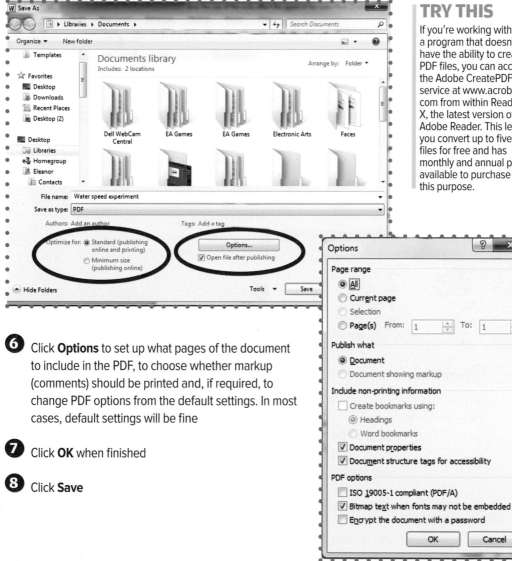

TRY THIS

If you're working with a program that doesn't have the ability to create PDF files, you can access the Adobe CreatePDF service at www.acrobat. com from within Reader X, the latest version of Adobe Reader. This lets you convert up to five files for free and has monthly and annual plans available to purchase for this purpose.

6 Click **Options** to set up what pages of the document to include in the PDF, to choose whether markup (comments) should be printed and, if required, to change PDF options from the default settings. In most cases, default settings will be fine

7 Click **OK** when finished

8 Click **Save**

▶ PDFs

DOWNLOAD A PDF FILE

PDF files are a common way of sharing information on the web and you may visit a website that offers PDF files for download – such as a menu on a restaurant's website. You may also receive a PDF file via email, such as a catalogue or leaflet.

Download a PDF file from a web page

1 Right click the web link to the PDF file

2 From the pop-up menu, choose **Save Link As...**

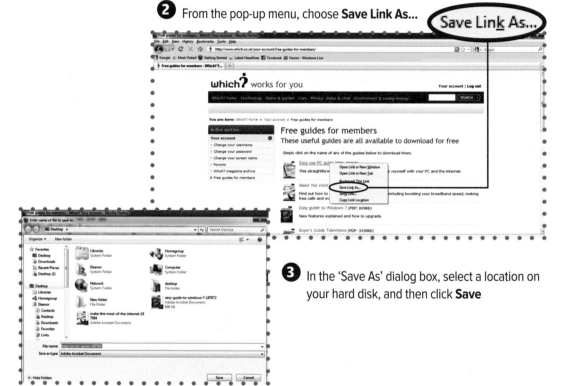

3 In the 'Save As' dialog box, select a location on your hard disk, and then click **Save**

Save a PDF file from an email message
In this example, the steps are based on Microsoft Live Mail, but they will be very similar in other email software

Open a message that contains an attachment by double-clicking it in the message list. In the message window, click the **File** menu, and then click **Save Attachments**. Select the folder where you want to save the attachments

OPEN A PDF FILE

Before you can open a PDF file, you need to make sure you have the correct software to read the file.

1 Click

2 In the search box, type 'Adobe Reader'. If it appears in the list, double click to open. If it is not already installed on your computer, type the following address into your web browser: http://get.adobe.com/uk/reader/

3 Click **Download now**, and follow the onscreen instructions to download and install the software

4 Once the software is installed, it should automatically open any PDF file that you double click on with your mouse

TRY THIS

If you have problems opening a PDF file with Adobe Reader, try right-clicking on the file icon, selecting **Open With** and clicking on **Adobe Reader** from the pop-up menu.

Open with Adobe Reader 9
Open
Print
Scan with AVG Free
Open with ▶
Share with ▶
Restore previous versions
Send to ▶
Cut
Copy
Create shortcut
Delete
Rename
Properties

TRY THIS

You can configure your web browser to open PDF files either within the browser window or in a separate window. Adobe's website (www. adobe.com) has detailed instructions on how to do so for different browsers.

PDFS

WORK WITH PDF FILES

When you're working on a document, presentation or spreadsheet with others, it's useful to get everyone's feedback before you finalise the file. With Adobe Reader X, you can make comments on a PDF file using the 'Sticky Notes' and 'Highlighter' tools. When you send the file back to the person who sent it to you or pass it on to someone else, they will be able to see your comments.

Unfortunately, you can't edit PDF files to make permanent changes using the free Reader. To do this, you need to buy Adobe's full Acrobat software.

Add a sticky note

The most common type of comment is the sticky note. This appears on the page as a note icon with a pop-up panel that contains your text message. You can add a sticky note anywhere on the page or in the document area.

1 Open the PDF file in Adobe Reader X

2 Select the **Sticky Note** tool from the top toolbar

3 On the document, click where you want to place the note, or drag to create a custom-sized note

4 Type text in the pop-up note. You can also copy and paste text from the PDF file into the note

5 Click the close button in the top right-hand corner of the note box to close the window. To quickly read a sticky note without opening the window, simply move your cursor over the note icon to display the associated text

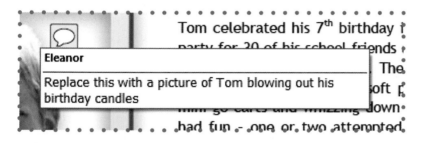

Edit a sticky note comment

1 Click the **note** icon to open

2 Make changes, as needed

3 To resize the pop-up note, drag the lower-left or lower-right corner

4 When you're finished, click the **minimize button** in the upper-right corner of the pop-up note or click outside the pop-up note

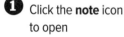

PDFs

185

PDFs

Delete a sticky note

 Select the **Sticky Note** tool

② Select the **note** icon, and press **Delete**

Highlight text

Another commenting feature available in Reader is the ability to add a highlight with a note.

① Open the PDF file in Acrobat Reader X

② Click the **Highlight Text** icon from the top toolbar

 Drag from the beginning of the text you want to mark up, holding down the Ctrl key and dragging to mark up a rectangular area of text. This is handy when marking up text in a column

ebrated his 7th birthday in style this month. We threw a
r 30 of his school friends at the Hertswood Leisure Centre
e indoor play areas. The children enjoyed two hours of
mbing through the soft play area, tearing around in the
carts and whizzing down the m
- one or two attempted the st
in some hilarious moments.

💬 ▾ **Eleanor**
22/06/2011 12:01:00

Hertsmere

as followed by a fantastic te
n - many thanks to her for all
ty Sam. Sandwiches, crisps, and
hed in a very short time by the

 To add a note, double click the highlighted text to add a comment in a pop-up note

PHOTOS & VIDEOS

By reading this chapter you will get to grips with:

- **Organising your digital photos**

- **Editing and sharing your digital photos**

- **Using video editing tools to create home videos**

▶ Photos & Videos

WINDOWS LIVE ESSENTIALS

If you use Windows 7 and are connected to the Internet, you can download Windows Live Essentials. This is a collection of free programs from Microsoft that make it easy to create and share movies and edit photos, as well as chat to others with email and instant messages.

Windows Live Photo Gallery and Windows Live Movie Maker are two key components of the Windows Live Essentials collection. Windows Live Photo Gallery provides tools to edit, organise and share your photos, while Windows Movie Maker lets you quickly turn video into polished home movies with easy sharing options.

Download Windows Live Essentials

1 Click

2 In the Search box, type Windows Live Essentials

3 Click on **Go online to get Windows Live Essentials**

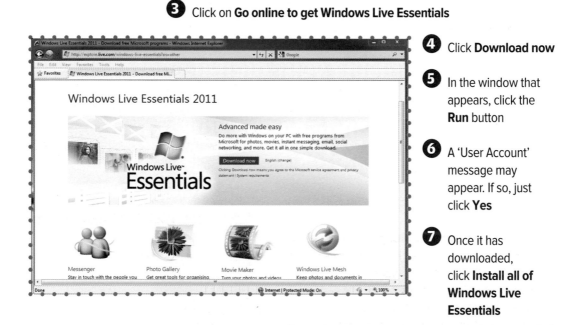

4 Click **Download now**

5 In the window that appears, click the **Run** button

6 A 'User Account' message may appear. If so, just click **Yes**

7 Once it has downloaded, click **Install all of Windows Live Essentials**

8 Once it's finished installing, you'll be prompted to restart your computer. Click **Restart Now**. All of the Windows Live Essentials programs will now be listed in the 'Start' menu

IMPORT PHOTOS USING PHOTO GALLERY

You can import your photos directly into Windows Live Photo Gallery from a digital camera, memory card reader, scanner, CD or DVD.

1 Click

2 Click **All Programs** and then click **Windows Live Photo Gallery**

3 Click the **Home** tab, and then click **Import**

4 In the 'Import Photos and Videos' dialog box, click the device that you want to use. If you're importing from a CD or DVD, select the CD or DVD drive. Click **Import**

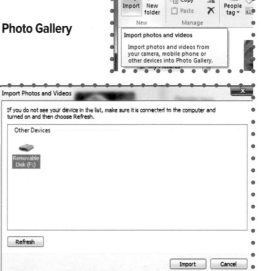

5 Select either **Review, organize and group items to import** or **Import all new items now** and then click **Next**

6 If you selected 'Review, organize and group items to import', you'll see a dialog box where you can choose and name the groups of photos or individual photos that you want to import. For example:

TIP

If you're in a hurry or want to organise your photos and videos later, click **Import all new items now**.

To see all of the photos in a group: click **View all items** next to the group name. Clear the check boxes for the photos that you don't want to import.

To name a group of photos that you want to import: click **Enter a name**, and then type a name.

To assign tags to a group: next to the group, click **Add tags**. Type one or more tags separated by semicolons, and then press **Enter**. When you're finished, click **Import**. Each group of photos will be imported and saved to a different folder.

▶ Photos & Videos

TRY THIS
Once you have downloaded and installed Windows Live Photo Gallery, you can simply double click on a photo anywhere on your computer to open it in Photo Gallery.

VIEW YOUR PHOTOS

Windows Live Photo Gallery works with your computer's Pictures folder, so that all photos in the Pictures folder will automatically appear in Photo Gallery.

1 Click

2 Click **All Programs** and then click **Windows Live Photo Gallery**

3 To see your photos, click the arrow next to **All photos and videos** in the left-hand info pane and then click **My Pictures**

View photos in gallery mode

You can navigate through thumbnails of your photos in a gallery view mode by using the buttons at the bottom of the window.

1 Your photos are initially grouped by date and as thumbnails, which are small versions of the full-sized photos. To see as many thumbnails as possible, click the **Maximize button** so that the Windows Live Photo Gallery window fills your window

2 Change the size of thumbnails by clicking the **Zoom** button at the bottom of the window and moving the slider up or down. Making thumbnails smaller lets you browse a large picture collection or making them larger lets you see more detail in each one

You can switch to the **Detail** view by clicking on the list button on the bottom right of the window to the left of the slider. This will show key information about each photo

 You can rotate a photo by clicking on the **Rotate** buttons at the bottom of the screen

View photos one at a time

You can also view photos one at a time at full size.

 To view a photo at full size, double click on it. The photo will now fill the Photo Gallery viewer window

2 To move to the next photo, click on the **right arrow** at the bottom of the window. To see the previous photo, simply click on the **left arrow**

3 To zoom into your photo for closer inspection, click the **Zoom** tool at the bottom right of the window

4 To return to the gallery view of all your photos, click **Close file** (the red cross symbol) on the top-right corner of the window

photos & videos

▶ Photos & Videos

ORGANISE YOUR PHOTOS
Windows Live Photo Gallery offers several ways to help organise your photos so you can quickly find those you want.

Change how your photos are listed
Photo Gallery organises your photos by date. You can, however, choose to view your images by other criteria, using various filters. Click the **View** tab, and select an option in the 'Arrange List' group. For example, click on **Tag** to see your photos listed by their tags.

Rename your photos
Your digital camera stores each photo with a numeric file name so they appear on your computer with unhelpful names such as DSC00267.JPG and P0000255.JPG. To rename each photo to something more recognisable can be time consuming, but Windows Live Photo Gallery helps you rename an entire group of photos at once.

1 Click

2 Click **All Programs** and then click **Windows Live Photo Gallery**

3 To see your photos, click the arrow next to **All photos and videos** in the left-hand info pane and then click **My Pictures**

4 Hold down the **Ctrl** key, and click the photos you want to rename

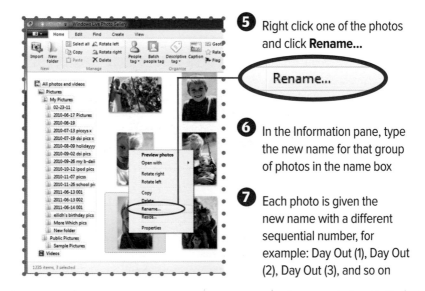

5 Right click one of the photos and click **Rename...**

6 In the Information pane, type the new name for that group of photos in the name box

7 Each photo is given the new name with a different sequential number, for example: Day Out (1), Day Out (2), Day Out (3), and so on

Tag your photos

Tags can be applied to single or several photos at a time, and you can add tags that name people in the photo or descriptive tags such as 'Snowy Day'.

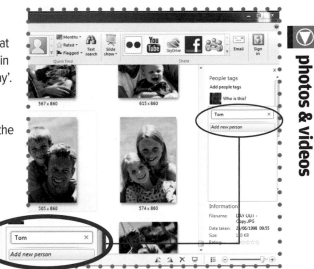

 To tag a person, click the photo. To select more than one photo at a time hold down the **Ctrl** key while you click photos

 In the people pane on the right-hand-side of the window, click either **Add people tag** or click, if shown, **Who is this** to identify a particular person in the photo. Type a name and press **Enter**

Rate your photos

You can also organise your photos by rating them on a scale of one to five. Five stars can be used to represent your favourite photos and one star for those photos you never wish to show anyone.

 To apply a rating to a photo, click the photo. To select more than one photo at a time hold down the **Ctrl** key as you click photos

In the 'Information' panel on the right, click on the number of stars next to 'Rating' to give the rating you wish. The more stars you give a photo, the higher the rating

Delete your photos

To delete a photo, simply right click on it and in the pop-up window click **Delete**. Alternatively, click the **Delete** button indicated by a red cross at the bottom-right of the window.

Photos & Videos

EDIT YOUR PHOTOS

With just a few clicks in Photo Gallery you can remove red eye, fix exposure problems, correct colour or crop photos for more impact.

Edit automatically

1 Click

2 Click **All Programs** and then click **Windows Live Photo Gallery**

3 To see your photos, click the arrow next to **All photos and videos** in the left-hand info pane and then click **My Pictures**

4 Select the photo or photos that you want to edit, then, at the top of the screen, click the **Edit** tab

5 There is one automatic option available: **Auto adjust**. Click this if you want Photo Gallery to automatically optimise the photo's brightness contrast and colour. Remember you can always click **Undo** if you don't like the results of this fix

6 Click **Close file** (the red cross) on the top menu to return to the gallery view

Crop a photo

1 Double click the photo you wish to crop

2 On the **Edit** tab, in the 'Adjustments' group, click **Crop**

3 If you want to change the photo's proportions to a common print size, such as 4 x 6, move your cursor over **Proportion** to see a list of proportions. Alternatively, click **Custom**, which lets you set any picture proportion. Or, click **Original**, which retains the proportion of the original picture

4 A frame will appear over the photo. What's inside the frame represents the part of the picture that will be retained when you crop it. Drag the edges of the frame to adjust it. To maintain the proportions of a crop frame, hold down the **Shift** key while you resize the crop frame

5 To rotate the crop frame so the picture is cropped vertically rather than horizontally or vice versa, click **Rotate Frame**

195

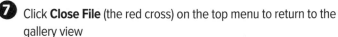
6 When you're happy with the frame position, click **Crop** and from the drop-down menu click **Apply crop**. You'll see the newly cropped version of your picture

7 Click **Close File** (the red cross) on the top menu to return to the gallery view

Remove red-eye

1 Double click the photo you wish to work on

2 On the **Edit** tab, in the 'Adjustments' group, click **Red eye**

3 Use the cursor to draw a small rectangle around the eye you want to fix. Repeat this for the second eye

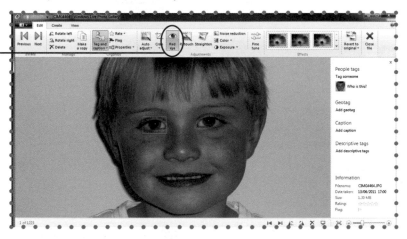

4 Click **Close File** (the red cross) on the top menu to save your changes and return to the gallery view

Straighten a photo
If you discover that a photo you've taken is at an angle, you can use Photo Gallery's straighten tool to adjust it.

1 Double click a photo to view it full size

2 On the **Edit** tab, in the 'Adjustments' group, click **Fine tune**

3 Click **Straighten photo** in the right-hand pane. To further straighten your photo, use the slider

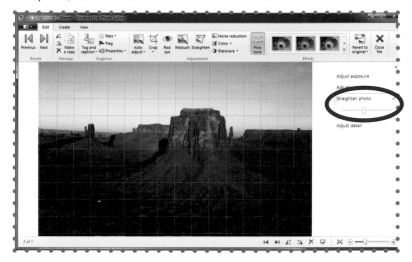

4 Click **Close File** (the red cross) on the top menu to return to the gallery view

Combine photos

You can use Photo Gallery's Photo Fuse to combine the best parts of two or more photos into one. This is handy for improving group shots, where someone might look better in one photo than in another.

1 Select the photos you want to fuse

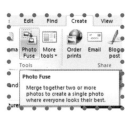

2 On the **Create** tab, in the 'Tools' group, click **Photo Fuse**

3 Click on the area of the photo you want to replace. Drag one of the points to adjust the size of this area

4 Click the replacement photo that you like best, and then click **Save**

⊳ Photos & Videos

TRY THIS
You need only go through the authorisation process the first time you upload to Flickr through Windows Live Photo Gallery.

UPLOAD TO PHOTO-SHARING WEBSITES

Windows Live Photo Gallery now has the ability to upload your photos and video directly to photo-sharing websites such as Facebook, Flickr and YouTube. Once uploaded, they can be shared with friends and family that you give permission to access and view the photos or video. To use this feature you need to have:

▶ A computer with an internet connection
▶ A Windows Live account
▶ An account with one of the photo-sharing websites

Upload photos and videos to Flickr

1 Select the photos you'd like to share from the gallery

2 On the **Create** tab, in the 'Share' group, select **Flickr**

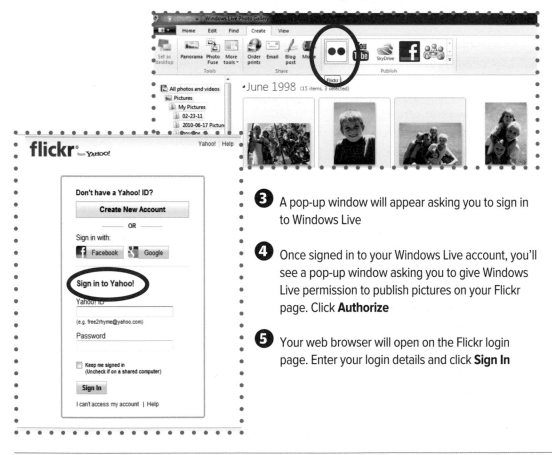

3 A pop-up window will appear asking you to sign in to Windows Live

4 Once signed in to your Windows Live account, you'll see a pop-up window asking you to give Windows Live permission to publish pictures on your Flickr page. Click **Authorize**

5 Your web browser will open on the Flickr login page. Enter your login details and click **Sign In**

Authorise the upload

1 Flickr will ask if this is a genuine attempt to connect to your account. As it is, click **Next** underneath the text that reads, 'If you arrived at this page because you specifically asked Windows Live Essentials to connect to your Flickr account, click here:'

2 Another window will ask you to authorize this request. Click the button that says, **OK, I'LL AUTHORIZE IT**. You'll then see a green tick saying you've successfully allowed Windows Live Essentials to publish photos to your Flickr page

3 Close this window and go back to Windows Live Photo Gallery. Click **Next** to complete the authorization process and start publishing your photos

Upload your photos

1 A pop-up box will ask you if you want to change any of the default Flickr settings, such as size and whether the photo will be viewable by everyone or only to people who are listed as contacts. Make your changes and then click **Publish**

2 Your photos will now be uploaded to Flickr

🔑 **Windows Live™ Essentials wants to link to your Flickr account.**

To ensure that this is a genuine request, please select from one of the following options.

| If you arrived at this page because you followed a link from an email, IM, twitter, or web page not associated with **Windows Live™ Essentials**, click here: | or | If you arrived at this page because you specifically asked **Windows Live™ Essentials** to connect to your Flickr account, click here: |

NEXT   NEXT

🔑 **Windows Live™ Essentials wants to link to your Flickr account.**

👤 This service is produced by a trusted Flickr partner.

By authorizing this link, you'll allow **Windows Live™ Essentials** to:

✎ **Access** your Flickr account (including private content)

✎ **Upload**, **Edit**, and **Replace** photos and videos in your account

✎ **Interact** with other members' photos and videos (comment, add notes, favorite)

Windows Live™ Essentials will *not* have permission to:

✘ **Delete** photos and videos from your account

OK, I'LL AUTHORIZE IT   NO THANKS

Your Yahoo! and Flickr passwords will always remain private, but **Windows Live™ Essentials** will have the permissions listed above until you revoke its link to your account. (You can revoke such links at any time in the Extending Flickr section of your account prefs.)

●● Publish on Flickr ✕

Publish to Flickr (1 selected)

You can change your account upload defaults at your Flickr account page.
Visit your Flickr account page

Flickr account:
mplayer75 ▾   Remove

Photo sets:
Don't add to a set ▾

Photo size:
Original size ▾

Permissions:
Public ▾

You've used 0% of your photo upload limit and 0 of your 2 videos this month.

Publish   Cancel

▶ Photos & Videos

UPLOAD FOOTAGE TO YOUR COMPUTER

A camcorder is great for capturing precious memories, whether it's a party or a special holiday. Sometimes, however, your footage may be too long, or include sections you'd rather cut. Using video-editing software, it's easy to make these changes.

Basic video-editing software is usually supplied with your camcorder. Alternatively, you can download Windows Live Essentials (see page 188), which includes Windows Live Movie Maker. This video-editing software works with Windows Live Photo Gallery so you can create good-looking home movies in just a few clicks.

Upload footage to your computer

Before you can start editing your footage, you need to get it from your camcorder onto your computer. Here's how:

1 Connect the camera or camcorder to your computer and then turn it on

2 Click

3 Click **All Programs** and then click **Windows Live Photo Gallery**

4 On the **Home** tab click **Import**. On the 'Import Photos and Videos' dialog box, click the device you want to import videos from, and then click **Import**

5 On the 'New photos and videos were found' page, click **Import all new items now**, type a name for the videos, and then click **Import**

Alternatively, click **Review, organize and group items to import**. You'll then see a dialog box where you can choose, name and tag the groups of photos and videos or individual photos and videos that you wish to import

7 In Windows Live Photo Gallery, select the check box in the upper-left corner for each photo or video you want to use in your movie

8 On the **Create** tab, in the Share group, click **Movie**

9 Now your photos and videos are in Movie Maker, you're can start making your movie

▶ Photos & Videos

WORK WITH VIDEO EDITING SOFTWARE

Once you've saved your video clips onto your computer, you can edit them using video-editing software to create a new, improved piece of video.

When editing, you can delete sections of video, move sections around and add special effects and transitions between clips. You can also add a soundtrack or narrative to your video, and even create a DVD, complete with a menu, for easy navigation on your TV.

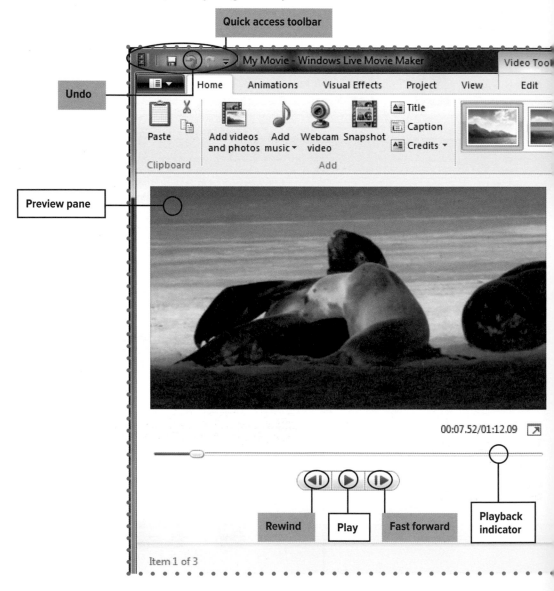

Quick access toolbar

Undo

Preview pane

Rewind

Play

Fast forward

Playback indicator

Ribbon

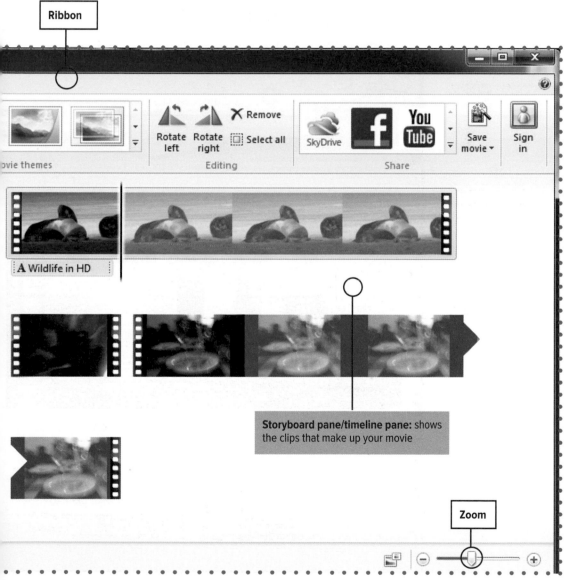

Rotate left

Rotate right

✗ Remove

▢ Select all

SkyDrive

Save movie ▾

Sign in

ovie themes

Editing

Share

A Wildlife in HD

Storyboard pane/timeline pane: shows the clips that make up your movie

Zoom

▶ Photos & Videos

Jargon buster

Timeline
The basic tool in video editing software used to build and edit a video project. The components of your video – video clips and photos – are placed in chronological order on the timeline, which runs horizontally across the window.

TIP
While you're editing your video in Windows Live Movie Maker, it's known as a project.

EDIT A VIDEO

Before you can start editing your video, you need to add the clips you want to use to the storyboard/timeline.

Get started

1 Click

2 Click **All Programs** and then **Windows Live Movie Maker**

3 On the **Home** tab, in the 'Add' group, click **Add videos and photos**

4 Select the video clip you want to add. Click **Open**

5 Your clip will appear in the right-hand pane and you can click **play** on the preview screen to watch it

6 Repeat steps 3 and 4 to add more video clips

7 This is the best time to put your clips in the order that you want them to be watched. Do this by dragging and dropping clips in the right-hand pane so they are in the order you require

Trim a clip

If some of your scenes are too long, they can be trimmed before being edited into a whole.

 In the storyboard pane/ timeline select the clip you wish to trim

2 On the **Edit** tab, in the Editing group, click **Trim tool**

3 On the playback indicator under the preview pane drag the left-hand slider to where you want the clip to start

4 Click **Set start point**

5 On the playback indicator under the preview pane drag the right-hand slider to where you want the clip to end

6 Click **Set end point**

Split a clip

If you want to add effects between scenes in a clip or change their order, you can split a video clip into smaller sections.

 Select the clip you want to split into two, and click the **Play** button

 Play the clip until it gets to where you want to split it, then click **Stop**

 On the **Edit** tab, in the 'Editing' group, click **Split**

4 This cuts your clip into two separate clips that appear on the right-hand pane

Add transitions

A video can look a little clunky if the scenes are just sandwiched together. You can avoid this by adding transitions, such as a fade-in or fade-out effect. These are placed between the clips on the timeline.

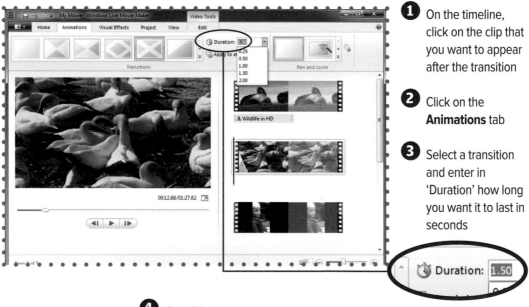

1 On the timeline, click on the clip that you want to appear after the transition

2 Click on the **Animations** tab

3 Select a transition and enter in 'Duration' how long you want it to last in seconds

4 Click **Play** on the preview monitor to see a preview of the transition

5 You can also add a 'fade in' and a 'fade out' by clicking on the **Edit** tab and then selecting one of these from the drop-down menus

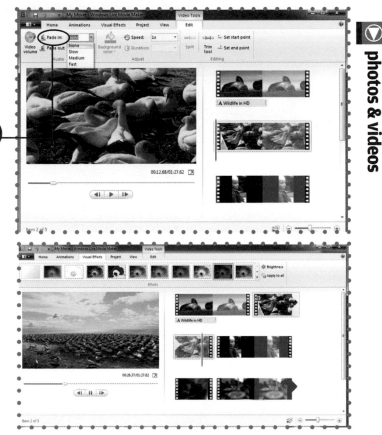

Add special effects

You can change the appearance of your video by using special effects. For example, using one of the black and white effects can give your video an old-fashioned look. Or you can use pan and zoom to create a close-up of someone's face.

1 On the timeline, click on the clip that you want to apply an effect to

2 Click on the **Visual Effects** tab

3 In the 'Effects' group, click the **down arrow** to see all effects available. Move your cursor over an effect to see a live preview of it in the preview pane. Click an effect to apply it your clip. To apply the same effect to all the clips in your storyboard pane/timeline, click **Apply to all**

Add titles and credits

You can choose to add a title at the start of your video, before or after a selected clip or at the end of the video, much like the end credits of a Hollywood film.

1 On the timeline, click where on the clip you want the title to appear

2 On the **Home** tab, in the 'Add' group, click either **Title**, **Caption** or **Credits** depending on which one you want to add at that point in the video. In this case, Title has been used

TRY THIS

You can tweak the properties of a project element – such as a clip, audio track, sound effect or transition – by hovering the mouse cursor over it and right-clicking.

▶ Photos & Videos

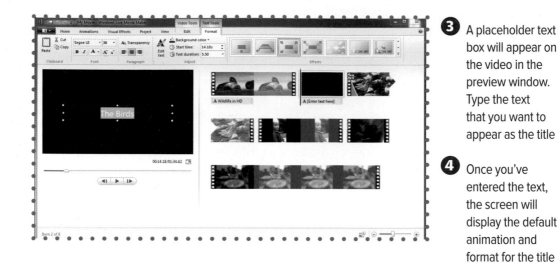

3 A placeholder text box will appear on the video in the preview window. Type the text that you want to appear as the title

4 Once you've entered the text, the screen will display the default animation and format for the title

5 To change the text, on the **Format** tab, click **Edit text**, and then edit or retype the text

6 If you want to change the font and colour of your text, click the **Format** tab. Here you can choose the font, font colour, formatting, background colour, transparency, font size and the position of the title

7 To change the animation effects – how the title appears and positions itself on screen – click the **More** drop-down arrow in the 'Effects' group to see the full list of animation effects. Move your cursor over an effect to see a live preview of the animation. Click an effect to apply it to your title

Add music

Adding a soundtrack to your video is easy in Windows Live Movie Maker. After you add music to the timeline, you can edit it so it plays just how you want.

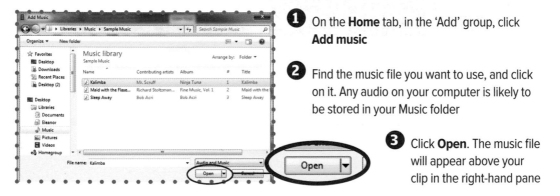

1 On the **Home** tab, in the 'Add' group, click **Add music**

2 Find the music file you want to use, and click on it. Any audio on your computer is likely to be stored in your Music folder

3 Click **Open**. The music file will appear above your clip in the right-hand pane

Change the start or end point of the music

You can trim the beginning or end of a piece of music, so only part of it plays in your video.

 Click on the music file in the storyboard pane/timeline

 On the **Options** tab, in the 'Editing' group, click **Set start point**

 Drag the playback indicator on the timeline to the point in the music where you want it to start playing in your video

 Repeat the above steps but this time in Step 2 click **Set end point** to set a new end point when the music stops playing

Fade music in or out

Adjusting the audio to smoothly fade in at the beginning and fade out at the end will make your video sound more professional.

 Click on the music file in the storyboard pane/timeline

 On the **Options** tab, in the 'Audio' group, choose one of the following:
- ▶ To make the music fade in, click **Fade in**, and from the drop-down list click the speed for the music to fade in
- ▶ To make the music fade out, click **Fade out**, and from the drop-down list click the speed for the music to fade out

TRY THIS

To change the volume of a piece of music, first click the music. Then under Music Tools, on the **Options** tab, in the Audio group, click **Music volume** and move the slider left to lower the volume or right to increase it.

▶ Photos & Videos

BE CAREFUL
Once you've published your video, you can't edit it. You can only edit the saved project, so make sure you're happy with it first.

SAVE YOUR VIDEO PROJECT

As you edit your video remember to save regularly to avoid losing edits should something unexpected happen such as your computer crash.

1 Click the down arrow to the left of the **Home** tab on the Ribbon

2 Click **Save Project As** if you haven't already given your project a name, name it and then click **Save**

3 If you've already given your video a name, simply click **Save Project**

Save and share a video
When you save your video project, it's saved as a Movie Maker Project file with the extension .wlmp. This means it can only be opened on a computer using Windows Live Movie Maker. In order to share your video with friends and family via email, on CD or to upload it to YouTube, Facebook or other websites, you must export it as a Windows Media Video or a .wmv file.

TRY THIS
If you prefer to set your own video settings such as bit rate, frame rate, width and height, click **Create custom setting...** in the 'Save movie' menu.

The easiest way to save your movie into a format that can be easily shared is to use one of the program's recommended settings. Windows Live Movie Maker 2011 will then look at the size and bit rate of your source videos and choose settings that will produce the best balance between file size and video quality.

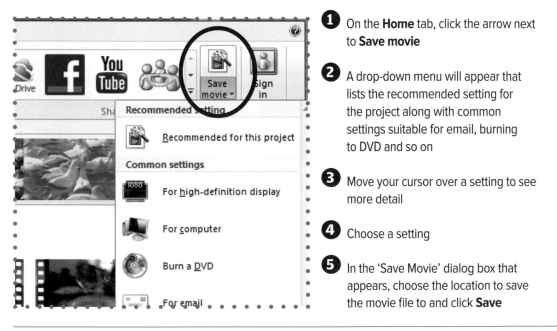

1 On the **Home** tab, click the arrow next to **Save movie**

2 A drop-down menu will appear that lists the recommended setting for the project along with common settings suitable for email, burning to DVD and so on

3 Move your cursor over a setting to see more detail

4 Choose a setting

5 In the 'Save Movie' dialog box that appears, choose the location to save the movie file to and click **Save**

SHARE YOUR MOVIE WITH SKYDRIVE

You can upload your saved movies to social networking websites such as YouTube and Facebook as well as Microsoft's own cloud computing system – Windows Live SkyDrive.

Upload a movie to SkyDrive

1 On the **Home** tab, in the 'Share' group, click **SkyDrive**

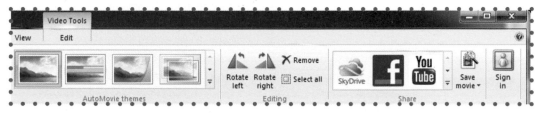

2 You'll now be asked to choose a resolution for your movie. SkyDrive has a file size limit of 50MB so if your movie file is larger than this, you won't be able to upload it. Choose the highest resolution without exceeding an estimated file size of 50MB (you can see your video's estimated file size detailed below the resolutions)

Windows Live Movie Maker

Choose the resolution of your movie

Your project may exceed the maximum size allowed by SkyDrive at some of these resolutions. If publishing fails at one resolution, try publishing again to a smaller size.

➔ **640 x 360 (recommended)**

Estimated size: 18.16 MB

➔ **426 x 240**

Estimated size: 8.75 MB

Cancel

Jargon buster

Cloud computing
Files and programs are stored remotely on connected internet servers rather than locally on your own computer. You can access your files from any device making it easy to share files with others who are authorised to access the same, shared storage space.

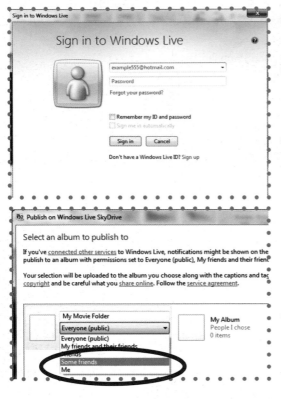

3 Enter your user name and password to sign into your Windows Live account

4 Choose an album in your SkyDrive where you'll upload your movie. If you haven't created an album yet, click **New album title**

5 Type a name for your album and then choose a sharing preference from the drop-down menu. Most options are self-explanatory except the last two:
– **Some friends** makes the folder available to all your Windows Live contacts, except those you've marked for limited access
– The **Me** setting means only those with a link can view the folder

6 Click **Publish** to upload your file. Once uploaded, you'll have the option to view it online

Share your movie

1 Go to Windows Live SkyDrive. Sign in with your Windows Live ID if necessary

2 Select the movie that you want to share and open the info pane by clicking the **Show information** button

3 Click **Sharing** and then **Send a link**

4 Click **To** – this will let you choose a contact you'd like to share with

5 Type the email addresses of the people you'd like to share a link with

6 Type a message and click **Send**

RESOURCES

▶ Jargon Buster

Application *see* Program

Attachment A computer file that is sent along with an email message. It can be any type of software file, and can be opened by the receiver if the appropriate software to view the file attachment is installed or available.

Backup A copy of your files or programs for safekeeping.

Bit rate Short for binary digit, a 'bit' is the smallest element of computer storage. Commonly used as a measurement for transferring data, 'bit rate' is the number of bits transmitted per second over a network, such as from the internet to your PC, and is usually abbreviated as bit/s or bps.

Browser The software that enables you to view web pages.

Card reader A device for reading data stored on Memory Cards, such as used by digital cameras.

Case sensitive Most search tools are not case sensitive or only respond to initial capitals, as in proper names. But as capital letters (upper case) retrieve only upper case, it's best to type lower case (no capitals) because lower case will always retrieve upper case letters too.

Cell In spreadsheet applications, a cell is a box in which you enter a single piece of information or data.

CD-R/RW Drive A Compact Disc Recordable or Rewritable can record data, images or music files onto blank discs.

Clip art Ready-made artwork that is included with your Office software or can be downloaded from the web for use in your documents and presentations. Clip art includes both subject-related illustrations and elements such as horizontal lines, symbols, bullets and backgrounds.

Cloud computing Allows files and programs to be stored remotely on connected internet servers rather than locally on your computer. You can access your files from any device making it easy to share files with others who are authorised to access the same, shared storage space.

Compression Digital files can be compressed using mathematical algorithms to create smaller files that take up less storage space and are easier to share. Digital photos, video, music files are commonly compressed.

Control panel A series of dedicated programs than adjust the computer's settings, such as passwords, internet access and accessibility.

Crop A photo-editing term that means removing a portion of a photo.

Cursor A cursor is the symbol on the screen that shows you where the next character will appear.

Desktop The main screen you see when you start your computer. From here you can organise and access programs and files.

Download To transfer data from a remote computer to your own computer over the internet.

Driver Software that allows your computer to communicate with other devices, such as a printer.

DVD-R/RW Drive Optical drive that can read and write to DVD discs.

Embed code Program code that's provided by some websites such as YouTube that lets you place their video or audio content on your own webpage. You copy the embed code and paste it into your website where you want the content to play.

External hard drive A storage device that plugs into your PC. Useful for saving copies of important files, or creating additional storage.

File extension The letters that appear after a file name. They show what type of document it is, and what type of program will open it – for example, a Microsoft Word document will end in .doc.

File format Refers to the specific way that information is stored within a computer file. The type of file format is shown by the letters that appear after the file name and these indicate what type of file it is and what type of program will open it – for example, a Microsoft Word file will end in .docx, while a Microsoft Excel file will end in .xlsx.

Filtering in Excel Excel allows you to filter – select specific – information in your spreadsheet columns so you can find values quickly. It's a quick and easy way to work with a subset of information in a range of cells or table. You can filter information by choosing a category of data or you can create filters to focus on specific data.

Flash drive *see* USB stick

Font A specific typeface in a specific point size and style.

Function A preset formula in Microsoft Excel.

Hyperlink A hyperlink can be either text or an image on a web page or in a PDF document that lets you jump straight to another web page when you click on it.

Icon A small picture that represents an object or program.

▶ Jargon Buster

Link Short for hyperlink and can be either text or an image on a web page or in a PDF document that lets you jump straight to another web page when you click on it.

Login Also called a login name, username or screen name, it is a unique name and password used to identify a person online.

Mail merge A feature of word processors, database software, and some e-mail programs that takes a common message and adds unique information such as email address, name, address to make it look unique to individual recipients.

Mathematical operator The symbol or sign that represents an arithmetic operation in an Excel spreadsheet formula.

Media type In computing and on the internet, media type refers to a type of digital content such as an application, illustration, photograph or a piece of video or audio.

Memory stick *see* USB stick

Memory card Removable storage device, which holds images taken with the camera. They come in a variety of sizes and there are several types including Compact Flash, Multimeda and SD cards as well as Sony's Memory Stick format.

MP3 The standard file format for digital music. The attraction of the format is that it is not tied to any one manufacturer in the way that AAC (Apple) and WMA (Microsoft) are.

Office suite A bundle of computer programs for doing common tasks such as writing letters and managing budgets. Typically includes a word processor, a spreadsheet program and presentation software.

Open source A program or file that can be freely modified by anyone. It is usually developed as a public collaboration and made freely available.

Operating system The software that manages your computer and the environment that programs operate in.

PDF (Portable Document Format) A file that captures all the graphics, fonts and formatting of a document, regardless of the application in which it was created. It can be opened on virtually any type of computer or mobile device.

Placeholder text Also known as dummy text. A piece of text – sometimes nonsense text such as lorem ipsum – designed to show the position, font, size and format of text in a layout.

Point Refers to the size of type – a point is the smallest unit of measure.

Pop-up A small window that appears over an item (word or picture) on your computer screen to give additional information.

Port A computer socket into which you plug equipment.

Red eye A strange red effect seen on person's eyes that can spoil a photo. It occurs when light from a camera flash reflects off the blood vessels in a subject's retinae.

Resolution The number of pixels in a digital image – usually expressed as two figures that represent the width and the height such as 1200 x 1600 pixels. The more pixels, the sharper the image will look.

Ripping Copying data from a CD or DVD to a computer.

Saturation How rich the colours are in a digital image.

Screen saver The image or set of images that appear when your computer is idle for a certain period of time.

Sharpness The clarity of detail in a photo.

Sizing handles When you click an object, such as a shape, image or clip art, in Word, a border with little white squares and circles will appear around it. These squares and circles are the sizing handles. You click on the squares to change the height or width, while the circles are used to make the whole object smaller or bigger.

Slide A single page of a presentation created with software such as PowerPoint.

Slideshow A display of a series of chosen pictures or slides.

SmartArt graphics A feature of Microsoft Office, SmartArt graphics are predrawn diagrams and illustrations that can be inserted into your Office documents. You can edit the diagrams and change the style without having to fiddle with shape size and alignment, as SmartArt graphics automatically adjust to maintain their overall shape and design.

Software A general term for programs used to operate computers and related devices.

Sparkline A miniature chart linked to a line of data, usually used to illustrate a trend.

Spreadsheet A spreadsheet is a collection of data arranged in rows and columns. A spreadsheet program lets you manage these electronically.

Tagging Process of adding descriptive keywords to a piece of information such as photo, to help search for it.

Taskbar The bar running across the bottom of your screen, from where you can open programs and access the main Windows functions.

Template A document or file with preset layout and formatting. A template is used as a starting point for a particular application so that the format does not have to be recreated each time it is used.

Thesaurus A book that lists words in groups of synonyms and related concepts.

Timeline The basic tool in video editing software used to build and edit a video project. The components of your video – video clips and photos – are placed in chronological order on the timeline, which runs horizontally across the window.

Toolbar A vertical or horizontal onscreen bar that's made up of small icons that, when clicked, will perform a task.

Transition A motion effect that applies when you move from one slide to another in PowerPoint or from one clip to the next in Windows Live Movie Maker.

Upload Process of sending files from your computer to the internet.

USB (Universal Serial Bus) A connection technology that allows you to transfer data easily between a computer and a device, such as a camera or printer. USB cables are used to connect devices and are plugged into a USB port on your computer.

USB stick Small, portable device used to store and transfer data. It plugs into a USB port and is sometimes called a USB key, flash drive or pen drive.

Video clips Short pieces of video, usually part of a longer presentation.

Windows Live Essentials 2011 A suite of free programs for your PC running Windows including tools for email, instant messaging, editing and sharing photos and video.

Wizard A software tool that guides you through the steps of a process or task by asking a series of questions or presenting options.

Word processor A program capable of creating, storing, and printing documents, sometimes abbreviated to WP.

⏵ Index

▶ Index

▶ Index

ABOUT THE CONSULTANT EDITOR LYNN WRIGHT

Lynn Wright is an editor and journalist with 20 years' experience in writing about computing, technology and digital photography.

HAVING PROBLEMS
WITH YOUR COMPUTER?

A few years ago **Which? Computing** launched an online Helpdesk service.
The team has a combined experience of over forty years and promises
to answer questions within two working days.

To date, the team has answered tens of thousands of queries from readers,
and there's no PC problem they won't tackle.

As a reader of **Using Your PC Made Easy – Office 2010
and More**, you can now access this indispensable service
absolutely free.

To submit a question for the Helpdesk*, simply go to
www.which.co.uk/computinghelpdesk

Enter your query and, where it asks for a membership number,
simply enter the code that you'll find in the Introduction.

*This service is only available online

ATHOLL DUNCAN

LEADERS IN LOCKDOWN

INSIDE STORIES OF COVID-19 AND THE NEW WORLD OF BUSINESS

Published by
LID Publishing Limited
The Record Hall, Studio 304,
16-16a Baldwins Gardens,
London EC1N 7RJ, UK

info@lidpublishing.com
www.lidpublishing.com

A member of:

businesspublishersroundtable.com

© Atholl Duncan, 2020
© LID Publishing Limited, 2020

Printed by Gutenberg Press, Malta

ISBN: 978-1-911671-01-5
ISBN: 978-1-911671-18-3 (ebook)

Cover and page design: Caroline Li

ATHOLL DUNCAN

LEADERS IN LOCKDOWN

INSIDE STORIES OF COVID-19 AND THE NEW WORLD OF BUSINESS

MADRID | MEXICO CITY | LONDON
NEW YORK | BUENOS AIRES
BOGOTA | SHANGHAI | NEW DELHI

BIG | BLACK
ISLE
GROUP

Black Isle Group (BIG) is a leadership development business based in the City of London and working with blue chip companies around the world. The philosophy of BIG is to help leaders maximise their personal performance and the performance of their teams. The business blends some of the world's best coaching with innovative Nudge technology to change behaviours and deliver long-lasting results.

CONTENTS

TACKLING INEQUALITY

GLOBAL COOPERATION

RESILIENCE

RESETTING THE SUPPLY CHAIN RESET

MAXIMIZING POTENTIAL

THE FUTURE

ACKNOWLEDGMENTS

I am extremely grateful to all 28 leaders in lockdown who gave their time freely to speak to me and share their wisdom for this endeavour. I would also like to acknowledge all my Black Isle Group colleagues – especially Jeremy Campbell and Ashleigh Evans – for their support. My thanks are also due to Martin Liu at LID Business Media for his faith in agreeing to set off on this venture in the first place; to Susan Furber for bringing order to my chaos; to Hazel Bird for her copy editing and her patience with my misuse of the comma; and to Aiyana Curtis for picking up the cudgels half way through. Last and by no means least I would like to thank the ever-patient Emily, my partner in life. It is unclear whether writing this book made things easier or more challenging for her as we hunkered down in close confinement behind our walls for 100 days of COVID-19. A time we will never forget.

INTRODUCTION

This is a story of leadership. It's set in an extraordinary period in history – a time when the world was hit by the greatest health crisis in the modern era and the global economy was brought to a standstill. It is centred on 28 interviews with 'leaders in lockdown'. All were conducted by videoconference over 100 days from mid-March to late June 2020. By the end of that period, more than ten million people had been infected with COVID-19, 500,000 had died,[1] 1.6 billion people were in danger of losing their livelihoods[2] and half of the world's countries had approached the International Monetary Fund for financial assistance.[3]

No CEO, chairman or board had been through anything like this before. The crisis was made all the more remarkable because for most of this time our business leaders were sat at home, many locked down at their kitchen tables – like champion thorough-breds shut in their stables. This was a state quite foreign to a breed who've spent most of their lives hurtling around on planes, trains and automobiles with barely a minute to spare. Working from home, they had time to reflect and cast their minds forward to consider the question, what next?

This book strives to do two things. First, it aims to provide a unique window into the insights, behaviours and actions of a pantheon of the world's most thoughtful business leaders through their inside stories of COVID-19. I hope this may help readers and leaders to learn, develop and be prepared better to tackle the crises of the future. As an INSEAD executive coach and chairman of the leadership development business Black Isle Group, my purpose is to help others to become better leaders. In Chapter 29, I provide some insights and analysis in order to stimulate personal reflection and leadership learning.

The second objective of this book is to look forward and analyse what will change in the world because of what we have been through. Looking through the crystal balls of the leaders in lockdown, I anticipate the megatrends that may emerge. I flag these throughout the book as the seven key themes which will come from the crisis.

1. The new age of purpose
2. The new world of work
3. Tackling inequality
4. Global cooperation
5. Resilience
6. Resetting the supply chain
7. Maximizing potential

I hope these themes will stimulate thinking and help leaders to prepare their strategies and business models for life after COVID-19. Each leadership interview is dated in case readers seek to understand at which stage in the crisis the views were gathered. Things changed rapidly throughout lockdown.

This is not a root-and-branch analysis of COVID-19. Nor is it a forensic investigation into how governments and public servants dealt with it, though some of our interviewees couldn't resist a few observations on some of their triumphs and failures. This is also not the story of the heroes of our health services.

Around the world, they displayed fortitude, bravery and compassion over many months. They strived to prevent every death and to care for every suffering human. The debt they are owed by society will never be repaid, but I leave it to others to tell their story more effectively and with greater insight.

In my career, I have been through more crises than most. As a BBC journalist, I was on the ground at Lockerbie in Scotland on the night in 1988 when 270 people died when a terrorist bomb blew Pan Am Flight 103 out of the sky. I was in Aberdeen, Scotland, when 167 people were killed as a result of the explosion of the Piper Alpha oil rig. I witnessed the scenes of grief in 1996 as a gunman shot 16 children and a teacher at a primary school in Dunblane, Scotland. I worked through 9/11 as the Twin Towers fell and witnessed every twist and turn of the global financial crisis in 2008. What did leaders and society learn from all these tragedies? What changed? Not enough.

The leadership learnings in this book will stay current as the memories of lockdown fade. They will be as relevant in the future as they were to the challenges of COVID-19. Developing, nurturing and improving our leaders is crucial for advancing humanity. There is a belief that the world and the businesses that sit at the heart of society are at a crossroads. We face many existential questions. How will our political leaders, our business leaders and our citizens deal with them? I hope you will find that our leaders in lockdown have some of the answers.

Our leaders in lockdown all spoke with admirable brevity, clarity and impact. They demonstrated this through their words of wisdom. There was no shortage of well-turned phrases that captured the moment and made me stop and think. As an aperitif ahead of the main course, I have pulled together some of these wise words.

"We need to inject humanity back into leadership." — Marian Salzman

"People will be staring into one of the defining challenges of our times, which is unemployment. We need to really lean into it and solve the social inequality." — Leena Nair

"My biggest message for business leaders is that another crisis is coming our way. Are we going to do anything about it? Or will it be just like COVID-19?" — Osvald Bjelland

"You have to make decisions when you haven't got complete information. That's really one definition of leadership." — Mark Thompson

"The community is not just another stakeholder. It is the purpose for our very own existence." — Nupur Singh Mallick

"The full impact of this is enormous. We are not returning to the past." — George Hongchoy

"You need to bring your boldest self to a crisis but don't do it on your own." — Richard Bevan

"I wish a revolution could be born out of this crisis." — Pocket Sun

"The one thing this proves is that trickle-down economics doesn't work." — Sacha Romanovitch

"I fear this may turn into public revolution and disorder, because when people become hungry, they become desperate." — Sir Brian Souter

"Women shouldn't have to do two things to succeed while a man only has to do one." — Vivienne Artz

"The virus has exposed the selfishness of countries and people far more than it has shown our ability to be compassionate internationalists." — Ho Kwon Ping

"What is that world we want to aspire for our children to live in? Can we try and build that one rather than the one we were destroying six months ago?" — Alison Martin

"Diplomacy for the next generation, if not several generations, is going to be redrawn." — Gary Liu

"There are a few organizations that sadly have leaders who are waiting to snap back in muscle memory and get back to the way it was. That's a false idea. There is no going back because your competition is going to a better place." — General Stan McChrystal

"We were the first out and we'll be the last back. But New York won't be back till Broadway is back." — Charlotte St Martin

"We never thought we'd see worse than 9/11." — Alasdair Nichol

"Nobody wants to go into an office. They are all petrified." — Andrea Murad

"We are judged as leaders not on what we are like when the going is good. We are judged as leaders on what we are like when the going is tough."
— Sir David Behan

"Don't go out and say you are a long-term investor … unless you have the stomach to live through the ups and downs."
— Clement Kwok

"With COVID-19, every single long-held belief has been thrown out of the window."
— Christian Lanng

"Globalization has made us better off, but better for whom? Better off for only 10%."
— Martin Gilbert

"Recessions are where small businesses and entrepreneurs really stand out. They are key to facilitating new ways of going forward."
— Mike Cherry

"Anything a human can do can be done by robots in the future."
— Li Tong

"I fundamentally believe that this moment in time will shift the way humanity thinks about health."
— Will Ahmed

"This is a reckoning, a moment of truth when organizations will be judged on giving purpose real meaning through action not words."
— Sally Osman

"How do you want to be remembered at a time when the world is paying attention?"
— Derek Deasy

"I hope we will be a more caring and kinder society."
— Pinky Lilani

MY LIFE IN LOCKDOWN

There is a place I sit on top of the sand dunes. It's a few minutes' stroll from where I live in North Berwick, a seaside town on the east coast of Scotland. It's a perfect spot to ponder.

I perched there one morning in mid-March 2020 just after sunrise. It was a tranquil, stunning scene. The view has hardly changed since the novelist Robert Louis Stevenson looked out from the same place more than 150 years ago and imagined *Treasure Island*. His inspiration was the little rock of Fidra, which sits 150 yards across a deep blue channel. It's one of four islands dotted in the waters of the Firth beyond the mile-long caramel sands. They were the backdrop to my life in lockdown.

Sitting in such a stunning place, it was hard to imagine the horror that was going on elsewhere – the gasping people in the hospitals of London, the mounting losses in Lombardy or the mobile morgues in the shadows of Manhattan's skyscrapers.

But it wasn't business as usual for me. Far from it. Each company I work with felt the full brunt of COVID-19. I chair Black Isle Group (BIG). It's a leadership development business that works with senior executive teams in blue chip companies such as

Barclays and Standard Chartered – in the City of London and beyond. Many clients cancelled or postponed their upcoming work with BIG within 72 hours of the crisis escalating. However, by the middle of lockdown, the more insightful had realized that there had never been a more important time to invest in developing leaders and improving the performance of their teams.

I also sit on the board of the British Horseracing Authority. It's the regulator and governing body for the sport of horseracing. The sport closed down in mid-March as the UK government made clear it was about to ban all large gatherings. The consequences for the 80,000 people who make their living connected to the sport were severe. The weeks of lockdown were consumed with efforts across the industry to get racing going again the moment government allowed. Every day that passed threatened more and more businesses that depend on the sport for their livelihood. Passions ran high. Thanks to a huge collective effort, horseracing was the first professional sport in the UK to return behind closed doors as lockdown was lifted.

I also chair the Scottish Salmon Producers Organisation, which represents companies that produce £1 billion of salmon every year. The salmon is the king of fish. The Scottish salmon is the king of salmon. The sector is the UK's largest food exporter. In 2019 the value of Scottish salmon that went to foreign markets – such as Europe, the US and China – was more than £600 million. The sector supports 10,000 jobs, mainly in rural communities. When COVID-19 struck, the overseas markets and the world's restaurants closed down. The impact on the sector was sudden and serious. The immediate challenge was keeping fish on the supermarket shelves in the UK. The closure of the overseas markets would cause pain for a lot longer.

I also sit on the board of a cinema business that includes the Edinburgh Filmhouse, the Belmont Filmhouse in Aberdeen and the Edinburgh International Film Festival. The week before the crisis broke, we had announced plans to build an ambitious new 11-storey movie theatre, 'a temple for film'. We were basking in the glory when the virus struck.

Box office takings slumped from £7,000 a day to £400 as people stayed at home. The last showing at the Edinburgh Filmhouse was the French movie *Portrait of a Lady on Fire*, which had just won Best Screenplay at the Cannes Film Festival. There were four people in the stalls when the curtain fell. None of us knew when it would rise again.

I also chair UK Coaching, which educates and champions coaches in sport at the elite and community levels. We work with national governing bodies and individual coaches to provide learning and development. We also help to inspire people to be more active. When the virus came, the commercial activity of UK Coaching ground to a halt. Suddenly a business that was already being reinvented by its executive was rapidly dealing with a whole new panoply of challenges.

Every one of these businesses was threatened by the crisis. Everyone had to face the harsh financial consequences. The people who work in these businesses were impacted deeply by both the health and the economic consequences of COVID-19. Over the weeks and months of the crisis, the senior teams and their boards would have to work together to ensure they survived. If we made it through, we all wanted to come out on the other side in better shape to face the post-COVID-19 world.

Businesses around the world, large and small, faced the same issues as we did. Their employees faced the same anxiety. How would they pay their mortgages? How would they feed their families? How would they cope if they or their families caught the virus? Would they have a job to go back to at the end of it all?

I also do a lot of executive coaching with CEOs and executive directors. This was a time of great stress and strain for these leaders. They needed time to reflect, time to stand back, and time to share their worries and to consider carefully the momentous decisions they were taking every day. There was never a more important time to be an executive coach. There was never a more important time to *have* an executive coach. Those who did not would not maximize their own performance.

In the early weeks of COVID-19, my working day fell into a routine. I felt a little guilty that it was not in the least unpleasant. I was bunkered in our home office in a converted garage a pebble's throw from the beach. Our COVID-19 bubble included my partner, Emily and our lockdown returning girls – Clara and Rosie. Rosie's boyfriend Leo had also snuck in. In normal times, I work mainly in London. That means commuting for a two- or three-day trip every week on the East Coast Main Line.

Instead of rushing south, when the alarm went off, I now ambled out most mornings for a gentle run. I padded alongside the lush fairways of the West Links, Archerfield and Renaissance golf courses. Then I'd jog on towards the hallowed turf of Muirfield, the scene of Open triumphs by the greatest names in golf.

After a while, with only a few curious deer for company, I would turn down to the beach. Glistening in the Firth of Forth all around were reminders of the economic crisis. Four Fred Olsen ferries moored in the bay at Aberlady, laid up for the duration. Oil tankers dotted on the horizon, lying empty with no oil to carry. Rigs standing idle off the shore of Fife with no need to drill. Golf courses with their flags removed – bereft of the tourists who spend millions round here and closed to the locals.

Then with the wind behind me, I would head home for breakfast, the chorus of the Fidra gulls my only company. The sea on my left-hand side. The sand under my soles. Sidestepping the occasional jellyfish. The breeze helping me back. No London Underground. No travel anxiety. No air pollution. Like many other leaders in lockdown, I began to question, what is corporate life all about?

CHAPTER 1

IN THE BEGINNING

WEDNESDAY 22 JANUARY 2020

The freezing temperature makes Donald Trump shiver as he walks through the icy morning air of Davos, Switzerland. He's among 3,000 of the world's richest and most influential people at the World Economic Forum. The agenda is focused on climate change. Trump doesn't want to talk about that. His focus is the stellar performance of the US economy, on which he intends to anchor his re-election campaign. But when he arrives for a television interview with CNBC's Joe Kernen, he's asked about another matter – the first case of COVID-19 in the US. "Are there worries about a pandemic?" probes Kernen. Trump's answer is brief: "We have it totally under control. It's one person coming in from China, and we have it under control. It's going to be just fine."[4]

THURSDAY 23 JANUARY 2020

Just after 11.20 am, the English Health Secretary, Matt Hancock, is at the despatch box in the House of Commons. Sandwiched between discussions on rugby league and Holocaust Memorial Day, he's here to give a ministerial statement. Several people have died in China after the outbreak of a virus in the city of Wuhan. Some cases are now being detected in other countries. There is none confirmed in the UK.

Mr Hancock tells the House, "The Chief Medical Officer has revised the risk to the UK population from 'very low' to 'low', and has concluded that while there is an increased likelihood that cases may arise in this country, we are well prepared and well equipped to deal with them. The UK is one of the first countries to have developed a world-leading test for the new coronavirus. The NHS is ready to respond appropriately to any cases that emerge. ... The public can be assured that the whole of the UK is always well prepared for these types of outbreaks."[5]

FRIDAY 24 JANUARY 2020

The Lancet is a globally renowned medical journal that publishes peer-reviewed articles from leading experts in the profession. Today it has released a piece titled 'A Novel Coronavirus Outbreak of Global Health Concern.' The paper notes that by 23 January 2020 there were 835 cases of a new virus in China. Twenty-five people had died. *The Lancet* article explains, "The increasing number of cases and widening geographical spread of the disease raise grave concerns about the future trajectory of the outbreak, especially with the Chinese New Year quickly approaching. Under normal circumstances, an estimated 3 billion trips would be made in the Spring Festival travel rush this year, with 15 million trips happening in Wuhan. The virus might further spread to other places during this festival period and cause epidemics, especially if it has acquired the ability to efficiently transmit from person to person." The experts conclude, "Every effort should be given to understand and control the disease, and the time to act is now."[6]

SATURDAY 25 JANUARY 2020

In Beijing, President Xi has convened an emergency meeting of his Politburo Standing Committee. Afterwards, he makes a rare public statement warning the Chinese public of the dangers of COVID-19. He describes it as a "grave situation."[7] The outbreak "must be taken seriously" and every possible measure pursued. Forty-one people have now died. Nearly 1,300 have been infected. President Xi places China on a war footing, locks down major cities and puts the People's Liberation Army in charge of disease control.

MONDAY 27 JANUARY 2020

In the boardroom of one of the City of London's largest investment firms, lunch is fast approaching. The board turns to 'any other business'. The CEO raises the issue of the COVID-19 virus given the stories that emerged from China over the weekend. "Should the executive take any action to adjust their positions and strategy?" Around the table sit women and men who have been through 9/11, the global financial crisis and everything in between. A careful and considered discussion takes place. It lasts ten minutes. The CEO agrees to keep an eye on the situation. No action is to be taken. High up in this glassy tower, the meeting drifts to its conclusion. Lunch is served.

THURSDAY 12 MARCH 2020

As the day dawns, things are noticeably different. My early morning flight from Edinburgh to London Gatwick, which is normally packed, is only a quarter full. I step off the train at London Bridge Station and I'm struck by the hush. The masses are streaming onto the station concourse but today they walk in silence. Sombre, sullen faces. People look afraid. Some with heads bowed, tucked into their coats against the biting wind. The clamour that normally fills the air of the City is replaced with quiet. Today London wears a worried frown.

I emerge from the station and pass the newspaper stands. The headlines hail a massive injection into the UK economy as a '£30 Billion War on Virus.'[8] "Whatever it takes," the Chancellor Rishi Sunak told the Commons.[9]

As the chimes of the City's clocks strike 8 am, I stride onto London Bridge and the stock market starts to plummet. The famous skyline emerges in front of me – the citadels of one of the world's greatest financial centres. Landmarks such as the Cheesegrater, the Gherkin and the Walkie Talkie tower across the horizon. St Paul's Cathedral pierces the blue sky away to my left, its dome a symbol of British fortitude and survival during the Blitz, its tombs the resting place of many British heroes, including Admiral Lord Nelson and the Duke of Wellington.

In their new shiny offices in the shadows of the dome of St Paul's, the journalists of the *Financial Times* are discussing Rishi Sunak's budget at their morning meeting when they are distracted by the market rout taking shape on the TV screens around them.

I walk on through the famous streets of the Square Mile. I pass Lombard Street, Leadenhall and Threadneedle Street. These cobbles have reverberated to many a stock market crash. They saw the South Sea Bubble of 1720. They felt the pain of the Wall Street Crash of 1929 and the Great Depression that followed. They saw Black Monday in 1987. They watched Black Wednesday in 1992, when the Conservative government was forced to withdraw the pound from the European Exchange Rate Mechanism. They observed the financial carnage in the aftermath of the terror attacks on 11 September 2001. They saw the torment of the credit crunch of 2008. Now they bear silent witness to the opening of another chapter in the City's history.

By the time I arrive at the destination of my meeting, another market crash is well underway. The World Health Organization has declared that COVID-19 is now a pandemic. Today is historic on Wall Street too. The Dow drops 10% – its biggest fall since Black Monday in 1987. It's the end of a bull market that has had an unbroken run since 2009.

By the day's end, Donald Trump has announced a ban on travel from Europe to the US, Boris Johnson has told a press conference that this is the "worst health crisis in a generation,"[10] and countries across Europe have started to close schools and take measures that are unprecedented in peacetime.

The newspaper *City AM* calls it the day of the 'Corona Crash.'[11] For many in the Western world, it's the day that COVID-19 hits home.

CHAPTER 2
LOCKDOWN

"There are decades where nothing happens; and there are weeks where decades happen," the leader of the Bolshevik Revolution, Vladimir Lenin, is reputed to have said.

Over a few days in mid-March 2020, the sheer scale of global events could have filled a decade. The death toll escalated at an astonishing rate as the virus spread like wildfire. The scenes in Italy were particularly dramatic. Thousands died. In Bergamo, soldiers were drafted in to carry coffins from warehouses to crematoria.

Countries began to enter lockdown across the world. Egypt, Germany, India, Ireland, Poland, Russia and many more told citizens to stay at home. New Zealand followed South Africa to declare a national state of emergency.

The first of the economic bailouts began. The US senate agreed a stimulus of $2 trillion. More than three million people signed on as unemployed in the US in one week alone. They were just the early adopters as the total figure rose to 40 million before lockdown eased ten weeks later.

Shortages of emergency medical equipment began to emerge. Doctors in Spain complained that they didn't have the kit they needed to save lives. New York pleaded for 30,000 new ventilators. The US Defense Production Act was triggered to get General Motors to start making them. New York City was fast becoming one of the world's epicentres.

The US surpassed China as the country with the most cases. Infections were now appearing across the States, although the president still thought the crisis would be short-lived, hoping businesses could be reopened in weeks. "I'm not looking at months," he said.[12]

As the terror of the virus spread across the West, China said it was past the worst. On some days it claimed the country had no new cases. But questions were beginning to be asked about the reliability of China's figures amid the first hints of another battle to come. The Tokyo Olympics were postponed for a year.

As hospitals began to fill up, the business world began to feel sick too. Ernest Hemingway's 1926 novel *The Sun Also Rises*[13] describes the process of approaching corporate death. "How did you go bankrupt?" asks one of the characters. "Two ways," comes the reply. "Gradually and then suddenly."

The business impact of COVID-19 was being felt suddenly across the world. The airline industry was one of the first to implode. With shops shut, many retail companies were also on the critical list. Hospitality, travel, pubs, restaurants and rental car companies fought to save their corporate lives. Car manufacturers took drastic actions. Chrysler, Fiat, Peugeot, Renault and Volkswagen all announced they were shutting factories across Europe. The global economy was being switched off.

One of the world's best-known investors – the 'Oracle of Omaha', Warren Buffet – has experienced his fair share of financial crashes. He has previously described economic recession with the words: "It is only when the tide goes out that you find out who has been swimming naked."[14] This time, even those who had been modestly well covered were in danger of being exposed.

The world of insolvency practitioners is notoriously discreet. Confidentiality is important, especially in the first stages of financial intensive care. So much is market sensitive. Rumours can hasten the death throes. One senior insolvency partner revealed to me what the start of COVID-19 was like for him: "The first few days made me realize what it must have felt like when the *Titanic* hit the iceberg – a scary number of companies, big and small, started stampeding for the lifeboats. The panic was palpable. They were drowning but we were drowning too. I thought how the heck are we going to cope? How will the insolvency world have the capacity to deal with such a tsunami of corporate failure?"

There were only 1,700 insolvency practitioners in the UK who could be appointed by courts to carry out administrations.[15] There were 17,000 corporate insolvencies in 2019.[16] Now it was predicted half a million companies were on the brink of going bust in the UK alone.

But insolvency leaders saw two opportunities. First, they would be one of the few industries to do well in the crash. Fees would be eye-watering by the time it was over. But this could also be a time to enhance the profession's reputation. The public saw them as the people who closed factories and made mass redundancies. They would prefer to be known for rescuing some of the world's best-known brands and saving thousands of jobs.

As the insolvency practitioners' phones rang off the hook, the directors of well-capitalized businesses with strong balance sheets sat quietly pleased with themselves. They had cash to see them through.

History tells us repeatedly that when the crisis hits the fan, the most important thing for every business is cash. We used to say, "cash is king." When COVID-19 hit, cash was God. Lack of it meant the death knell for those who had been living on borrowed time. It also threatened good, profitable businesses faced with an unprecedented reduction in revenue. No matter how healthy your future order book, if you don't have cash in the bank to pay the wages and the bills, you go bust.

The truth is that a large number of small- and medium-sized enterprises only ever have a few weeks' working capital. The only answer in an economic situation of this magnitude was for the government to bail out entire industries in a way that had never been done before.

On Friday 20 March 2020, just after 5 pm, the UK Chancellor did just that. "The economic intervention that I'm announcing today is unprecedented in the history of the British state," he told the House of Commons. Rishi Sunak had only been in post for 36 days. "Getting through this will require a collective national effort, with a role for everyone to play – people, businesses and government. It's on all of us," he said.[17]

His measures were worth £350 billion – more than ten times his announcement of the previous week. For the first time in British history, the government would pay the wages of workers in what became known as 'the furlough scheme'.

The Chancellor went on, "We want to look back on this time and remember how, in the face of a generation-defining moment, we undertook a collective national effort – and we stood together."

It was a hugely powerful moment for all those watching on television or listening on the radio. Many commentators said it was reminiscent of wartime. At this moment, it was a war against an unseen virus doing unseen damage to unknowing people right across the world.

Within a few weeks the British state would be paying the wages of around nine million workers. As always, the devil is in the detail of a government scheme. Immediately, some felt left out, especially the self-employed. That would be remedied.

Seventy-two hours later, on the evening of Monday 23 March, the UK Prime Minister, Boris Johnson, sat in Downing Street, the Union Flag hanging by his side. His task was to address the British public through a national TV broadcast.

"Without a huge national effort to halt the growth of this virus, there will come a moment when no health service in the world could possibly cope; because there won't be enough ventilators, enough intensive care beds, enough doctors and nurses,"[18] he explained.

He announced the unprecedented peacetime measure of locking down Britain. People would only be allowed to leave their home for very limited purposes. Essential workers could travel to their work. People could shop for basic necessities and take one form of exercise a day. Otherwise, they should only leave their homes for any medical need or to provide care for the vulnerable. Public gatherings of more than two people were banned. Nearly all shops would close, with supermarkets, grocers and pharmacists the exceptions. All social events were outlawed as well as weddings and baptisms. Funerals would be allowed but attendance would be restricted. There would be a necessity to bury the dead.

The prime minister concluded, "In this fight we can be in no doubt that each and every one of us is directly enlisted. ... To protect our NHS and to save many many thousands of lives. ... the people of this country will rise to that challenge. And we will come through it stronger than ever."

The headline on the front of Britain's *Daily Telegraph* the next morning bellowed 'The End of Freedom.'[19]

We now know that the UK economy contracted by 25% in March and April 2020.[20] Never before in history had we seen such a drop. Hundreds of thousands of businesses were facing bankruptcy. Unemployment was heading for unprecedented levels. The people's future was more uncertain than at any time since 1945. The country had moved from shutdown to lockdown. In a few days, we had witnessed more momentous events than we'd seen in decades. The capitalist system had been laid low by COVID-19. Even Lenin could not have imagined anything like this.

THE NEW AGE OF PURPOSE

In the 28 leadership interviews carried out for this book, everyone agreed that things would never be the same again. How much would change was a matter of varying opinion. Seven key themes emerged:

1. The new age of purpose
2. The new world of work
3. Tackling inequality
4. Global cooperation
5. Resilience
6. Resetting the supply chain
7. Maximizing potential

Most leaders covered every one of these themes while more passionately advocating for those they felt most strongly about.

In the next three chapters, the leaders interviewed touch on a wide range of insights as they tell their stories of lockdown. There is a common thread that runs between them – their passion about purpose. Marian Salzman's view is that "purpose is no longer a line or two to emblazon on a website and forget about."

Leena Nair's company, Unilever, has been in the vanguard of leading with purpose in recent years. It's at the heart of what they do for the benefit of their customers, employees and a much wider range of stakeholders. Leena explains that throughout the period of lockdown, "purpose [was] truly elevated." Focused by their purpose in July 2020 Unilever became the most valuable company in the FTSE 100.

Osvald Bjelland sees large corporations with purpose at their heart as the way to tackle the many serious issues facing the world – from climate change to inequality to poverty. The contention is that we have been talking a good game in the corporate world but not delivering. Now, post-COVID-19, it's time to get serious and create the new age of purpose.

CHAPTER 3

MARIAN SALZMAN, SENIOR VICE PRESIDENT, GLOBAL COMMUNICATIONS, PHILIP MORRIS INTERNATIONAL

LOCKED DOWN IN PROVIDENCE, RHODE ISLAND, US, 3 APRIL 2020

Marian Salzman is covered in sanitizer and hunkering down in her beach shack in Rhode Island when we speak. She's sharing the modest space with her husband and her two beloved Golden Retrievers.

It's from this isolation outpost that she's running her team of 700 – the women and men at the front line of efforts by the world's largest tobacco company to create a smoke-free future. A future free of cigarettes.

She's ten days into the 14 she needs to be sure she hasn't contracted COVID-19. She was tested back in Switzerland, where Philip Morris International (PMI) is based. "The test is no pleasure," she says, squirming as she remembers the invasion of her nasal privacy. The result was negative. Still, she's taking no chances.

As we talk, the National Guard is retreating from Marian's beach hut after a visit to check things out. The state of Rhode Island has been exceptionally vigilant in ensuring potential carriers of the virus remain under a two-week quarantine.

Marian is a serious player in global corporate life. She's the senior vice president of global communications for PMI, charged with making the company – once famous for the Marlboro Man – into a respectable corporate citizen as it continues its transformation away from cigarettes. It's a task fit for her.

She has been described as a charismatic power blonde – "think Carrie Bradshaw mixed with Hillary Clinton"[21] – and her COVID-19 uncertainty has not taken the edge off the sharpness of her opinions.

"One thing we need to do on the back of this," she tells me, "is inject humanity back into leadership. We've had enough of all these layers of hubris. We have underestimated the importance of being a decent human being.

"I did something provocative," she admits. Marian sent a very personal note to each one of her 700 employees, asking everyone to get in touch "if you want to talk." The response was powerful. First, a co-worker who was pregnant and all alone reached out. Then a colleague in Italy unable to attend the funerals of family members who had died.

Marian has spent much of her life in the testosterone-fuelled atmosphere of New York City advertising. She is the generation which followed the era depicted in the TV series *Mad Men*. Just as that world changed, now she thinks we will emerge from COVID-19 with a complete rewriting of the rules.

"An entire generation will be shaped by this in the way that many Americans were shaped by 9/11," she says. It took a long time after those terrorist attacks before Marian, then living in Manhattan, would venture above the lower floors of any skyscraper.

One of the changes she loudly predicts is that more and more, "all life will be local. The pioneering spirit may end." She also foresees fewer barriers between work and home life. "We will have to answer, what is work? Where is work? If I were in commercial real estate, I would be terrified. An office is going to become a luxury – and a liability."

Marian says WPP CEO Martin Sorrell once suggested she "get a thicker skin." Now she thinks, "Maybe we will have to teach people how to face fear." Much of her leadership thinking is around how to help the younger generation. She is concerned about the consequences of home schooling for the poor and those who have chaos in their homes. While there is much opportunity in a new way of educating young people, there is a great danger it will further widen the socio-economic divide.

With an Ivy League education, she also sees big implications for the most famous American cathedrals of learning. "What will become of Yale and Harvard?" she ponders. Then there are the countless millions who are losing their jobs right across the US economy.

"We are facing a lost generation. How will they fit back into the workplace? Maybe we will have to enlist our juniors and reinvent national service." As someone who has inhabited the corridors of corporate power most of her life, she remains confident that the new world order will not see a crucifixion of corporations.

"The big corporates are being hugely generous. I believe the bigger well-run companies will be the glue that holds communities together. I have never been more grateful to work for a large company – and not just because of the healthcare."

Marian sees a significant merging of brand strategy and corporate philanthropy. "Corporate purpose is no longer a line or two to emblazon on a website and forget about; it now sits at the heart of the business, serving as a guide for big decisions." She points to a list of corporate examples.

"When a company sets up a fund to cover the basic needs of its employees and their families during the crisis – as Booz Allen, Comcast and others have done – is that philanthropy or a new form of employee-based universal basic income?

"When Crocs donates 10,000 pairs of shoes to healthcare workers, is it philanthropy, product placement or a thank you to some of its most loyal customers? When Rolls-Royce, Airbus and Microsoft team up to produce ventilators, is that philanthropy or an evolution of the sort of private–public partnerships we haven't seen since GE teamed up with NASA on Apollo 11?

"When Indian start-up Oyo Hotels & Homes offers accommodation for free or at sharply reduced rates to healthcare workers battling the COVID-19 crisis, is that philanthropy or PR? When Starbucks pays workers for 30 days, even if they don't show up for work, is it philanthropy or an expansion of sick leave? When Zoom gives its video platform to K–12 schools for free, is it philanthropy or smart early acquisition marketing to a next generation of business customers? Or is it the birth of a new utility infrastructure?"

There are a number of reasons we should listen to Marian Salzman. Her website describes her as having "a brilliant knack for spotting trends before they go mainstream." One commentator called her "an octane-fuelled, 100-ideas-a-minute bunny."[22] In the current crisis, she sees major shifts in the corporate landscape and in behaviours across society.

"I am encouraged to see so many individuals and organizations being their best selves. People are helping each other – neighbours and strangers – in ways big and small. Companies are filling gaps left by governments. It's ironic that it's taken our enforced physical distancing to bring people closer together.

"Let's keep talking, keep experimenting, keep learning, keep sharing. Maybe, just maybe, we'll emerge from all the devastation as a more civil society."

The latest edition of Marian Salzman's annual trends report, published at the end of 2019, was titled *Chaos: The New Normal.*[23] She doesn't claim it was a premonition. But in her final words to me, she couldn't have been clearer.

"There is so much need now for doing things differently."

CHAPTER 4

LEENA NAIR, CHIEF HR OFFICER, UNILEVER

LOCKED DOWN IN LONDON, ENGLAND, 9 JUNE 2020

Fighting pandemics is written into the history of Unilever. William Lever set up his soap factory in Warrington, England, in 1884. His Lifebuoy carbolic soap saved tens of thousands of lives by stopping cholera, typhoid and dysentery spreading through Victorian slums.

More than 130 years later, soap was back on the front line of a pandemic. We were all urged to keep COVID-19 at bay by washing our hands. Hygiene was the first line of defence.

"This is the kind of moment that Unilever was born for," Leena Nair tells me from her home in the London suburbs. The company has a handwashing programme aimed at helping one billion people. It has taken on an increased importance given COVID-19 and has distributed millions of bars of free soap. Unilever contributed €100 million to help the fight against the pandemic through donations of soap, sanitizer, bleach and food.

Unilever employs 155,000 people in more than 100 countries. The global scale of its business presented a unique challenge.

"We were all in the same storm, but we were not in the same boat," says Leena. "The challenges in Kenya were different from India, were different from China, were different from the UK.

"Every single day, because of the global nature of my role, I was confronted with completely different issues. Every government responded differently to the crisis. We had to create our own pathway that was uniquely Unilever."

Unilever is one of the world's largest consumer goods businesses. It has around 400 brands in its corporate cupboard. It would be a challenge to go through a day without consuming one of its products. These include Ben and Jerry's, Dove, Hellmann's, Knorr, Lipton, Persil and Vaseline, to name just a few. Thirteen of its brands top more than €1 billion each in sales. Unilever's total revenue was a whopping €52 billion in 2019.

Their response to COVID-19 was of a scale and intensity the company had never seen before. "The impact was unprecedented," says Leena. "It has been the most stretching period of my working life but the most fulfilling."

Unilever has been at the forefront of creating a purpose-centred business in recent years. When the crisis hit, its response was to build on what it was already doing. "Our three beliefs are: companies with purpose last, brands with purpose grow and people with purpose thrive," says Leena.

Unilever has 45,000 employees in Kenya, which only had 177 intensive care beds at the start of the crisis. So, Unilever converted its warehouses into intensive care units. It bought a quarter of a million COVID-19 tests and donated them to the poorest countries where it operates. In Chile and Ecuador, it converted company vehicles to ambulances. It made ventilators on factory lines.

"Purpose has truly been elevated because when you are anxious, when you are worried, when you are not sure, the only thing that keeps people going is this higher purpose of doing meaningful work in the world. This time has elevated purpose like no other," says Leena.

Unilever offered €500 million to help cash flow across its extended value chain. That gave support to its most vulnerable suppliers and small-scale retail customers to help them protect jobs. The company pledged to protect its workforce from sudden drops in pay for up to three months. This covered its employees, contractors and anyone else who worked on its sites full time or part time. It formed an alliance with General Motors in Argentina to share manufacturing operators. This both helped to enhance the skills and technical knowledge of workers and helped to ensure that the local operations were able to continue to supply essentials to their communities.

Unilever Food Solutions was affected as restaurants closed, but sales of sanitizers and cleaning products soared. Smart HR systems helped to move 8,500 staff from areas where demand was falling to brands that needed to increase production. "We learned to redeploy at scale," Leena says. "This redeployment allowed us to keep people in jobs and ensure business continuity."

Leena Nair moves at pace. Her leadership style is high energy. I suspect her enthusiasm and passion move through the company faster than any pathogen would dare. So, what did she observe was the recipe for success across the Unilever leadership group in the crisis?

"The inner game of the leader matters as much as the outer game," she says. "Purpose, sense of service, learning agility, resilience and personal mastery. Leaders who strengthen their inner game deliver high performance and get the business to grow. What a time to show that's so true. The leaders who stepped up were the ones who had a greater meaning. This has endorsed what we believed in."

Unilever – like the other big corporates – moved huge numbers of people to homeworking at breakneck speed. Leena thinks the new ways of working have broken down hierarchies. "It has created a level playing field of inclusion. It has given us a peep into people's families. I see their pets, their dogs, their children, their struggles. Suddenly you see the whole person."

In the future Leena reckons companies will reduce their office spaces as fewer people commute to their buildings. She believes there will be a blended approach to office and homeworking. People might spend two days a week in the office and three days at home. She thinks that the virtual world we lived in during lockdown can be improved upon.

"We should not over-celebrate it. We don't yet know the long-term impact of large-scale remote working on human connections and our social capital. Work is a collaborative process. We don't want to lose that, so we need to find the right balance.

"People will still need to come together to discuss ideas. People do greater things together because you trust each other. You respect each other. We have to tread carefully and take what we've learned and make sure we keep the diversity of thought and experience."

So, what does Leena think will be the greatest challenges as the world emerges from the crisis? "People will be staring into one of the defining challenges of our times, which is unemployment. We need to really lean into it and solve the social inequality. It is my hope that we will tackle these issues head on.

"My fear is that organizations might just go back to bad behaviours. A vaccine comes along and people go back to doing things we did in the past. There is a hope and a fear. The jury is very much out on which will win out."

Unilever is getting ready. They're looking at how they can help society to deal with the deep economic impact of COVID-19. They have been piloting new employment models. They've been rethinking new ways of giving employees skills and new ways of creating jobs. "We want to influence governments and industries in all these areas. My hope is that these issues will get centre stage."

Leena believes there will be a need for people to come together in a joined-up response to the economic fallout. "Big businesses have to step in along with government. Systemically, people have to get together to solve job creation, job placement and matching skills. This is the time when safe havens will stand out – companies that stand for purpose and taking care of people."

Leena began working for Unilever 28 years ago as a management trainee in India. She's moved onwards and upwards in the company ever since. Her enthusiasm is inspiring. "I'm living my purpose every day. My purpose is to ignite the human spark to build a better business and a better world. It is a humanitarian crisis. It is about the human spirit. It is about valuing human beings. It is about valuing human life. At the same time, it is hugely stretching."

Leena genuinely sees COVID-19 as a watershed for leadership. She believes it has exposed the 'Superman' leader as a relic of the past and that it may usher in a new era of compassionate leadership. She describes the attributes which worked in the crisis and sees them as the template for the future.

"Being kind. Being compassionate. Being empathetic. Being inclusive. No longer is the leader the one who has all the answers. The first thing they do is listen and acknowledge the pain and the answers will follow. Empathize, walk in their shoes. Lead with no hierarchies. Be willing to be humble and curious. These are the leaders who are succeeding at this time. We have undervalued these things in the past because we liked leaders chasing for growth and talking up profit and adopting the Superman style of leadership."

Leena Nair has one final thought on the new kind of leader she wants to see post-COVID-19: "Remember, the more you give the more you get."

CHAPTER 5

OSVALD BJELLAND, CEO AND FOUNDER, XYNTEO

LOCKED DOWN IN THE WEST OF NORWAY, 24 APRIL 2020

Osvald Bjelland talks to me from the kitchen table in his farm in the west of Norway. It sits alongside the glassy waters of a sparkling fjord. You can only get there by boat. His family has grazed sheep on the pastures for more than 500 years.

Osvald doesn't make his living on the farm any more. Now he advises global leaders in many of the world's largest corporations.

Early this morning, he's not quite the crisp corporate sharpshooter displayed on his slick company website. His hair is dishevelled from the brisk winds billowing outside. (I know by now that many leaders in lockdown don't do their hair.)

Osvald's demeanour is not that of a boardroom schmoozer and rather much more a wise uncle who should be listened to. The kind of sage you might find in one of those Norse legends.

He pulls no punches. "This growth model has ended up on the rocks. The conflict between humans and nature is untenable. We can no longer avoid the conflict between the few and the many with more and more money in the pockets of the few.

The intergenerational stress between young and old and between short term and long term needs to be seriously addressed.

"In one way we have seen that our economic growth model has produced enormous progress and lifted millions out of poverty. However, due to rather fundamental problems, there's a risk that overall we will hand over a less positive future to the next genera- tion than we inherited ourselves."

Many of the global companies Osvald works with are in deep shock. He relates one example in a blog written a month before we talk. "This week, a senior business leader I have worked with for many years told me: 'the company I work for has lost over 60 per- cent of the market value built up over 120 years, tens of millions of people will lose their jobs where I live, and millions will lose loved ones to a premature death'.

"He then asked me a critical question: 'While this is playing out, how does one keep a keen eye on other, equally important issues over the medium and long term, like gross inequality and climate change?'"[24]

In Norway, the impact of COVID-19 has been less severe than elsewhere. During the COVID-19-induced shutdown, Norway had a little more than 8,000 cases. Around 230 died.[25] Many put that low mortality rate down to the high number of tests that were conducted and a good health system. Norway was also quick to shut down many aspects of society, close businesses and seal its borders. When Osvald and I speak, Norway is about to begin a phased opening of schools, kindergartens and some shops. This is well ahead of most other European countries.

But the country won't cure its economic ills as quickly as it recov- ered from the virus. Norway is very dependent on oil and gas. The collapse of the oil price has hit its economy hard. As the minister for trade put it, "Norwegian business is in its toughest fight ever."[26]

Osvald believes the transition away from carbon-intensive energies is of enormous importance and long overdue.

Even though all around where he sits today lie the traditions and history of his family farm, Osvald doesn't spare that community from their responsibilities. "Some people are very reluctant to face up to what is wrong with farming. People are stuck believing farming is great."

Around the world, two thirds of our food comes from nine plants. Biodiversity has been reduced. Osvald believes it is time to rethink how we grow and supply our food.

"The virus will burn out. But when it comes to how we are polluting our waters, our air and our food systems, that will still be with us. We are not facing up to this."

Before the lockdown, Osvald worked far from his family's fjord. Xynteo has projects in India with Unilever and Tata. It also works extensively with other big multinationals, such as Scania, Shell and Mastercard. So, what is he telling his clients as they come to terms with COVID-19?

Osvald is married to a leading Norwegian politician, Thorhild Widvey, who has at various times been the country's minister of energy, minister of culture, deputy minister of fisheries and state secretary in the ministry of foreign affairs. So, he understands more than most the pressures on leading politicians. He points out that governments have played a huge role in handling the crisis, and he says they will play an equally important role in decarbonizing heavy industries and reducing the footprint of our lifestyle in general. But, for now, most of his work is focused on large corporations in the private sector.

"Out of the 100 largest economic units in the world, 67 are private companies. So, in order to change the world, I focus on large multinational companies like Shell, Unilever and Mastercard. Can Scania reinvent transport? Can Shell change the world's energy? Can Unilever reform the food supply? This is the route to change."

At the centre of so much of Osvald's work is the critical question, "How do we reinvent growth?" He believes part of the problem is that "We've trained our people to optimize the parts rather than look at the system.

"We have lived on an illusion of customer choice. The whole issue of broader responsibility of what you bring to the market is a long trend which we need to address. Changes in food and energy need deep cooperation. This may well bring about far greater cooperation between private companies and government."

Times may be tough in Norway for a while. Some think it could be the worst economic patch since the Second World War. Unemployment has already shot up. Osvald believes a more frugal life would not necessarily be a bad thing. "Maybe we can live very fulfilled lives with a much more modest lifestyle. To have less debt, and be in a financially sound position, might be more attractive."

But a bit like in one of the Norse folk tales, Norway has a store of riches that it can turn to in its dark moment. The country has the world's largest sovereign wealth fund – a testimony to its prudence in saving some of the bounty from its long-running oil boom. That fund will provide much-needed finance to help bolster the Norwegian economy as it fights to recover.

Osvald, like many others of the leaders in lockdown, bemoans the lack of global leadership at a time when it is needed most. Norway is not a member of the EU. Its population declined in two public votes. But it is part of the European Economic Area – the internal market. COVID-19 has also brought challenges to European unity. But Osvald ponders whether the continent's politicians could be playing a greater role in global leadership.

"There are very few people in politics at the moment who have a broader view and take people with them. We desperately need international cooperation. Trump is trying to torpedo every organization he doesn't control. We have a very profound leadership deficit, which spans both government and business. At its best, leadership is about uniting people to collaborate on building towards a shared future. There is a glorious opportunity here for genuine leaders to pull people and organizations together, in the right direction – to recover better."

Some corporate leaders are often imagined as 'masters of the universe'. COVID-19 has humbled many of them. Their organizations could have reacted well when the virus reached their shores, but many were caught in the headlights and didn't see it coming.

We all wonder why. Now, the talk in many corporate boardrooms will be how to build in greater resilience and agility, and a stronger balance sheet. Those may be the measures suggested by the risk managers. Osvald is clear corporations need to be better prepared next time.

"My biggest message for business leaders is that another crisis is coming our way. We're just not sure which one. We know there is a crisis of climate. We know that there is the possibility of a mass migration of ten million from sub-Saharan Africa to Europe. We know that these crises are coming, but are we going to do anything about them? Or will it be just like COVID-19?"

Osvald Bjelland is passionate about nurturing the next generation of leaders. Most of all he believes this crisis is an opportunity we shouldn't waste. "Individuals can have a greater impact than we often imagine. We need a new generation of high-capacity leaders who can bring people together. Psychologically, this is a time for reflection on what really matters. We may never get this moment again in our lifetimes."

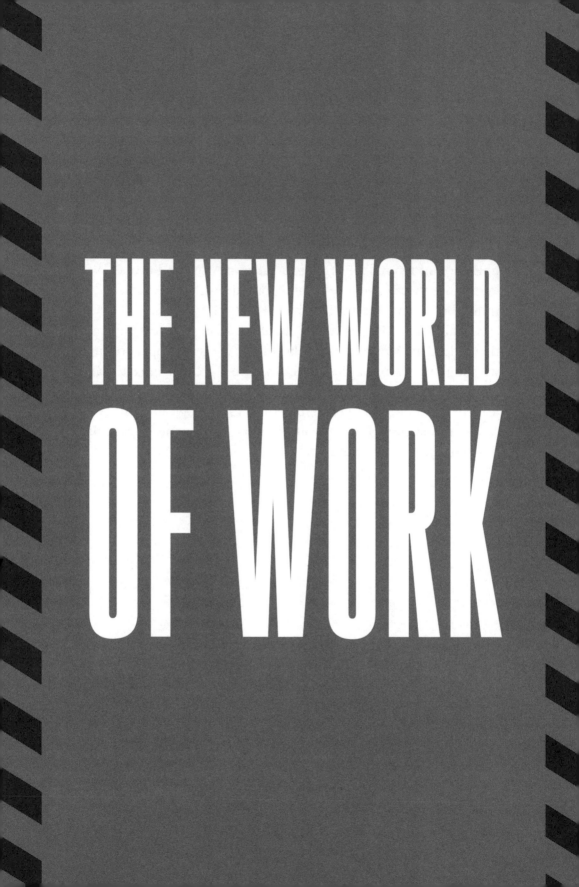

THE NEW WORLD
OF WORK

The second major theme on which there was strong agreement among the leaders in lockdown was that post-COVID-19 there will be a new world of work. This means an existential change in the way we work. It has implications for offices, scheduling, commuting, business travel and productivity. Presenteeism is dead.

For many the new world of work that the virus has forced means a fundamental reconsideration of how they do business. That means reconsidering governance, structures and business models that have been exposed by COVID-19 as not being financially sustainable or fit for the future.

In the next four chapters our interviewees share stories and insights on nearly every aspect of the crisis. But they all address, in their own compelling ways, the new world of work.

We hear from Mark Thompson, the CEO of *The New York Times*, who questions the future of skyscraper offices and concludes that it's time to reimagine the workplace. Nupur Singh Mallick tells us how her company, Tata (which is also an interesting case study on purpose), moved 600,000 workers from offices to homeworking in an astonishing piece of corporate logistics. She also explains how all of Tata's businesses are resetting their strategies around a new age of digital and automation.

We hear from George Hongchoy, whose business owns large office buildings in Asia. He believes people will return to the office environment. However, in the longer term he wonders whether a new way of working might see offices move closer to home rather than being packed together in the central business districts of the world.

Having moved entire populations to remote working, many companies have since realized that it isn't working as well as they first thought. Post-COVID-19, they are looking to adjust and reshape remote working into something that looks very different from what was seen during lockdown. Leaders will need to be trained much better in the skills of managing remote teams. Organizations will need to adjust structures to blend remote working, flexible working and office working to the best effect.

Richard Bevan works in the football business. COVID-19 exposed concerns about governance, sustainability and business models across many companies and in many sectors. Football was just one of them. Richard advocates that the crossroads created by the pandemic has created a time to change. His new world of work is about systemic change in order to be fit for the future. Many other leaders are on the same journey.

Our leaders in lockdown are in no doubt that COVID-19 will accelerate a new world of work.

CHAPTER 6

MARK THOMPSON, PRESIDENT AND CEO, *THE NEW YORK TIMES*

LOCKED DOWN IN MANHATTAN, NEW YORK, US, 18 MAY 2020

On 6 May 2020, the CEO and president of *The New York Times* had just concluded his first quarterly earnings call with Wall Street when he decided to hop on his beloved Brompton fold-up bike.

Still inside the building, Mark Thompson pedalled off across the vast floors of Times Tower. He surveyed the savannah of empty desks. He trundled past the potted plants, the small framed photos of smiling loved ones and an abandoned cardigan. Three thousand people normally pack the Eighth Avenue headquarters. Now fewer than 20 were in the building. The sight of the cycling CEO caused little stir.

"It was like going around an empty milking parlour," Mark tells me. "I wondered why we'd had all these people sitting in rows staring at computers." He imagined his teams comfortable at home, getting more work done and pondered the ways of corporate America. "I thought, there's a big question mark over the office as an organizing principle of cities and I wondered whether it makes sense any more. It made me wonder: should you sell your skyscraper?"

Mark decided hoisting the 'for sale' sign might be a step too far. But he does believe it's time to reimagine the workplace in the wake of COVID-19.

"We must get a new sensible settlement about how we all work together that is more family friendly, more planet friendly, more practical. It will mean we use offices and collective workspaces better and give people more freedom to plan their lives."

When I talk to Mark, he's at home on the Upper West Side of Manhattan. Coffee is bubbling in the kitchen next door. He's relaxed but a little frustrated about being grounded. He's having a good war. His mission in his eight-year tenure has been to move *The New York Times* from a regional city newspaper to a global leader in digital news. In March 2020, his team recorded 240 million unique users. The paper is now one of the most widely read news sources in the world. The business, which was valued at $1.3 billion in 2012, is now worth $6 billion. Even a 50% forecast fall in advertising revenue for the second quarter of 2020 can't take the shine off progress.

"The newspaper advertising will come back," Mark says. "Some may come back as digital. But the main thesis of the business model is digital subscription. In that first quarter, in three months, we added more digital subscribers than the entire UK industry has got."

Mark has been a leader for a long time. He was appointed editor of the BBC's *Nine O'Clock News* in 1988 at the age of 30. He's been a CEO continuously for 18 years. He had the top job at Channel 4 in the UK before an eight-year stint as director general of the BBC. He then crossed the Atlantic to *The New York Times* in 2012. He's old enough and wise enough to admit he's evolved his approach to leading the big beasts of the media.

"I've learned not to push ideas into an organization or insert my strategy. The trick is to pull it out and then it comes from them. Because if it comes from them, they own it."

Those tactics shaped his approach when he arrived in the slightly brasher surroundings of Manhattan armed with his English accent and his BBC ways.

"The great trick at *The Times* was to say, 'Let's look at what you do. Let me examine with you what you do. Let's have a process of intellectual inquiry. What do you believe in? What are your values? What are your strengths?' Then, when we've done that – the strategy is theirs's not mine."

Mark is one of the few CEOs who actually knows what it's like to have COVID-19. Along with members of his family, he was laid low for a relatively short period with mild symptoms. It didn't faze him. Not a lot does. Mark T, as he was affectionately known at the BBC, has been through choppy waters before.

"I have been through a few storms," he says, with a sense of understatement and a sardonic grin. He was the director general of the BBC who had to face up to a series of editorial breaches in 2007. One involved misrepresenting the Queen. In another, BBC staff faked competitions on game shows. He had to act decisively and restore trust. So, he knows the value of calm heads and experience when a crisis hits.

"It's like being the captain of the ship. If you haven't been through a couple of really terrible storms, you don't know. There's no way you can know till you go through one. There is a great benefit to everyone if you have one or two leaders who have been there before because they can give people the calmness and confidence that we are going to get through it."

At least half the staff at *The Times* are millennials. "They look to see what's happening at Silicon Valley, Google, Facebook and in Elon Musk's companies," Mark tells me. "So, you have to move at pace."

The Times cleared all of its buildings of people and moved everyone to homeworking in a matter of days. No one really knew if it was possible to run a 24/7 global newsroom from thousands of apartments and houses scattered across the city. No one knew how they would get everyone back.

"You have to make decisions when you haven't got complete information. That's really one definition of leadership. Are you capable of making coherent decisions even when common sense says,

'We don't know enough? Don't take the chance? Let's gather our thoughts?' You can't respond quickly enough to a crisis or changes in technology and society if you do that. You are constantly having to use your judgement to make bets. The bets this time were pretty big."

Several times in our conversation I offer Mark the opportunity to say something about the American president, but each time he lets it float gently past. Trump has frequently lambasted *The Times* as "false" and "the enemy of the people." Still, 30 years at the BBC have taught Mark to choose his words carefully when discussing politics.

"It is very easy to point to the United States and the current president as examples of poor leadership," he tells me. "I think what is really shocking is how universally poor leadership has been everywhere in this crisis. It is very hard to come up with countries who have taken a generous, open-minded, collaborative approach. Even the EU has shown remarkably little support within the Eurozone core. It is universal across the world and it is very disheartening. It reinforces that the post-war multilateral world is not really working any more, and it is each country for itself.

"It all started with the fall of the Berlin Wall. Before then there was a lot more logic around the need to sit down with your friends and sit down with your enemies and do things like regulate global trade through the World Trade Organization (WTO) or support global health through the World Health Organization. It is all getting very ragged now.

"The mutual hostility and rivalry between the US and China feels like it is moving really quite dramatically. The Sino-US tension and rivalry could well be one of the themes for the next few decades, maybe even the next half century. This could be as big as the Cold War."

As an Englishman in New York, Mark has forthright views on how things have gone back on the other side of the pond.

"It looks like the UK has had one of the worst track records of anywhere in the world. I think there is going to be some God almighty inquiry into what happened. My sense is they were very slow to respond. I had a crisis team going in January. We were laying our plans in February. We went to our own lockdown on 11 March and many people had been homeworking a week earlier. The UK didn't really lock down till towards the end of March. The question for the UK government and the question for Trump is what happened in February?"

Mark Thompson was once ranked at number 65 in the *Forbes* list of the 'World's 100 Most Powerful People'[27] – not that far behind Steve Jobs and Osama Bin Laden. That probably embarrasses him. (Though he might point out he's outlived both.) As CEO of *The Times*, he also has a leadership role to play in New York. Alongside the global digital path that he's set for *The Times*, it remains the newspaper of the Big Apple. So, how does he think the city will recover from being the place that COVID-19 hit as hard as anywhere else in the world?

"New York has been written off many times before. The logic and the opportunity in the city mean it bounces back. But I do think it is going to be hard this time. Live entertainment, Broadway, the arts organizations – what is going to happen there? How quickly will that come back? The crazy real estate prices may come down. But it is going to make worse this appalling contrast we have been between rich and poor, side by side."

The poor need their next meal to survive. The rich need their companies to survive. Mark is pretty clear what the winning formula will be in corporate America – which companies will pull through and which won't make it.

"The main thing for company leaders is – it is the subtle, flexible, responsive ones who will survive and thrive. People who are too slow to respond are going to be toast. That is a first-order thing. It is agility and listening that are the key things."

Mark sees COVID-19 as a "massive accelerant" of previously visible trends in the media sector. It will accelerate on demand services, it will accelerate streaming and it will put more pressure on linear broadcasters. He's got good and bad news for the broadcasters he left behind in Britain.

"If you're the BBC, the virus is good for you because people have been reminded about how important you are. If you are ITV, this is very tough because the question is will the advertising ever come back?"

On the day we talk, the American president has started a new narrative. He's suggested the figures that show the COVID-19 casualty numbers to be significantly greater in the US than anywhere else may be exaggerated – even manipulated by political opponents. Mark Thompson smiles when I ask him about this latest development.

"In the battle between truth and lies, the people on the side of untruths will still try and chance their arm. But the virus is a very hard opponent," he says.

"What is – is. You are going to get found out, if you try and pretend what is – isn't."

CHAPTER 7

NUPUR SINGH MALLICK, GROUP CHIEF HUMAN RESOURCES OFFICER, TATA GROUP

LOCKED DOWN IN MUMBAI, INDIA, 5 MAY 2020

"I'm not sure whether I'm working from home or living at work," Nupur Singh Mallick tells me with a smile and a laugh. She's calmly sipping a large cup of tea at her desk at her house in Mumbai.

In a few minutes, she will join Tata's 4 pm daily videoconference for senior leaders. They've come together at this time for every one of the past 50 days. But they don't meet to focus on the internal matters of one of India's greatest companies. They meet to focus their business resources to help fight COVID-19, right across India.

Ratan Tata, the scion of the famous family, pledged, "Tata has in the past risen to the needs of the nation. At this moment, the need of the hour is greater than at any other time."[28]

In the early stages of the crisis, the company donated $170 million to fight the virus. Its efforts span a huge range of assistance: building beds; donating food for cattle; distributing water; sourcing and manufacturing personal protective equipment (PPE); masks and ventilators; and unleashing the expertise of its software and IT specialists. It's also helped with healthcare infrastructure and digital testing solutions; provided millions of meals for doctors, nurses and healthcare workers; and rolled out online learning for children and students.

Nupur tells me, "Since its inception, the Tata Group ethos has stood for the fact that the community is not just another stakeholder. It is the purpose for our very own existence. We know why we exist. We are here to live up to our values and our purpose. What comes from society should go back to the people. It's all about helping the people and helping India."

The numbers involved in Tata's COVID-19 support efforts are massive. But this is India. It is a land where the scale of everything is not easy to comprehend. The population is nearly 1.4 billion. Almost as many as China and four times the number of people in America.

Tata Group is made up of 30 companies with a combined market capitalization of $113 billion. They have more than 700,000 employees. They are structured in ten divisions, including infrastructure, aerospace and defence, financial services, automobile, consumer, retail and IT. They own airlines, hotels and Tetley tea.

When Nupur and I talk, COVID-19 is taking its toll across India. Lockdown has been strict and is likely to be extended for weeks ahead. The infection is spreading in the densely packed slums of the sprawling cities and the assumption is that India will be hit very hard by the pandemic.

Tata moved 600,000 employees to homeworking in days. The sheer scale of that task is something that would have been unimaginable in normal times.

"It tells you how flexible people are and how advanced the technology is," Nupur says. "Before COVID-19, all of us were reluctant to adapt to work from home at this mass scale. "Now there is much more collaboration. People are productive and more punctual in meetings. People are also a lot kinder and accepting than before."

Nupur is a leader who believes in moving at pace. Before lockdown was declared, 70% of the company's employees had been shifted to homeworking. Its leadership training, which had traditionally been delivered through attending the Tata Management Training centre in Mumbai, was switched to virtual with similar speed.

"We saw immediate decisions had to be taken. It was not a time for waiting and watching." Nupur believes that as a group, Tata "will not return to old ways of working."

She adds, "You want to come out of this much stronger. We are seriously considering by 2025 whether we could have only 25% of our people working in an office. We will not go back to where we were."

Nupur agrees that issues still need to be solved around home-working. "It is not something that can just be mandated. When you come up with a new way, the people need to be at the centre of the design. We don't want to create division between the work-from-home group and the work-from-office people.

"We must also take great care of the mental wellbeing of our people and do more to tackle loneliness. Loneliness is not just for people who live alone."

Nupur joined the company as a trainee 23 years ago. Now she is group chief human resources officer working closely with the 60 other HR directors across Tata. "I can hear the conversation right across the group. Now every company is recalibrating their business plans and digital will be at the heart of everything we do going forward."

That digital ambition is laid out in a vision for India written by the chairman of Tata Group, Natarajan Chandrasekaran, in his recently published book *Bridgital Nation*.[29] It's described as a blueprint for a prosperous India that will include everyone. It aims to bridge the huge chasms between rural and urban and rich and poor through a combination of artificial intelligence, cloud based and automated learning. The Tata chairman believes that this could create and impact 30 million jobs by 2025. COVID-19 might slow the pace of that ambition or accelerate the need.

In India in April 2020, 122 million people lost their jobs. More than 90 million of them were small traders and labourers.[30] The true economic impact will be long lasting. Tata will feel the ill winds of the global recession right across its business. In the UK the company had to seek government support to keep the steel industry going. For the Tata leaders, Nupur states that communicating effectively with their people has never been more important. Throughout the crisis her message has been consistent and it will remain so in the future.

"People don't have clarity. Often leaders want to hide and wait till they get clarity. I say, 'Please don't hide. Go and talk to your people. Be honest; be hopeful.'"

That is a theme for Nupur as she looks after the massive human resources of Tata.

She tells me, "The conversation has to be honest but always with a sense of hope because when you lose hope it's over. When we talk about the future, we have to give hope."

Tata is clearly preparing for a major reset to be fit for the post-COVID-19 world. Its group human resources officer will be a champion of change across its 30 companies. But, Nupur tells me, not everything is up for grabs.

"While ways of working and business models might see a paradigm shift, our values and culture at the Tata Group are what bind us all together. The only thing that shouldn't change is who we are."

With that, Nupur Singh Mallick is off to join her Tata senior team to continue helping with India's fight against COVID-19.

CHAPTER 8
GEORGE HONGCHOY, CEO, LINK ASSET MANAGEMENT

LOCKED DOWN IN HONG KONG, 22 MAY 2020

"I'm not a pessimist or an optimist," George Hongchoy tells me. "I'm just a realist."

He's the CEO of Link Asset Management Limited, the largest real estate investment trust in Asia. COVID-19 has put a bit of a dent in his company's portfolio. It's had major implications for the sector too. "The full impact of this is enormous. We are not returning to the past," he says.

George has just released a profit warning, has launched an HK $300 million (US $38.69 million) support scheme to help tenants with their rent, and is now getting ready to protect his shopping malls from another round of Hong Kong protests.

Yet he maintains a commendable air of calm and control as he tells me, "There are worse things than what you are dealing with right now. Count your blessings."

Before the crisis, Link's portfolio was valued at HK $220 billion (US $28.36 billion). This has been marked down to HK $193 billion (US $24.8 billion) because of COVID-19 – a reduction of 12%.

The company has 132 properties in Hong Kong, Beijing, Shanghai, Guangzhou, Shenzhen and Sydney. That's around 14 million square feet of real estate. In late July 2020 they announced the US $487.5 million acquisition of The Cabot office building on Canary Wharf – the London headquarters of Morgan Stanley.[31]

Their properties include shopping malls, offices and car parks. Link has also got the famous Hong Kong fresh markets, where rows of traders sell meat, fish and fresh produce from stalls. They're a hugely important part of Hong Kong culture and tradition. The company has invested in renovating and reimagining more than 40 of these markets over the past decade.

"We've made them a safe and hygienic place to shop," George tells me. They remained open throughout the health emergency. Link installed air conditioning and improved the facilities, putting them on a par with supermarkets, and this brought in younger customers in greater numbers. During the crisis, they added hand sanitizers, distributed rubber gloves and increased the use of electronic payments. So, people don't need to handle cash.

George says trade in supermarkets and fresh markets went up 20% during the crisis. People were buying more food to cook at home rather than going to restaurants, which had restricted their capacity as the Hong Kong government introduced social distancing. It was a different story for the retail tenants in Hong Kong's vast malls. Many asked for rent relief. Some benefitted from Link's HK $300 million relief fund. In China, lockdown was relaxed in May. Shoppers returned to the malls but initially business was slow. George says footfall was 80% of what it was before the crisis, but revenue has so far only come back to 50%.

"In the near term, people have gone back to a simpler way of life," he adds.

Link has been a business success story – all be it stalked by local political grumbling over rents at its properties. It recently made its first acquisition outside Asia when it bought a ten-storey office block in Sydney's Central Business District for AU $683 million (US $469.5 million). Things had been going well.

Protests against the government had quietened down. Then the virus hit.

"Things are manageable," George assures me. "We will shore up our balance sheet and prepare ourselves for the bigger storm to come. Prepare for the worst and hope for better."

Link is a big business. Its revenue is around HK $10 billion, which is roughly US $1 billion. With a portfolio of that scale it's keen to understand the changes that might emerge in the wake of COVID-19. Hong Kong and China have witnessed a huge shift to homeworking just like elsewhere. But George doesn't see this as an acute trend, as predicted in other regions of the world.

"It depends on the function and the nature of the roles. I still think that work and social interaction go together. Employers will become more flexible. We'll need more space for each individual. But I think most people will go back."

However, over the longer term he believes there may be a move away from the concept of the central business district.

"Town planners have discussed this for many years. Maybe you don't need a central business district. Maybe you need employment nearer to people's homes and an end to the idea of commuting. An end to everyone going to one place."

In the short term, there will be changes in the retail world too. Shops and malls will be cleaned much more often to keep them free of germs. There will be more integration between online and offline. "We have given everyone in the world forced training in online shopping," George tells me. "Retailers are smarting up." He suggests customers could select fashion online and arrive in store to try clothes on. Gyms in China are asking clients to book in two-hour time slots. The exercise areas are given a deep clean after each session. It all shows retailers are innovating to live alongside the virus for the foreseeable future.

He explains how Hong Kong has tackled COVID-19. Many will ask why other countries couldn't have followed Hong Kong's example. "I don't think the word is 'lucky'," he says. "But in Hong Kong we did have SARS [severe acute respiratory syndrome] in 2003 and that has helped us. Tracking and tracing. Doing tests. Everyone given their wristband with bluetooth. We also built quarantine centres to ensure the health system wasn't overwhelmed."

As the health crisis starts to pass, it is time to reflect on how people coped. George deployed his three 'Cs' in crisis management – collaboration, communication and care. He sums up this formula as follows: "Collaborate – don't solve the problem on your own. Work with people. Communicate – you can never communicate enough. And care – think about your people."

Now, as the COVID-19 crisis recedes, the economic crisis arrives and the protests return, once again the staff of Link will be called upon to safeguard shoppers and tenants of its shopping malls in Hong Kong.

"We are civilians. We are not trained to deal with violent actions. We are all on standby every night. It's tough. If I think of our daily operation, we have had a dress rehearsal with the massive number of protests we had last year. What will test us now is having to handle both the virus and the protests at the one time. I feel for our tenants – they have just got their heads up above the water to breathe again and now their businesses will suffer once more."

The uncertainty around the protests in Hong Kong's shopping districts adds another difficulty to agreeing new leases and terms.

"When it becomes hard is when we have to negotiate with tenants despite finding it difficult to read the future. It is hard when you don't know."

On the day that George and I talk, China has announced it will introduce a new security law in Hong Kong. This will increase tensions and reignite protests. Some businesspeople are weary with the disruption and disorder.

Within 48 hours of our conversation, thousands of protestors are back on the streets of Hong Kong. The police respond with tear gas, pepper spray and water cannons. It is just the start of another period of demonstrations that will run and run.

George Hongchoy has collected a number of accolades in his ten years as CEO of Link. He was named one of *Harvard Business Review*'s '100 Best-Performing CEOs' in the world in 2018 and 2019, and won the EY Entrepreneur of the Year China Award in 2017.

Real estate in Hong Kong and China has its fair share of challenges. George seems to take most of them in his stride. Before we finish our call, he tells me his son has reminded him, "There is no such thing as half empty. There's only half full of water and half full of air."

George concludes, "I think most of us are very lucky. We're sound and healthy." Sounds like the realist has become an optimist.

CHAPTER 9
RICHARD BEVAN, CEO, LEAGUE MANAGERS ASSOCIATION

LOCKED DOWN IN MANCHESTER, ENGLAND, 5 JUNE 2020

Richard Bevan's business is sport. He's CEO of the League Managers Association (LMA), which represents more than 500 professional football managers in the UK and across Europe. He is also chairman of the Caribbean Premier League, which is a fast, brash T20 cricket tournament. It's one of the swiftest-growing leagues in the world of cricket.

COVID-19 stopped sport in its tracks. Everything from the Olympics to the US's National Basketball Association was postponed or cancelled. The financial impact will be severe and long lasting. Richard explains the state of play in football: "We are facing a global crisis unlike any that we have known. Sport is proving to be one of the high-profile business casualties of the pandemic. There are far-reaching economic, social and structural consequences for future revenues from elite to grassroots and from governing bodies to promoters. Every organization will be affected. There will likely be significant effects for the next two to three years."

The crisis has also exposed structural and cultural issues, which Richard believes need to be addressed. He says, "Today many clubs face the stark prospect of administration and winding up petitions and the unexpected and unwelcome impact of COVID-19 has made things dramatically worse. There need to be strong checks and balances on financial management in football with accountability, transparency and strong leadership."

Richard tells me that the impact of COVID-19 has been very different depending on the level at which you are playing the game. At the top, between 50% and 60% of football's income comes from the broadcasters. "In the Premier League it is about completing the season, maintaining the integrity of the competition, and limiting the losses and the financial rebates."

At the lower end, 80% to 90% of revenue comes from the gates, food and beverages, and local sponsors. "These are the clubs that are in a really serious condition," Richard says. "For them it is not about whether they will complete this season but actually whether they will start next season at all."

In 1992, 22 of the biggest clubs in England broke away to form the Premier League. Some argue the structure has been fragmented ever since, as the split left the rest of England's 72 professional teams under the banner of the English Football League (EFL). The Football Association was left to run the national teams and be the overarching governing body. As the EFL emerges from COVID-19, it has a monumental black hole in its finances. Richard believes the crisis has exposed the need to change the shape of the game.

"In a crisis you get clarity," he tells me. "The chairman of the EFL has already said the structure isn't fit for purpose. It's like working in a PLC with no head office. My biggest learning from the crisis is if the sport wants to be successful going forward, it needs a head office. That's about centralized thinking, centralized revenues, centralized messaging and making sure everyone is on the same team bus. That needs to be the focus.

"What the pandemic has shown is that the frailties of short-termism both on and off the pitch do not provide a sustainable platform for the future. Circumstances are forcing everyone to take a long, hard look at how things are done. There is an appetite to change and change for the better. There is huge support for reform, and we have a huge resource of talent to draw on to redraw the face of football governance for the benefit of everyone involved, both in the short and the long term.

"We need to unite together to care for all the different stakeholders in the game, especially our fans and the different communities we serve. I hope all the stakeholders take the opportunity to step up and show the game the way forward through better governance, through improvements in the way that performance is reviewed, and by promoting sustainable, forward-looking business plans."

More than 40 professional football clubs have gone into administration since 1992. That's a warning signal for the next period and a reason for systemic change. "We need to ensure we have a clear working framework for the future and, where necessary, an independent regulator to support the decision-making process," Richard says.

Richard also believes that the crisis has reminded people of the original principles of what the sport of football is all about – especially at a time when it is being played behind closed doors. "It's about the fans. Without the fans we don't have a game."

The LMA has dealt with a huge volume of issues since the pandemic began. "Health is the guiding principle for every decision," says Richard. When the furlough scheme was introduced, clubs messaged coaches, managers and staff causing widespread uncertainty about their futures. "We decided not to email but to pick up the telephone." He wanted members to know the LMA was "here to help." One of the LMA's legal team spoke to 51 managers on one day. "We were driven by the members and their needs rather than the ideas of someone in head office." That led the LMA to provide medical advice to managers' families on issues as varied as testing and wellbeing. It engaged five doctors from its network to help. "Communications, clarification and consistency of message" was the mantra.

Richard offers sage advice on how to lead in a crisis: "Football is managing through what sometimes feels like a permanent state of psychological crisis."

Not surprisingly, he advocates a team approach when the going gets tough, "You need to bring your boldest self to a crisis but don't do it on your own." He points to the examples of great international football managers. Dutch manager Johan Cruyff "changed the identity of a country. But he didn't do it alone." The French international manager Didier Deschamps likes to have three captains in his team – a physical captain, a technical captain and a psychological captain. Richard sees this model as applicable and effective in business too.

"You need to build the spine of the business. So, I want leaders in all parts of my team. I want to have around me good finance and good legal advice. You need to recruit really well – have a leadership team and a shadow leadership team for each part of your business. You need diversity and a growth mindset."

Back in the 1990s, as a young man, Richard joined the Professional Cricketers' Association. Although it didn't have any money or any staff, it did have the legendary English cricketer Colin Cowdrey as its patron. He had more than 114 caps for his country and a natural ability to network. He invited Richard to a test match against India at Lords. "I was expecting to turn up, have lunch and meet a couple of people," says Richard. But Lord Cowdrey took him on a tour of the hospitality boxes and introduced him to the chairmen and CEOs of nearly every major FTSE 100 company. That led to a five-year deal with Mitsubishi and Richard's career in the business of sport was launched.

"That taught me that building relationships is the biggest focus, in business and in sport," he says. His advice to young leaders is to make 20 really good contacts every year. "Before you know it you will have a network of 200 who will become friends, business partners, connectors and clients."

There are interesting parallels between leaders in sport and leaders in business. One of the most famous managers of recent years is José Mourinho, dubbed 'the special one'. Mourinho's view is that great leadership is founded first on great knowledge.[32]

Richard has observed the leaders in business and the leaders in football. "Football managers are the most important people at a club," he says. "They are also the first people that get the sack when things go wrong." On average, a professional football manager is out of work every 12 to 15 months. Arsène Wenger is one exception. He survived for 22 years as Arsenal manager. He cites culture, values and behaviours as the keys to his longevity. "You have first to create a culture, a sense of who we are as a unit, what makes us different from other people, how can we create something that is common to all of us."[33]

"Managers have a great ability to stay calm, to think clearly," says Richard, "They work in a very volatile industry. They are able to recognize how to be resilient and absorb the negative stress and turn it into positive energy. When they do get sacked it's a very public business. That keeps them grounded. They have a presence about them which gives them consistent beliefs. They have a certain style and integrity about what they say and do. They practise that more than they realize. When you have chaos going on all around you, the manager has to instinctively make decisions. They are great instinctive decision makers.

"If you look at the great leaders in football like Arsène Wenger, Howard Wilkinson and Bobby Robson, who I have had the privilege of working for all three in the LMA, you find they share one attribute – their first answer is normally the correct one."

One change that Richard advocates is that the government should regard sport as an economic driver rather than a pastime. He believes a sports minister should be on the main cabinet rather than in one of the lesser offices of state: "The government needs to recognize that sport is one of the UK's top ten exports and has such an influence on health, education and many other areas on their agenda."

Richard, like many leaders in lockdown, thinks that like high performers in sport, high performers in business must take steps to maximize their own physical and mental performance. Post-COVID-19, this area will become essential, not optional. "We need to make sure that we are mentally and physically fit to do the job. We've learned in the pandemic not to be reactive about our health but to be proactive."

Richard saves one of his most sage observations for last. He thinks COVID-19 has highlighted a gradual change in management style in the corporate world. Command and control is dead.

One of the most famous managers in football, Sir Alex Ferguson, observed the same.[34] Richard says, "The traditional command and control style of management is changing. We are moving from a demanding role to a convincing role."

Richard Bevan believes the crisis has hastened this change. "The really exciting companies are those that manage from the bottom up and that has been accelerated by this crisis.

"Coaching is the golden thread through football and business. Learning and adapting is the golden thread of how to come through the crisis in the best shape you can."

The third theme which our leaders in lockdown voiced was tackling inequality. The pandemic exposed inequality in so many ways. The virus was unequal in who it killed – targeting ethnic communities, the poorer in society, and our eldest and most vulnerable citizens. The white middle class avoided the worst.

The economic consequences of COVID-19 will hit the poorest the hardest. The most vulnerable will be squeezed even more in the next few years as unemployment rockets. The emerging economies will be blighted by debt as their finances flounder. The richer economies will sail on. The move towards virtual in schools, colleges and universities will widen the attainment gap.

The killing of George Floyd in the US sparked widespread rioting and highlighted racial inequality in America and the rest of the world. Racial injustice is raw and unresolved. Gender inequality has been brought into even sharper focus. Remote working exposed a new set of issues which disadvantage female employees. It revealed inequality in how parents divide responsibilities at home to the detriment of working mothers.[35] COVID-19 also highlighted how access to public healthcare is not a given right for so many – the great health divide.

In the following four chapters our leaders take a whirlwind journey around their lives in lockdown. Their stories cover a lot of ground. But the common thread between these leaders is that each has a passion around tackling inequality.

Pocket Sun is a young and dynamic entrepreneur determined to break down the door of the male-dominated world of venture capitalism and release the potential of female leaders. She tells us she wishes "a revolution could be born out of this crisis."

Sacha Romanovitch traded her role as CEO of one of the UK's largest accountancy firms to help fight for fairer finance for the poor. She explains how, because of COVID-19, "People who are already in vulnerable circumstances are being put in an even worse position overnight."

Sir Brian Souter is a hugely successful entrepreneur and one of the UK's leading philanthropists. He covers many aspects of the impact of COVID-19 and tells of his fears for the poorest in society – especially in Africa and Asia, whose countries do not always have robust welfare systems for their citizens to fall back on.

Vivienne Artz is President of Women in Banking and Finance. She points out that if we can move armies of staff to homeworking overnight, then why can't we move at the same pace to advance the gender agenda? Progress on gender equality remains glacial.

The truth is that the corporate world has stalled in tackling inequality. Some progress has been made but so much remains to be done. Post-COVID-19, it's time to move from recognizing inequality to tackling it.

CHAPTER 10

POCKET SUN, VENTURE CAPITALIST AND CO-FOUNDER, SOGAL

LOCKED DOWN IN SINGAPORE, 6 MAY 2020

"Most of our portfolio companies are doing well and some are really thriving," Pocket Sun tells me from her apartment in Singapore. This is not what you expect to hear during the biggest crash in the modern history of capitalism. Pocket is only 28 years old. She's bucking the trend.

A young woman born in China, she is far from what you might expect in venture capital (VC). She's determined to change the VC world. She wants to redefine the next generation of entrepreneurs and investors. So far, she's been making a difference.

She's driven by a simple observation. "The VC industry has been very dominated by men and has stayed a small and exclusive network. It is only available for people who already have a foot in the door." She cites the statistic that in the US only 2.8% of VC funding went to female entrepreneurs in 2019.[36]

"It was a closed-door, exclusive place for people in the same social networks and the same golf club."

Her answer has been to build her own powerful alternative network. Through the SoGal Foundation, she has brought together 100,000 female entrepreneurs in 50 chapters across five continents. "There has been a big mismatch between the demographics of entrepreneurs and investors. The entrepreneur coming to us looks colourful and diverse."

Pocket's first fund has now invested in 31 companies. She has enlisted support from 94 investors around the world. They've put their money into companies that are aiming to enable "how the future generation lives, works and stays healthy."

The businesses she's backing include an at-home health-testing company, a start-up that makes custom wedding dresses online, a business changing the face of death care and a New York-based venture redesigning mental healthcare, launched during the COVID-19 crisis.

The healthcare company – Everlywell – created the world's first at-home test for COVID-19. "They turned it around in eight days," says Pocket. The mental health venture – Real – completely changed its business model when the virus hit. "It took ten days for it to go online and become fully digital."

The wedding dress start-up prospered when traditional wedding shops were forced to close in lockdown. "This company is experiencing rapid growth, with a record high single-day sign-up of 10,000 brides," Pocket tells me in a modest, matter-of-fact manner. "It was built on digital from the get-go. With this business model it is winning tremendously." The company's expertise in the Chinese supply chain also allowed it to source high-quality surgical masks, which it donated to healthcare workers in the US.

Pocket believes that the winning ingredient in her portfolio of companies is the diversity of the founders. "It is because we deploy gender lens investing. Women are adaptive and very fast executors. Women entrepreneurs have never been capital rich to begin with. They are used to being scrappy and bootstrapping to survive. They are also more sensitive to cash flow and profitability. They pay close attention to the changing needs of their customers."

Pocket says she was mentally prepared for COVID-19 before many others. In late January, she had to abandon a trip to China to see her parents for Chinese New Year. "I knew what was coming when I followed daily what was happening in China."

Even when the crisis was at its peak, SoGal did not slow down. If anything, it grew. "When everyone else was suddenly triaging their portfolio, we were closing multiple new deals. Most of our peers stopped doing that. It is about evolving with agility and embracing change. We are constantly thinking about what the next thing will be and where our capital should be deployed. What do people need right now and in the future? How big can it be? Is this the right team? Who else is out there? Is this the right time to enter the market?"

Pocket's business partner is Elizabeth Galbut. Elizabeth began investing while still at university, creating a student-led VC firm at Johns Hopkins, a university in Baltimore. After helping healthcare incumbents digitize and bringing in $200 million of new business at Deloitte, Elizabeth teamed up with Pocket to form SoGal Ventures. But how did a young woman from China end up trying to change the male-dominated world of American VC?

"The honest truth is I stumbled upon it," Pocket tells me. She received a master's degree in entrepreneurship and innovation. Then she did a programme at Stanford University in California, focused on investing in Silicon Valley. That prompted her to challenge the status quo.

"It struck me that if you didn't look like Mark Zuckerberg, you were going to have a much smaller chance of getting VC funding. There was a big shortage of women role models. The idea of starting a VC firm was super-scary at the time, because it was such an intimidating world, full of insider talk. If you didn't already have a way into the network, it was almost impossible to break into. This is what we aim to change with the work we do at SoGal."

Pocket's appetite for change is not just confined to the VC world. The COVID-19 virus has focused her attention across a range of issues from consumerism to capitalism to how we treat the vulnerable. "I wish a revolution could be born out of this crisis," she says.

"This period is such a great opportunity for reflections on the whole system that we're living in."

Much of what she wants to challenge is related to the way we work in the modern corporate world. "I think we are in late-stage capitalism. Now that we cannot travel, it makes me think, why do we need vacations so much? Is it because we feel a 10-day island getaway can save us from another year of the daily struggle? Is this how humans are meant to live on earth?"

Pocket noticed that her friends who lost their jobs during COVID-19 seemed to feel an identity loss at the same time. "They told me without the daily routine, they didn't know who they were any more. Their whole life was centred around waged work and everything outside that seemed to be secondary. I found it strange that everyone was talking about being productive from home when the whole world just fell 'sick'. We really should be collectively taking a step back and figuring out the level of trauma we are experiencing."

She challenges the current system of consumerism. "Do we really need all that stuff? Why are we convinced that our worth is associated with these things?"

Pocket points out how the virus has weighed so much more on the poor. The tens of thousands of infected foreign workers in crowded dormitories in Singapore are just one example of that. She has recently visited India and seen 15-person families living in the same room. Can we change how we care for our vulnerable people as a consequence of what we've been through with COVID-19?

"Rich people are a lot more protected from the virus," she tells me. Even though she commends Bill Gates for his contributions to global health, she questions how we are relying on him to help with developing a vaccine. "Society shouldn't be saved by billionaires."

A conversation with Pocket Sun gives you hope for the future. It makes you optimistic that transformational change might just come from the grim reality of COVID-19. If we are really to reset the world, we need people like Pocket, her entrepreneurs and her investors to lead the way.

CHAPTER 11

SACHA ROMANOVITCH, CEO, FAIR4ALL FINANCE AND FORMER CEO, GRANT THORNTON

LOCKED DOWN IN EXMOUTH, ENGLAND, 24 APRIL 2020

"I've gone a bit more Devon," says Sacha Romanovitch, her gentle burr[37] floating over Zoom as she lapses back into her local accent. She's been at home in Exmouth, 200 miles from London, on the southwest tip of England, since the crisis began.

In a different time, as the CEO of the accountancy firm Grant Thornton, she might have been helping the UK's largest corporates to steer their way through the financial maze of COVID-19. Instead, she's focused on how the most vulnerable in society will survive the crisis.

Sacha is now the CEO of Fair4All Finance. It's a business whose mission is to make life easier for those with very little money. This group of society is excluded from the financial basics. Its members find it impossible to access the complex world of financial services.

"Everyone needs to be able to access the fundamentals to take part in society," Sacha tells me. "We need to address the fact that mainstream finance is largely designed for people with predictable lives and predictable incomes. The crisis just heightens all of these issues. People who are already in vulnerable circumstances are being put in an even worse position overnight."

She displays all the characteristics of someone who has just aligned their passion with their job. The problems that she and her colleagues are dealing with are a million miles from the world of corporate finance or the trading floors of the City. She is on the front line with the real victims of the economic impact of COVID-19. None of them has a SIPP (self-invested personal pension) or a portfolio to fall back on. Their need is to access affordable credit to see them through the dark financial months.

"Sixty per cent of the people losing their jobs right now are on low incomes," Sacha says. "We're talking about people who barely have a can of beans. Society's answer is an Elastoplast of support rather than a proper safety net."

Sacha is a grammar school girl brought up in Surbiton, in southwest London. She won a place at Oxford. Her early career moved at pace. She became a partner at Grant Thornton at 33 years old. That's a high achievement in the accountancy profession. She then rose to become the first female CEO of a major UK accountancy firm, running a £500 million business with over 5,000 UK employees. She also sat on the global board of Grant Thornton, which has oversight of more than 40,000 people in 140 countries.

As you might expect, numbers come easy to her. She tells me that 11.5 million people in the UK have less than £100 of savings to see them through the crisis. Seven and a half million have significant debt. Many can't get access to cash during their lives in lockdown. Around 1.3 million people don't have a bank account and 1.9 million households can't afford a washing machine.

"The one thing this proves is that trickle-down economics doesn't work. Much of caring for the most vulnerable has been delegated to charities. What we are seeing with the fallout from COVID-19 is that it's the most vulnerable who are being squeezed the most."

But Sacha isn't despondent. Instead, she sees the current situation as an opportunity for change. "What we are seeing is that financial services are only a microcosm of the problem. So, how can we use this situation to accelerate the changes we need in the longer term?"

One way she intends to do that is by viewing the current crisis through a "moral spotlight." Take the issue of unauthorized overdrafts. Some banks were due to hike their rates for those overdrafts up to an eye-watering 40%. Those who have less would have had to pay a whole lot more. Careful lobbying changed that. Now, for at least the period of the pandemic, most banks will not charge anyone for going up to £300 overdrawn. A modest amount but a lifeline for many. Fair4All Finance has also launched £5 million of support for affordable credit providers to help them scale up their efforts to support more vulnerable people.

Sacha believes that the moral spotlight should shine across the business landscape.

"People notice who is pitching in to help right now and they see who is trying to squeeze every last buck out of the situation if they can. I hope people will remember that," she tells me. She sees the period of the crisis as crucial for achieving change for those in vulnerable circumstances.

"It is vital that we accelerate our work to ensure that significant harm isn't done by governments or financial services businesses."

Sacha has been reading the Hilary Mantel novel *Wolf Hall*, a tale of Tudor intrigue. In it, Thomas Cromwell returns home to find that his wife and his two daughters have all died of the 'sweating sickness'. It's a timely reminder that the ills we face are not new.

The challenge in the modern era is what happens when the sweating sickness passes. Can we achieve systemic change in the aftermath of the crisis? Sacha is a whirlwind of ideas on that front. A quick scan of her social media confirms that. In the week that we talk, she has revealed how she was "dumbstruck" when she was shown the siloed organizational design of the NHS. She supports myriad comments re-enforcing the need for climate and social justice. She likes the news that due to COVID-19 we have been able to rehouse thousands of rough sleepers. But why couldn't we have done that in normal times?

There are other big targets to be shot at, too. There is what she describes as "reinventing what industries and trades do." She adds, "First off we need to reinvent retail with thought to the circular economy. What's the point in us buying new stuff we don't need while throwing perfectly good stuff into landfill?"

She sees this as a moment when government and business could "step up to a metalevel." Her thinking is reminiscent of the Marshall Plan, through which the US provided $15 billion to rebuild Western Europe after the Second World War. Similarly, the New Deal was brought in by President Roosevelt in 1933 to rebuild the US during the Great Depression. Could we take the COVID-19 crisis as the cue to envisage 'the Great Reset'? Looking right across sectors, could we evolve a new industrial strategy and a new talent strategy to match?

The NHS was a child of the Second World War. The time was right for that big idea. Now this restless CEO believes that reform of the way we support the poorer in society could be an essential part of the Great Reset from the pain of COVID-19.

Like many others, Sacha also sees this as a golden opportunity to redefine work. In her own routine, she is quite enjoying being able to base herself in the next room to her son. She realizes that so many hours spent travelling to London or further afield have often been wasted time. Change in these areas would also have the twin benefits of being kinder to the planet and giving a greater flexibility to those with caring commitments alongside their professional life.

But she is uncomfortable about how the digital divide will affect the many who can't have what most of us in lockdown take for granted. "What about the parents and children who can't afford a computer? Those who can't afford broadband? They're stuffed." This leads her to advocate a proper digital transition as another theme for major change, levelling up access to money and services.

The enemy of change may be the human tendency to just go back to being busy again when a problem passes. "We really need to create space for insight and reflection," Sacha says. "People must have the opportunity to appreciate – what has been different about their lives over these months and what do they want to be different in the future? It may be a zillion little changes by individuals that create the new normal. But we need to actively redesign our lives in this new context."

With that, Sacha Romanovitch signs off from our call to check on her son's schoolwork. Then, from her tight home office in Exmouth, she will resume her hectic schedule. Her crusade to help transform the lives of the vulnerable is only getting started. She sees COVID-19 as the burning platform for change. But she is under no illusions about the pragmatic pitfalls that stand in her way in the weeks ahead.

As Hilary Mantel writes in *Wolf Hall*, "It is all very well planning what you will do in six months, what you will do in a year, but it's no good at all if you don't have a plan for tomorrow."[38]

CHAPTER 12

SIR BRIAN SOUTER, FOUNDER OF STAGECOACH, ENTREPRENEUR, INVESTOR AND PHILANTHROPIST

LOCKED DOWN IN PERTHSHIRE, SCOTLAND, 1 MAY 2020

Forty years ago, Sir Brian Souter worked weekend shifts as a bus conductor while he trained as a chartered accountant. Then he decided to swap the world of debits and credits for tickets and timetables. He founded the bus business Stagecoach with his sister, Ann Gloag. Their first excursion was from Dundee to London on 9 October 1980.

From that humble beginning, the company, fuelled by Prime Minister Margaret Thatcher's deregulation in the UK, grew into an international transport business. At its peak the company was worth around £3.5 billion. Its buses have plied routes in every corner of the world. It's run ferries in New Zealand and railways across Britain. It won the UK's first rail privatization contract, South West Trains, and partnered with Richard Branson's Virgin on the east coast and west coast mainlines. It founded Megabus, bought Coach USA, and ran buses in Africa, Australia, Europe and New Zealand.

But today more than half its buses are parked up and thousands of drivers have been furloughed. Some 90% of its passengers are sitting at home. The nation's bus stops are deserted. The government has had to step in with hundreds of millions of pounds to keep Britain's bus companies on the road.

Sir Brian tells me, "Things will never be the same again."

He remembers an industrial dispute in the 1970s when he was working as a bus conductor. Services stopped for nearly two months. "When we got going again, 15% of our passengers never came back."

He believes that in the aftermath of COVID-19 the transport sector will be changed forever.

"We are going into uncharted territory. We will see accelerated social change. Volumes and patterns will be different. The high street will be struggling. How many shops will be left? As long as there is a threat of the virus, people may be reluctant to go on public transport and just prefer to use their car."

Sir Brian is a self-confessed bus fanatic. His father drove buses and young Brian often jumped on for the ride. His life took a different route when he trained as a chartered accountant and joined Arthur Andersen. He humbly claims that he was never very good with numbers, unless there was a pound sign in front of them.

His financial forecast today is not for the faint-hearted. "As we come out of lockdown, things will get horribly worse. There is going to be an enormous number of redundancies. We are facing a 1930s-type recession. In some cases where the government has bailed out businesses, we'll be left with zombie companies owned by the state."

Sir Brian sees the world of COVID-19 from several perspectives.

For starters, he is one of the UK's most generous philanthropists. In October 2019, he announced a donation of £109 million to charity.[39] That's in addition to the £100 million that he's channelled to good causes through the Souter Charitable Trust over the past 13 years.

He sometimes describes his business model as, "I make the money and my wife gives it away."

His sister Ann's Gloag Foundation supports children's homes in Kenya, health projects across Africa and the Mercy Ships initiative, which sends floating hospitals to help in the poorest regions of the world.

"It is going to be terrible for the poor," says Sir Brian. "It could have awful consequences, especially for the poor in Africa and Asia, many of whom don't have a robust welfare system to fall back on. I fear this may turn into public revolution and disorder, because when people become hungry, they become desperate."

He has an alarmingly simple response to the fact that homeless people have been sheltered in empty hotel rooms during the crisis: "If homeless people can be taken off the streets now and given accommodation, why were we not doing that before?"

Sir Brian also views the world through the eyes of a significant private equity investor. Souter Investments currently has stakes in 28 companies. Many others have been bought and sold in the past. His portfolio has outperformed the stock market by 55% over the past 12 years.

"When it comes to buying companies, a big head of steam had built up before the crisis. People were paying too high a multiple. So, in private equity this adjustment could be welcome. There will be lots of opportunities where businesses will need to be recapitalized or taken out of administration. Whereas in the past we were looking at high-growth, high-quality businesses, we will now be looking at opportunities that arise from the crisis."

Sir Brian also sees that in the aftermath of COVID-19 there will be a new age of digital transformation across the business landscape. "We are going to be living in a digital world even more than before. We need to see what that means for the high street. At the end of the day, a lot of what Stagecoach does is it takes people into town to do their shopping. How will that change if there are hardly any shops left?"

He also sees that the current crisis will bring to the surface a major issue which has been festering for a while – the lack of tax paid outside the US by the big digital corporations Facebook, Amazon, Apple, Netflix and Google.

"We can't seem to get taxes from them. I know it's a complex international tax issue. But for governments to pay their way out of this the digital giants will need to start paying their way for hospitals, roads and schools." Some of that money might even be able to find its way to sustaining the high street too.

Another issue Sir Brian is mulling over is what this means for local versus global.

"There is a huge carbon issue with trailing stuff halfway across the world. Maybe there could be fiscal incentives for local production? I am not saying I am an advocate for it but maybe we could consider how to be a more self-sufficient economy as long as we could link the incentive with environmental benefit."

Like several other leaders in lockdown, he bemoans the lack of true global leadership.

"We need to work together to tackle global problems. If we had three or four people of Angela Merkel's quality, that would make a difference, and now is the time to bring the nations together in a united effort."

Sir Brian's family have returned to the nest from London and Africa. Like many others, they've been brought back together by COVID-19. He is adjusting nicely to virtual communication rather than face to face.

"But we need the human contact. We need to have friendship, fellowship and fun as part of the elements of life."

We talk about a time when we were on business together in Toronto and we visited one of Sir Brian's bus garages. Within an hour he had met every member of staff in a whistle-stop tour. He'd posed for pictures with the cleaners, jumped into the back of a double-decker to help the mechanics mend an oily engine and reviewed the Toronto to Montreal timetables. No hand was left unshaken. A masterclass in employee engagement!

"You can't do that on Zoom," he tells me.

There's a lot of turmoil in Sir Brian's business world. Forty years after he formed Stagecoach, it's facing its biggest challenge yet. The problems in his charity work are of a different realm. The task there is to help save lives as the poorest in society face up to the economic consequences of COVID-19.

"This will definitely refocus our priorities in many ways," he says. "Most of all, many people will rethink what it really means to be contented."

Stretched out on his sofa, Sir Brian Souter has plenty to think about. Forty years after founding Stagecoach, he looks ready for the next stop on his journey.

CHAPTER 13

VIVIENNE ARTZ, PRESIDENT, WOMEN IN BANKING AND FINANCE AND CHIEF PRIVACY OFFICER, REFINITIV

LOCKED DOWN IN KENT, ENGLAND, 14 MAY 2020

"We need to have a new relationship with data." That's the view of Vivienne Artz, a leading authority on privacy, when I speak to her in lockdown at her home in Kent. Her enthusiasm is only briefly punctuated by the snoring of one of her dogs stretched out at her feet, oblivious to the data debate.

The pandemic has brought Vivienne's subject and her expertise into the mainstream. In the past, many of us have ranked data privacy alongside risk management and audit in the pantheon of less-than-sexy corporate issues. Not now. "It's so exciting," Vivienne tells me.

Data could hold the key to saving lives in the new world of track and trace. But it could also threaten personal privacy and data security.

The strategy of testing, tracing and isolating is seen by many as a game changer for combating COVID-19. Contact tracing is crucial. It has been used successfully in several places through a mobile phone app. Germany, Hong Kong, Singapore and South Korea have deployed it to good effect.

Google and Apple partnered to develop a tracing app. Some governments went with them. Others went their own way. Privacy campaigners were concerned that contact tracing could place into the computers of the state more private information than ever before – including where we've been and who we've met.

"The holy grail of data is health data. When you put that together with location data, that's when you get a mixture which people are most sensitive about. This is where the big debate is now," says Vivienne.

Privacy advocates point to the danger of 'mission creep' in governments' use of personal data. The thin end of the wedge. An editorial in the *Financial Times* captured the dilemma. "Much of the discussion around human rights and coronavirus has centred on autocratic states using the pandemic as cover for anti-democratic steps. It is just as important to recognise that civil liberties can be eroded through well-intentioned decisions by democracies. Governments must be as vigilant in restoring personal freedoms and privacy once the crisis is over as they are in tracking and combating its spread."[40]

Google and Apple hoped their system would become the global standard. The UK promised its own app as part of a "world beating"[41] tracing system to be in place by 1 June 2020. But, after trials on the Isle of Wight, it played down the importance of an app and suggested it might be ready "for winter"[42] or abandoned completely. It decided to rely on a manual, call-centre-based system for tracing those who might have come into contact with virus carriers.

The principle of contact tracing apps is that they work by sending signals between mobile phones. If someone whom you have come into contact with then develops symptoms of COVID-19, the app sends you a message and urges you to isolate and be tested.

Around 20% of people in the UK don't have smartphones[43] – most of them in the oldest generation, who are the most vulnerable to COVID-19. So, the app wouldn't help them. The idea of mandating such tech is highly unlikely for most countries with privacy laws. There is also a range of views over whether the use of such technology could eventually become an 'all clear' COVID-19 passport to allow people to use public transport or access bars and restaurants. An ethics advisory board was set up by the UK government to help it wrestle with these myriad issues. Attitudes vary significantly from country to country.

"Some jurisdictions are very willing to sacrifice privacy. In China, for instance," Vivienne explains. "To others privacy is absolutely paramount. Take the Netherlands and France. In France, it's quite difficult to even ask an employee if they've had COVID-19. In the US, there is a different standard in every state. In the EU, they are looking at contact tracing and location data. But are they going to share that data outside the EU? The concern would be that we end up with an EU solution in the EU that only works in the EU."

Vivienne is a lawyer by profession and a veteran of the data debate. She praises the practical approach of the UK Information Commissioner's Office as being an "enabling regulator." She believes it could play a highly influential role in finding global solutions. Most of all, she's "a pragmatic modernist" in her approach.

"You must ask yourself, 'Are we trying to protect something that's gone?' You can no longer be invisible. If you never try something, you never progress. What we need to do is have a new understanding around what is responsible use of data.

"We need a grown-up debate about data for good. This pandemic has highlighted that we have to process sensitive data. That is not just by governments – we are going to have to allow the private sector to process sensitive data too. The pharma companies need access to data so they can innovate. They need it to find out what they don't know. There's a regulatory challenge in that too. You can't seek permission to find out what you don't know or what you might find out as it is not sufficiently specific."

Those on the cautious side of the privacy debate say there needs to be more clarity from governments about what data will be collected, how it will be stored and when it would be erased. As Vivienne is quick to point out, governments have not always been at the leading edge in terms of data security.

"There is a big concern about the ability of government bodies to secure data. Their systems can leak like a sieve. The worry is that this could become some sort of hackers' paradise."

The international discussions and negotiations are extremely active. But will they be able to move at the pace required to implement international contact-tracing solutions quickly enough? Or, as has been the case in so many other areas in the pandemic, will countries turn inwards for their own bespoke solutions that don't integrate across international boundaries?

Data moved up the agenda as the pandemic spread across the globe. The privacy issues are complex and not easily solved. But the technology is seen by many as vital in moving the world forward in the wake of COVID-19.

Vivienne has also focused much time on the implications of the big shift to homeworking.

"I'm not sure it's a long-term solution to work from your kitchen. There is a high risk of confidentiality and security being compromised."

She is also keen to highlight the new challenges in regulating a workforce that is spread around thousands of homes rather than located in one office. The regulatory system will have to be reimagined to cope with the shift to remote working.

Vivienne is also the president of Women in Banking and Finance – a volunteer not-for-profit networking organization. She points out the inequality that arises from women working at home.

"Women do up to ten times more unpaid work than men – whether that's caring or food shopping or looking after children.[44] Remote working will just further highlight such questions – why do women pick up so much of the unpaid work, and why is it not shared more equally with men? Remote work cannot be adopted in order to allow women to lead two lives. Women shouldn't have to do two things to succeed while a man only has to do one."

Vivienne's observations on the female leadership in the COVID-19 crisis will resonate with many. She observes that the female political leaders – Jacinda Ardern, Angela Merkel and Nicola Sturgeon – look like they are doing a better job than their male counterparts.

"A woman's mind works very differently. They are thinking 'what's the impact?' on so many different levels. Women think of not just the issue, but they think of what it means for society as a whole. The result is a greater empathy with the people."

Vivienne powerfully articulates the need for wider change in the wake of COVID-19.

"If we can do a 'lift and shift' of most of our workforce from the office to home in three or four days, we can do that to fix other issues around equality of opportunity. When there is an imperative, we can do it. There is an imperative now to fix these other things too."

Vivienne Artz sees this as an opportunity to reset the working world and tackle current inequalities.

"We shouldn't focus on getting back to where we were. We need to make sure we take away all the lessons we have learned and create a better and more equal world of work."

GLOBAL COOPERATION

Many of our leaders in lockdown were concerned about the lack of global leadership throughout the COVID-19 crisis. The pandemic did not bother about borders. The response should have been a coming together of international leadership for the sake of humanity. Instead, the behaviours showcased antagonism, narrow minds and parochialism. The China-US tensions epitomized this.

Countries fought with their neighbours to source face masks. An international bun fight kicked off to find a vaccine. There was a focus on protectionist trade policies from 'America First' to Brexit to China. At a point when the world needed to be collaborating, governments were looking inwards – down their own silos.

In the following three chapters, our leaders cover a plethora of views, anecdotes and insights. But they each have an interesting perspective on the need for global leadership. Ho Kwon Ping tells us, "The virus has exposed the selfishness of countries and people far more than it has shown our ability to be compassionate internationalists."

Alison Martin highlights the need to come together to create a better world for our children. In particular, she is passionate about how we must tackle climate change as we emerge from the crisis. She tells us, "You need all governments and businesses around the world to work together."

The CEO of The *South China Morning Post*, Gary Liu, has a ringside seat observing the China-US tensions. He believes, "This was the opportunity for them to set aside the conflict that has been escalating … for the good of the world." But they chose a different path.

Some companies did come together for the 'good of the world'. The big pharma businesses partnered on vaccines. Google and Apple joined together their efforts on contact-tracing apps. Surely there should be much more of this in the future?

Post-COVID-19, business leadership has a crucial role to play in trying to rebuild international alliances. Our leaders in lockdown saw the urgent need for global cooperation. They didn't hold out much faith in our politicians to lead this in the immediate future. So, corporations and their leaders will have to play their part, more than ever before, in coming together to solve global issues for the sake of humanity.

CHAPTER 14

HO KWON PING, CO-FOUNDER AND EXECUTIVE CHAIRMAN, BANYAN TREE HOLDINGS

LOCKED DOWN IN SINGAPORE, 4 MAY 2020

Another day in lockdown. Another leader whose business has been hammered by COVID-19.

Ho Kwon Ping founded Banyan Tree Holdings along with his wife, Claire Chiang, 25 years ago. It all started with a single boutique resort in Phuket, Thailand.

The group now owns or manages five brands, 47 hotels, 64 spas, 72 shopping malls and three golf courses. The business spans 24 countries. It has plans to double its footprint, with another 46 hotels and resorts in the pipeline.

Tonight, I find the co-founder and executive chairman in a philosophical mood.

"My business is shot through because of the virus. I have to rebuild it."

His hotels and resorts have had to shut their doors one by one, following the wave of the virus as it spreads around the world. Yet he's is optimistic that his luxury hospitality brands will bounce back.

"I think you will see less of the big package holidays with thousands of people cramming into hotels, like they do in the Mediterranean. I think people will be more niche-oriented in their approach to leisure travel. Business travel will be impacted. But I don't think you will see an end to leisure travel. I think it will take 12 months for us to get back to normal. It will not allow us to bounce back this high season. But next year's high season we should bounce back almost completely."

Kwon Ping has had a distinguished business career. He has been chairman of Singapore Power and sat on the boards of major corporates including Diageo, Singapore Airlines and Standard Chartered. He is also the founder of Singapore Management University.

Singapore was lauded for the way it handled COVID-19 at the start of the crisis. Learning from the experience of SARS, it used testing, tracing and circuit breakers well.[45] That was until the virus began to spread inside the camps for migrant workers. They flock to the wealthy city state from places like Bangladesh and India. They work on construction projects and in manufacturing. Suddenly, Singapore had the most infections in South East Asia. Nearly all of those infected were in the camps, exposing a side of Singapore that is at odds with its international reputation.

"Singapore had coped pretty well," Kwon Ping tells me. "We got congratulations for the way we dealt with COVID-19 and then we were wrong footed with the migrant workers. We didn't realize that the virus could spread so rapidly when there are such dense living conditions. These migrant camps are not unique to Singapore. If anything, they have warned us of the damage the virus will do in the densely populated slums of Indonesia, the Philippines and India."

Singapore is well placed to bounce back from the economic impact of the virus. The government has a very solid base of reserves – unlike some of its neighbours, who will be saddled with high levels of debt. Kwon Ping believes that COVID-19 will bring into sharper focus the need to change the shape of the ASEAN (Association of Southeast Asian Nations) economies.

"The problem that all of South East Asia has is that we either export intermediary products to China or we assemble a lot of products and ship them to the US. We are going to have to generate our own consumption demand. It is there. Six hundred million people beginning to join the middle class. In the last 20 years, the ASEAN economies have never really been integrated. There is a true ASEAN common market now. We see removal of tariffs. More intra-ASEAN trade. The moment has come to really generate our own growth rather than rely on exports to China and the US."

Kwon Ping was born in Hong Kong and educated in Thailand, Taiwan and Singapore and also at Stanford University in California. He has spent a lifetime observing the shifting sands in relations between China and America.

"We are seeing an entire paradigm shift in civilizational relationships now," he says. "Americans cannot accept the idea that America will not be the supreme military and economic power. Even its own civilizational values and its soft power will no longer be globally dominant. It's just inconceivable to Americans. At the same time the Chinese are very nationalistic now. So, I am not optimistic that this tension will decrease.

"There is a general consensus across the entire American policy establishment that China is an existential threat to American supremacy. China is a big threat to America in artificial intelligence, in robotics and in so many other leading-edge areas. China is a bigger threat than Russia ever was, because even at the peak of the Cold War, Russia was a failed state. It offered no alternatives to sustainable economic growth. You are not going to find China collapsing the way that the Soviet Union did."

Kwon Ping has been through several major crashes like this one. So, experience tells him we might overestimate the amount of change that will emerge. But he believes that major advances will come in science and healthcare.

"Every major crisis accelerates nascent trends. It doesn't start anything. It just accelerates," he observes.

"The whole world is nearing the frontiers of how much more we can do in terms of electronics-related technology. It is going to be in healthcare that the most fundamental frontiers of science are going to be broken into. It is in medicine that we are going to make the really revolutionary advances in the next 20 years. There won't be that much more in the move from 5G to 6G to 10G. Those changes are going to be increasingly marginal. But in terms of life expectancy, prolongation of life, cures for cancer, immunotherapy, cloning, DNA – the COVID-19 crisis has pushed much of this forward."

Asia dealt with SARS between 2002 and 2004. So, Kwon Ping believes that these countries were psychologically better prepared than those in Europe and the US. But he cautions against focusing too much effort on preparing for the next pandemic.

"We will overexaggerate the lasting impact of this crisis – unless we have another pandemic in a few years' time. They usually occur every 70 to 100 years. We will have a lot of excitement about pandemic-related technology. Then, because the memory of private equity funds is pretty short, if we don't have another pandemic in seven years, nobody is going to fund these things. So, I don't see a lot of breakthroughs in terms of technology related to pandemics."

Like some of our other leaders in lockdown, Kwon Ping believes that COVID-19 will bring about changes in supply chains. He even sees a trend, helped by the rise in robotics, which will shift some manufacturing back from Asia to Europe.

"People have now seen for real the problems of supply chains that are built on purely economic efficiencies and do not take into account geopolitical reasoning and geo-health politics. COVID-19 is just accelerating a trend in which it was already increasingly understood that supply chain decisions can no longer be made purely on the basis of cost, productivity and efficiency. They will have to be made on political grounds too."

Kwon Ping has never been afraid of speaking his mind. As a young man he was detained by the Singaporean authorities for writing articles they didn't like. He was held in solitary confinement for two months. His fire to speak truth to power is undiminished.

"COVID-19 has shown that all this talk of multilateralism is wishful thinking or political posturing. The whole idea of we are 'all in it together' is false. In reality, the result of this is that it has exposed the selfishness of countries and people far more than it has shown our ability to be compassionate internationalists."

Kwon Ping likes spending time with the younger generation, especially at the university he founded. It invigorates him. More and more, he finds younger people would prefer to start social enterprises than to be the next Mark Zuckerberg. He also believes the crisis has encouraged other fundamental rethinking.

"I think that this has sparked a keen awareness among ordinary folks about some important questions. This will lead to more people wondering – what is the purpose of work? It will lead to more people wanting to find more meaning in life than just getting a salary."

In Ho Kwon Ping's garden stand three overlapping banyan trees. They were planted by him and his wife for each one of their children. Now he is a proud grandfather who ponders an unexpected benefit of lockdown for him and his family.

"You begin to value the little things. My whole family has come together in a way that we haven't for years. We've had a lot of time for conversation."

The virus has also made many wealthy and powerful people confront the concept of time. Kwon Ping is one of them.

"You have to deal with time," he muses. "This has made a lot of people wonder – what is life all about? You ask yourself – what do I want to do with my remaining years? Of course, I want to rebuild my business. But it also reminds you that purpose is at the very heart of living. And that is a great discovery."

CHAPTER 15
ALISON MARTIN, CEO EMEA, ZURICH INSURANCE GROUP

LOCKED DOWN NEAR ZURICH, SWITZERLAND, 25 MAY 2020

"I am an optimist – which is a benefit and a flaw," Alison Martin tells me.

Maybe that's why the CEO displays such soothing calm when I ask whether COVID-19 will result in the biggest insured loss in history. "We are capitalized to withstand those sorts of losses. That's what we do for a living," she tells me in a way that makes me feel well and truly reassured.

The numbers seem astronomical to me. It's said that the Tokyo Olympics was insured for $2 billion. Insured losses for the entire insurance industry could be more than $100 billion. Losses that weren't insured could be double that. No one really knows yet. Alison explains, "This is still an unfolding event. It would be a bit like trying to measure the impact of a storm as it moves across the Atlantic before it hits land."

Alison is CEO EMEA and Bank Distribution for Zurich Insurance Group. The company has set aside $750 million so far. But Alison sees far more reaching implications from COVID-19 than just payouts. "This is an opportunity for a huge wake-up call to be heard. This could be the reset year for all of us to say – what is that world we want to aspire for our children to live in? Can we try and build that one rather than the one we were destroying six months ago?"

Zurich has signed up to the United Nations' Business Ambition for 1.5°C along with 216 other businesses with a total market cap of $3.6 trillion. The aim of the campaign is to limit global warming to 1.5°C. In a sector that takes great care over the small print, Alison believes the bigger picture matters more than ever.

"Our role in society is to be there for our customers, our people, our partners and the planet. We have a much broader societal responsibility.

"In this transition right now, we have the capability to support customers to move much quicker in changing to be more consistent with a pathway towards achieving the UN's global warming temperature limit. That is much more beneficial for society at large."

Zurich is already flexing its influence to encourage large commercial customers to reduce their impact on the environment. For instance, it can stop dealing with carbon-intense businesses unless they come up with credible transition plans. Alison sees the climate emergency as a risk that is crystallizing faster than many realize.

"The horse has bolted out of the stable already. The impacts of climate change and of a global pandemic both know no national boundaries. You need all governments and businesses around the world to work together to manage the situation and work out how each industry needs to transition. What does the new world look like and what is the path to the future that is fair and acceptable to all of us?"

Zurich is nearly 150 years old. It has customers in 215 countries and has been recognized as one of the world's top 100 brands. Alison leads 20,000 people. She lives outside Zurich with her husband and her five- and six-year-old girls. He leads on childcare. "A challenge even for a former major in the British army," she tells me.

Working from home is relatively comfortable compared to what some of her colleagues have endured in other countries, especially as "everything works in Switzerland."

The fallout from COVID-19 for the insurance sector hasn't been quite so ordered. The *Financial Times* reported that a third of small businesses in the UK might stop buying business interruption insurance in the future.[46] They are angry about the failure of some insurance companies to pay out.

"The UK has been extreme in its vitriol against the industry," Alison explains and points out that the sector is viewed much more favourably in other countries. She says there's good reason that many policies haven't paid out.

"It's a small proportion of businesses that would have had wording in their contract that could have covered this kind of pandemic scenario. This is for the simple reason that the insurance industry would not typically look to provide wide-scale pandemic coverage because we do not have the capital to do that."

However, throughout the crisis Zurich has provided support including premium rebates, payment holidays and extensions of coverage. It has also helped commercial customers by providing advice on how best to manage risk and protect their employees and customers.

Checking the small print of an insurance policy is something that everyone should know to do. But it is an issue that boils to the surface when a big crisis hits, especially when the claims are so large and widespread.

"There is a big lesson for us in the industry; making sure that it is absolutely crystal clear what cover people do and do not have. The insurance industry's challenge – and it has been perennially – is how do we help people understand what they have and have not got coverage for?" This is an issue the sector will try to address again post-COVID-19. "We will continue to see simplification of the actual underlying products that people are buying. We will simplify language so it is as clear as we can make it about what is and is not covered."

Other systemic changes are being considered.

"Maybe we need a pandemic pool system going forward – so it is very clear that we share the risk between the industry and governments and the underlying insured. The current situation is very unfortunate for everybody. For the people who might have thought they had cover and they don't. For the government, which ends up picking up the tab. For the reputation of the insurance industry, it's not good not paying out for claims. From a regulator's perspective, it's critical that the insurance industry is only obliged to pay for claims that it was contractually bound to pay for. As soon as you step beyond that, the insurance industry is insolvent and won't be there to pay for all the other everyday claims. A solution for this has to be found going forward."

As someone who has spent much of her life assessing and managing risk, Alison is well positioned to take a view on why the virus came as such a surprise, especially to politicians and some businesses in Europe and the US.

"As individuals we have a risk notion that unless an event is very real and proximate to us, we don't believe that event is going to occur."

What is very real now is the impact on the economy. So, what does Alison hear from her customers? "It depends on the sector. It ranges from people who are trying to avoid near-death experiences to ones who have more work than they ever imagined. It is very different. There are more in the former camp than in the latter. The longer our economy has the brakes on, the more people will go into that struggling camp."

COVID-19 will accelerate much-needed digital change in the insurance sector. The more established companies have been criticized for being slow to modernize, especially compared to insurtech businesses.

"The insurance industry was typically perceived as lagging behind the banks. This crisis has accelerated the digital transformation," Alison says.

Zurich's approach is to "digitize where the customer wants." For instance, that would mean making it easier to make small claims on car insurance by allowing customers to upload pictures of the damaged vehicle on their phone or sign their insurance policy digitally. It could even mean completing a virtual medical check when buying life insurance.

Alison is clear that some customers will still want to see an adviser. "It will be a blend. It will be different in different markets. But some people will still want to deal face to face or talk to an empathetic human being."

She's concerned about countries turning inwards in the crisis. She fears that the widespread desire to simplify the supply chain and bring manufacturing home will have consequences. "A risk of COVID-19 is that it increases our existing inequalities, and if we retrench to incredibly national provision, then we are writing off the ability of many in the developing world to grow."

Alison reflects on her own leadership style and what she has observed in others during the crisis. Her starting point is refreshingly simple: "You need tone from the top. We need to do everything we can to look after the people who work for us." She sees empathy and compassion as non-negotiable. "You have to give a bit more" – especially in a crisis in which so many have suffered.

Alison Martin firmly believes in humanizing leadership, particularly in the new world of remote working, where people are "bringing work and home and humour together". She adds, "It has been really tough and for some people this has landed in an incredibly difficult way. Part of the role of leadership is to be able to provide people with optimism. Sometimes it's not that easy but you have to lead with a smile on your face."

CHAPTER 16
GARY LIU, CEO,
SOUTH CHINA MORNING POST

LOCKED DOWN IN CAUSEWAY BAY, HONG KONG, 18 MAY 2020

This has been the most challenging time for the *South China Morning Post* (*SCMP*) since the Japanese invaded Hong Kong in 1941. As the Second World War raged, the invaders took over the newsroom and turned it into a propaganda factory.

The virus posed a different threat to the *SCMP* and Hong Kong. It may well create an equally historic legacy.

"This is really a pivotal moment for the world. It is existential in so many ways," *SCMP* CEO Gary Liu tells me from his office in the Causeway Bay district of Hong Kong. He's a 30-something new world tech leader catapulted into one of Asia's oldest and best-known newspapers. He's worked at Google, Clickable, AOL and Spotify. Then he became CEO of the news aggregator Digg, where he tripled revenue and traffic.

His arrival in Hong Kong in 2017 brought Silicon Valley to Happy Valley. It also stated an ambition to build the *SCMP* as a global digital news brand, as well as the English-language newspaper for Hong Kong.

Gary exudes Harvard-educated charm and articulacy. He looks the part too, dressed in a smart plaid shirt, grey zipped hoodie and Apple AirPod earphones. He sips coolly from a designer water bottle as a hint of Hong Kong skyline sneaks out of the corner of his Zoom screen. He's not Zuck nor Beaverbrook.[47]

The Chinese ecommerce multinational Alibaba owns the *SCMP*. They bought the newspaper group for $266 million in 2015. When Gary first sat behind the CEO's desk in January 2017, the *SCMP* had a total audience of around 4.3 million, around a quarter of which were in Hong Kong. Three years later they have 50 million monthly active users, and more than 95% of them are spread across the globe.

"It's been skyrocket growth," Gary tells me. "We're proud of it but it brings with it a lot of responsibility to get the story right. Because the world needs to understand."

While digital eyes soared, advertising revenue fell. COVID-19 accelerated that trend.

"The revenue that has declined is not going to come back even after COVID-19 dissipates," Gary explains. "This is a one-directional shift. It has given advertisers an excuse to change their own behaviour and they are not likely to change back."

This is a defining moment for newspaper companies across the globe. "If news organizations are not able to bridge the gap over another 12 months and they can't react fast enough and shift to new revenues, then they are going to be part of significant consolidation across the markets."

At the *SCMP*, Gary and his team see this as more an opportunity than a threat. They are laser-focused on digital revenues.

"Over the last several years we had already been undergoing a transformation to prepare ourselves for a moment like this," he tells me. He adds with a flourish, "We had the rain catcher in place for the deluge."

The *SCMP* was on the ground in Wuhan from the start of COVID-19. Their insights and expertise have been deep in covering the China-US trade war. They were as close as anyone in reporting the military encampment of China in the South China Seas. In one sense, the *SCMP* is in the right place at the right time. In another sense, it has made its own luck.

"This whole situation has validated the bet that we took several years ago, which was that the story of China and its rising impact on the world would be *the* story of our lifetime. The *SCMP* is now a global organization that covers China in depth more than anyone else, with the nuance and intimacy that's necessary."

Gary is churning inside about the whole fake news phenomenon. He wants Google and Facebook and their peers to start taking responsibility for what appears on their platforms. He describes them as "the world's largest publishing companies" and thinks they should be held accountable in the same way as media businesses like his own. During the crisis, he's encouraged that for the first time they've started controlling "misinformation and disinformation."

"The internet platforms have been resistant, claiming that all they are is a conduit – a pipe –and that the accountability rests with the people who are posting the information and publishing online," he tells me with an indignant look. "Now they have taken on the accountability of saying this is truth and this is not because it is a global health crisis. The question is whether or not this accountability will last beyond COVID-19. Hopefully this is going to be the pivot point for what they believe their responsibility is."

Hong Kong has dealt well with the health crisis. When Gary and I talk, there have only been four deaths.[48] This is remarkable for such a densely populated city. There hasn't been a complete lockdown like elsewhere, but a highly stringent system of contact tracking and tracing has been in place. Gary explains how Hong Kong has benefitted from having systems that were built on the back of the SARS epidemic in 2003.

"The infrastructure was already there. There was a collective community response. You didn't have to teach an entire population what they were supposed to do. People just very naturally went into defence mode and that allowed a city like Hong Kong to fend off a deep impact of contagion in a city as dense as ours very, very quickly."

With the COVID-19 crisis controlled, Hong Kong's attention has inevitably turned back to the demonstrations that have rocked the city since June 2019. They started with opposition to proposed legislation to allow extradition of 'criminal suspects' to China. They soon developed into a 'pro-democracy movement' opposing the Hong Kong government, the influence of China and the authority of the police.

"The issues behind the protests are going to be a chronic low-grade fever for the city. The overall distrust that now exists in Hong Kong is here to stay," Gary explains. He sees the lack of trust in the police as quite a turnaround. He's certain that the attitudes of the mainly young protestors are undiminished by COVID-19. "The sentiments of an entire generation seem to be set and those are going to be very difficult to change."

The question that the protestors are really asking is: who is in charge – Hong Kong or Beijing? The answer is that China increasingly wants to pull Hong Kong back into the fold. Gary sees that and tells me, "The influence of Beijing on the city will be more and more apparent. I honestly don't know what that means for the city. I am optimistic about the recovery of Hong Kong, although I recognize it will be a different city than before the protests."

Gary's comments are prophetic. Within a few days of our conversation, China declares that it will impose new national security laws on Hong Kong. Some see this as the end of Hong Kong as we knew it and the death of the 'one country, two system' structure. This immediately leads to an upsurge in demonstrations and sharp diplomatic responses from the UK and the US.

Looking outwards from Hong Kong's harbour, Gary predicts big shifts in three other areas – travel, automation and education. With universities flipping to virtual, he predicts that digitization of content will mean "societies and governments are going to recognize the value of being able to democratize education." That will mean there is "no good reason not to make high-quality education accessible to everyone."

He forecasts that in the post-COVID-19 recession a need to cut costs will accelerate the next era of automation, potentially causing a "massive displacement in the workforce." He thinks there will be major implications for global tourism and hospitality because of the virus. It will be a "convenient excuse" for protecting domestic populations from disease. That will turn into "a different level of protectionism of borders."

As a leader whose business is owned by a Chinese company, he observes more closely than many the signals and thinking from Beijing. He is acutely aware of how global power structures will shift.

"Diplomacy for the next generation, if not several generations, is going to be redrawn. China and the US were presented with an opportunity to decide whether cooperation or conflict would be the way forward. This was the opportunity for them to set aside the conflict that has been escalating because of the trade war and say 'for the good of the world we are going to do x', and both sides decided to not only stick with conflict but to also escalate it further. That is the pattern for the future."

He cites how the virus highlights how access to public health-care should become "a basic human right." But he knows that the search for a vaccine will increase global inequality rather than reduce it.

"We are going to see the rich countries dominate access to the vaccine and the poor countries have almost none. The speed to get to the vaccine is going to determine the speed of economic recovery because getting everyone back to work the way that we've had in the past is going to require a fully vaccinated population. There are going to be countries that come out of this many years faster than other countries. And the countries that are going to come out of this faster will be the ones that are already developed and economically stronger. So, the inequality issue is going to be so much larger."

Gary Liu thinks carefully about leadership and values. He hopes "that conviction is going to become central to quality leadership in the future in a way that it hasn't been before."

It could also accelerate progress towards the moment when corporate behaviours is dictated far more by consumer sentiment. This has been predicted before but has not materialized.

"There has been a generation of talk about voting with your wallet. Unfortunately, we have disappointed ourselves as a society over and over again. At this moment in time there's a recognition that truth and collective sacrifice matter deeply. Hopefully, that will change consumer behaviour."

When Alibaba bought the *SCMP*, some feared it would become muzzled by Beijing's influence, even though the company stated it would not seek to interfere in editorial matters. The same concerns have been directed at other owners and leaders of the *SCMP* in the past. When you meet the company's current CEO, you realize he is not the sort of guy to be anyone's poodle. His words echo those of good journalists down the ages. He's passionate about speaking truth into power.

"Sources of truth are extremely important," he tells me. "Not only in moments of crisis but for the overall progress of human society."

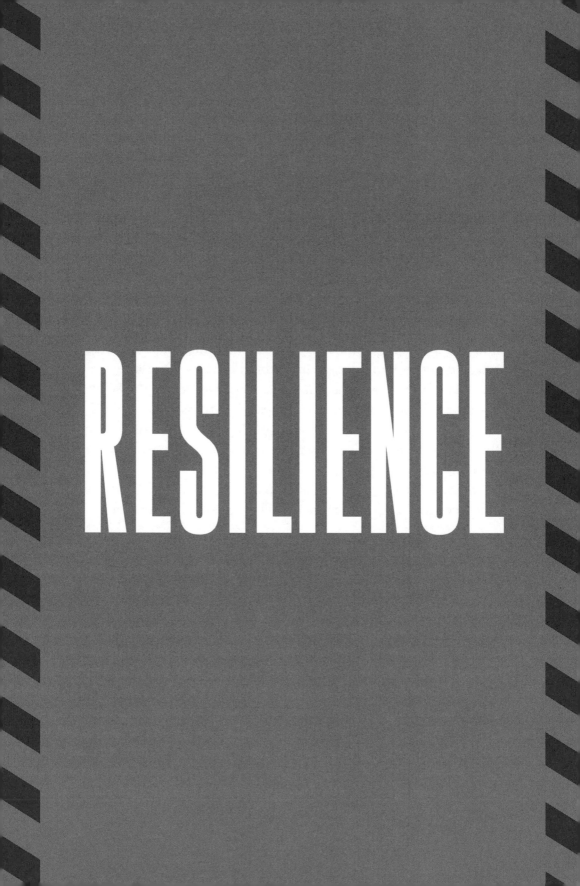

RESILIENCE

Resilience was a major theme for our leaders in the crisis. This was a test of stamina in so many ways. The physical and mental toll on leaders was immense. Parallels were often drawn with wartime. It was also a test of the resilience of organizations themselves. Which had built in the financial resilience to survive such an extreme event? How robust were the balance sheets against such a drop in revenues? Which businesses had the capacity to deal with the extraordinary response that had to be put in place? Which had the continuity arrangements that would maintain services to customers and keep operations running?

Resilience had never been more important. In the following four chapters we hear from leaders who demonstrated resilience in a variety of different ways.

General Stan McChrystal is one of the most famous military leaders of recent times. He shares parallels from the conflict zones of Iraq and Afghanistan on leading in the COVID-19 crisis. He also challenges the corporate world for not being better prepared – for not building more resilience into its DNA. He says, "We need a different culture in organizations for how we are prepared for uncertainty."

Three New Yorkers paint a picture of how they and their city coped with becoming one of the worst epicentres of the virus anywhere in the world. Their stories capture the resilience of a city and its people when faced with a challenge that they could never have imagined.

We hear from Sir David Behan, whose staff showed exceptional resilience in the most traumatic of circumstances. He is executive chairman of a care home company that saw four of his staff and more than 1,000 residents die. His story demonstrates leadership at every level in his business. As Sir David puts it, "We are judged as leaders on what we are like when the going is tough."

Hongkong and Shanghai Hotels is another story of resilience. The company has survived many a crisis in its 150-year history. The company's CEO, Clement Kwok, explains his take on financial resilience. He describes what long-term investment means for him as follows: "Don't go out and think you are a long-term investor ... unless you have the stomach to live through the ups and downs." COVID-19 will, once again, refocus attention on the danger of the short-term mindset and the value of long-term thinking.

The theme of resilience ran strongly through the months of COVID-19. It will become even more relevant in boardrooms as we emerge. Who will act now to ensure they are better prepared for the next crisis?

CHAPTER 17

GENERAL STAN MCCHRYSTAL, JOINT SPECIAL OPERATIONS COMMANDER IN IRAQ AND AFGHANISTAN

LOCKED DOWN IN ALEXANDRIA, VIRGINIA, US, 31 MARCH 2020

Three weeks into the COVID-19 crisis, General Stan McChrystal sits in front of white wooden shutters in the study of his home in Alexandria, Virginia. He looks straight down the camera on his laptop and addresses 500 businesspeople in the City of London.

He is surrounded by the framed memorabilia of one of the most outstanding military careers in modern history. He may have moved tent from the sweltering dust of Afghanistan and Iraq to the relative calm of home, but his style and steely command are the same.

An old wooden rifle is mounted on the wall to his side. The fatigues of a four-star general are replaced with business smart casual. The man once described by US Defense Secretary Robert Gates as "the finest warrior and leader of men in combat I've ever met"[49] is now fixed on his mission to help business survive the battlefront of COVID-19.

Stan has only ever done straight talking. Legend has it he runs eight miles a day, gets by on one square meal and only needs four hours of sleep. He commanded the men who captured

Saddam Hussein in Operation Red Dawn. He was behind the mission that led to the death of the leader of Al Qaeda in Iraq and personally identified the body in the bombed-out hut. He's not scared of the virus.

He's also no stranger to performing in front of the camera. In 2003, while serving at the Pentagon, he gave daily televised briefings to the people of America on the war in Iraq. He announced the fall of Baghdad. With a mastery of understatement, he told millions watching, "I would anticipate that the major combat engagements are over."[50]

For the next hour, people more used to board packs and spreadsheets are spellbound by the military commander. From the very start, he's on the offensive. "People say we could never have predicted a situation like this. They're wrong. Of course, we could have predicted a pandemic. And what follows a pandemic? A financial and economic crisis. We should have predicted this, and we should have been better prepared."

The general founded McChrystal Group in 2011. Along with 150 colleagues, he now advises major corporations and senior executives on complex change. The group assembled for this Zoom conference are seeking to quell their own anxiety. For most, 9/11 is something that happened long before they hit the executive suite. For others, the crash of 2008 came before they rose to the level of serious decision-making.

The question most are seeking to answer is, how do you lead in a situation that is so different from the normal experience of corporate life? "This is a different kind of crisis. It is difficult for us to get our arms around it," the general tells us. "The reality is that you know we will come through it.

"But like in any battle, when the first bullets fly, the younger people look to their leaders to see how they are going to respond. That's when you need to be courageous, focused and businesslike. Act how you want others to act.

"Every soldier sees the battle from their own foxhole. You got to listen across your organization. You've gotta give clear direction.

Tell them this is what we've decided to do. Then people need inspiration. We need someone to tell us that what we're doing matters. Someone to tell us that people care and someone to tell us we're doing a good job."

The general's battle plan for COVID-19 is probably not that different from the one he put in place for the fall of Baghdad or fighting insurgents in Afghanistan. He advises that we must start with clarity of information. We need to understand the crisis and how it will affect us and our businesses. Then create a clear plan and make sure that plan is visible to the people in our organization. Be out there with your people – even if that will have to be done virtually rather than face to face.

"Be honest with your words," he urges. "Don't hunker down. Be prepared to give up authority. Be compassionate. Be synchronized."

Being synchronized was an essential of the general's military command. He urges the business leaders he addresses today to make that idea a much bigger focus compared to normal times. He started every day in Afghanistan by bringing together 100 military personnel in one meeting. "Information flows when you bring people together that might not have flowed otherwise," he tells his virtual audience.

However, he warns that in these gatherings all eyes are on the leader and any small action can be misinterpreted. He tells of one day when he took his glasses off and, fighting tiredness, wiped his face. The action sparked concern across his command. "What's the matter with the old man? What's he mad about?" The general continues, "I just wanted to wipe my face, but I sparked a reaction that was not intended. The little things that you do as a leader are sometimes of great importance."

Another issue that the 'old man' feels passionate about is how the corporate world seems to be in dereliction of its duty in failing to prepare. His view is that the world will continue to be rocked with predictable regularity through modern history and we should be ready for it.

"In the next ten years there will be another painful crisis. We need a different culture in organizations for how we are prepared for uncertainty. Organizations need to adopt a boxer's stance. Right now, there's so little spare capacity. So little cash on the balance sheet. The pressure is all about maximizing profit in the short term. You need to trade short-term efficiency, so you have agility.

"It is going to be a period of uncertainty for a long time. The new normal will not be the old normal. There will be a different set of operating rhythms. But we have to get better suited to responding to a crisis."

So, what of the future? How does Stan think this will change the corporate world? He has certainly adapted well to working from home and enjoyed avoiding the wasted energy of travel. This is his 12th videoconference today. Is this the end to corporate globetrotting?

"It is going to vary. Some people will go straight back to the way they were. But they are not going to be as effective as they can be. There is a certain amount of this done because people like to globetrot. There is an inefficiency built into travel and some people like that.

"But the clever leaders will work out everything we can do virtually and learn what has to be done face to face and they will carefully, strategically go and do that. The rest of the time they will get a tonne more done."

He is of the belief that many will build on the unprecedented change in ways of working that have been established around the world in such a short period of time.

"Boom, the crisis comes. The inertia in organizations is overcome. Suddenly, we are moving. The key is to get an organization moving. There are a few organizations that sadly have leaders who are waiting to snap back in muscle memory and get back to the way it was. That's a false idea. There is no going back because your competition is going to a better place. Anyone who gets caught going back to the rear is going to pay a terrible price."

With those words of warning ringing in our ears, General Stan McChrystal bids us good luck, turns to his old rifle and ends our call. A masterclass in leadership from a man who has moved his sights from the killing fields of military conflict to the battle-front of business.

CHAPTER 18

CHARLOTTE ST MARTIN, PRESIDENT, THE BROADWAY LEAGUE; ALASDAIR NICHOL, CHAIRMAN, FREEMAN'S AUCTION HOUSE; AND ANDREA MURAD, FINANCIAL JOURNALIST

LOCKED DOWN IN MANHATTAN, NEW YORK, US, MAY 2020

New York has been hit harder by COVID-19 than any other city in the world. More people have died there than in most countries. New Yorkers epitomized resilience.

Charlotte St Martin lives on the Upper East Side of Manhattan, near the Metropolitan Museum of Art. It is normally a noisy, crowded place. "It is so eerie now," she tells me. "I sit out there, and I feel like I'm the only person in the world because I hear nothing. It's very surreal living here."

Charlotte's office is on Times Square. She's president of The Broadway League, which represents 700 theatre owners, operators and producers on the most famous street in world theatre. But it too has fallen silent now.

Broadway is big business. It employs 97,000 people and has an economic impact of more than $15 billion.[51] It sells nearly 15 million seats a year, 65% to tourists from out of town. The curtain fell on Broadway in early March 2020. Shows are cancelled for the foreseeable future.

Broadway won't operate with social distancing. They say it just doesn't work in 100-year-old theatres. There isn't the space for the cast, the staff or the audience. "It wouldn't be fun. It wouldn't be entertainment," Charlotte tells me. "Part of the joy of theatre is sharing the emotions, the laughter and the tears, and being for those two hours in a room with 1,500 people laughing and crying, sharing your emotions with them. It is an experience unlike anything else."

It is unlikely the theatres will get a bailout. "If we got government money, it would be the first time in our history," adds Charlotte. "We're totally commercial."

Despite the hardship experienced by the people on Broadway, they have shown great spirit. "The sense of community has been incredible," Charlotte says. "I didn't know how strong it was until this happened."

Broadway stars are addicted to performing. Many are appearing online or on TV to raise money for charity. But it may be a long time before they tread the boards again. "We were the first out and we will be the last back. But New York won't be back till Broadway is back."

From Alasdair Nichol's apartment in the West Village he can see the Empire State Building lit up in red every night – a sign of support for the health workers. It's a comforting sight in a landscape that has become increasingly unfamiliar.

"It's bizarre. It feels like you are in a science fiction novel. There is nobody about. There's no traffic on Sixth Avenue. At the hospital around the corner there are refrigerated trucks outside as mobile morgues. It's just *not* New York."

But New Yorkers are an inventive breed. Alasdair picks up speciality cocktails 'to go' from a nearby bar when he's walking his dog. The manager at the famous Keens Steakhouse drops off a juicy rib-eye every now and then. Cocktails and steak distract from the grim reality.

Alasdair is the chairman of the oldest auction house in America. Freeman's of Philadelphia was founded in 1805, the same year as the Battle of Trafalgar. It specializes in fine art and jewellery. It's sold a lot over the past two centuries, even Benjamin Franklin's desk. Its people are not going to let COVID-19 bring the company down.

"We've been doing it for 200 years. We've been through wars and pandemics. The key to our company is we're adaptable," Alasdair says. Like many of our other leaders in lockdown, COVID-19 has accelerated the move to virtual for him and his team.

"The first big online auction we did, we had a really successful sale. We sold 96% of the lots and 70% went over the top estimate. We now have a lot of new buyers," says Alasdair. He's still unsure how online bidding will be sustained for the most prestigious high-value pieces he sells. "I think people who are paying big six-figure sums for a work of art still really need to stand in front of it and see it for themselves."

He is optimistic that business will remain brisk as the crisis rolls on. "I don't know how long it's going to last but there is a lot coming onto the market. They say, 'When times are bad people sell and when times are good people buy.' I prefer to think of it as the people who have the money still have the money."

Andrea Murad lives not far from Alasdair – a little bit further up Sixth Avenue. She's a financial journalist who has been in New York City for more than 20 years. She arrived around the time the Long-Term Capital Management hedge fund went bust. It lost $4.6 billion in four months – a lot of money even by Wall Street's standards. She was pretty cut up about 9/11. She was on the subway not far away when the Twin Towers were hit. She witnessed them collapse as she walked home. But, for her, this has surpassed even that.

"We never thought anything could be worse than 9/11. But with this, I don't know anyone who hasn't lost their minds."

The street below her apartment is quiet, bereft of traffic and people. The silence is a contrast to the first few weeks of COVID-19. In the city that never sleeps, you couldn't sleep. The sound of sirens pierced the air from morning till night.

A few sights have brought home the surreal nature of what's been happening in Manhattan. First, there was the hospital ship arriving in New York Harbor. Then there was a field hospital being built in Central Park. Neither facility was any great use in the end. But the sights numbed the senses.

Andrea tells me that Facebook is like "one long list of obituaries." Her 85-year-old uncle is one of them. Many of her friends have been laid low. The reality is horrible. "Fever of over 100 degrees for days and days on end."

In New York, at 7 pm every night, people cheer and clap and bang on pots to thank the health workers. Each night the cheers get louder and louder. "It's a great uniting thing," Alasdair tells me. "It really brings us all together."

Another emerging ritual is the lengthy queues for food stamps, which wind round corners – reminders of the immediate and escalating poverty. The incredible wealth of some New Yorkers is surrounded by deep poverty. Now an economic black hole has been cast upon the city. So many people in New York live from pay cheque to pay cheque. With bars, restaurants, taxis, hotels and retail all now shut down, many don't know where their next meal is coming from.

Some 420,000 people have fled the city. That's 5% of the total population. In the wealthiest blocks, nearly 40% have left town.[52] Many have gone to their second homes in the Hamptons, Long Island or even Palm Beach in Florida. Rentals became hard to come by in these areas as the upmarket refugees flocked out of Manhattan. Students and young professionals have left too, often going back home to their families. But the poor had no option, accentuating the inequality. Twice as many African Americans and Hispanics have died than whites.[53]

In the centre of this dark scene is Governor Andrew Cuomo. His news conferences are a 'must watch' for many. Now some want him to run for president – a suggestion he had to quash in a TV interview with his brother, Chris Cuomo, who is an anchor on CNN.

Andrea tells me, "He is just so calming and soothing. He tells you it as it is. He says, 'This is what's happening. This is what we need. This is our plan.'"

Alasdair agrees: "He is such a counterpoint to what is coming out of the White House. New Yorkers just want the facts. He's a straight-talking New Yorker. He's having his moment."

Some moms can't get enough of Cuomo. They are apparently "crushing on him" and describe his briefings as their "daily fix," according to the *New York Post*. One tells the newspaper, "For me, it was when I heard him say, 'My mother is my light and joy.'"[54] New York humour doesn't go amiss.

Like in many other places where the virus has hit hard, homes for the elderly have seen some of the worst casualties. Nearly 5,300 residents and staff died in New York care homes between March and mid-May 2020,[55] and 98 people died in one home in Washington Heights, Manhattan, in just six weeks.[56]

And as in every other major city impacted by COVID-19, the recovery will take a long time. But will the scale of the trauma here change New York forever? Or will the tough-talking, indominable spirit of the New Yorker bounce back quicker than anyone could imagine? Right now, Andrea Murad believes fear is on top.

"Nobody wants to go into an office. They are all petrified," says Andrea. New York City has the most expensive commercial real estate in the world. But Twitter has told its entire staff they can work from home forever in an "era defining moment."[57] Other professionals I speak to say they don't expect to darken the doors of their New York headquarters again in 2020.

What will that mean for areas such as Chinatown, whose hundreds of restaurants rely on white-collar workers at lunchtime and in the evening? Will it become a wasteland blighted by the scars of COVID-19 and the march of the Zoom revolution?

Another New York business leader I talked to cited the Marshall Plan, the $15 billion US investment to rejuvenate Western Europe after the Second World War. "What we need after this is a Marshall Plan for Manhattan. I really fear for the economic future of the City."

New York City has reinvented itself before. Alasdair Nichol believes it will do so again. "New York has been through a lot. We never thought we'd see worse than 9/11. People are champing at the bit to get going again. It might be a different New York when we come out of this. But it will still be the best city in the world."

Three miles away on the Upper East Side, Charlotte St Martin is thinking about the night the curtain rises again on Broadway. "I think there will be a sense of joy, excitement and exuberance. There may be masks but there will be a lot of hugging. It will be pretty wonderful to be here when we're back up."

The show must go on.

CHAPTER 19
SIR DAVID BEHAN, EXECUTIVE CHAIRMAN, HC-ONE

LOCKED DOWN IN TUNBRIDGE WELLS, ENGLAND, 19 JUNE 2020

Perhaps no private business was hit harder with the human consequences of COVID-19 than the care home company HC-One. More than 1,000 of its residents died and four members of staff lost their lives.

"The sheer scale brings it home in a very vivid and real way. We've been fighting such a deadly killer," says Sir David Behan, the company's executive chairman.

"I've been working for 42 years in public service and never imagined we would have to deal with a set of circumstances like this. I realize now that over the years, I've used the phrase 'unprecedented' completely inappropriately and incorrectly. This is a virus that is truly unprecedented."

HC-One has more than 300 homes around the UK and employs 24,000 people. Sir David has spent his life working in care. As a 16-year-old he volunteered to help the homeless, and he's been helping ever since. "I wanted to make a contribution to a more socially just society," he says.

Between 2006 and 2012 he was the senior Whitehall civil servant for the sector. He's also been chief executive of the industry's regulator, and he's now the chairman and CEO of Britain's largest care home company. He's "been humbled and inspired" by the way his staff responded to COVID-19.

"People who work in health and social care are driven by a set of values around wanting to help people, wanting to make a difference, and wanting to make a contribution," he tells me.

When I meet him over Zoom from his home in Kent, he is nursing his own bruises from being knocked off his bicycle. But they are mere flesh wounds and are nothing compared to the anguish his staff and residents have experienced.

"At the beginning of the pandemic, staff were very frightened and anxious that they would pick up this virus and take it home and that it would affect their loved ones. That was very real."

HC-One has had no shortage of major issues. In May 2020 it faced legal action over the running of one home in Skye, Scotland, where ten people died. A regulatory inspection revealed "serious and significant concerns." Improvements were made.

Despite his background as a mild-mannered former civil servant, Sir David simmers a little over some media coverage that he believes implied that care homes and the staff who work in them had "been to blame" for what transpired across the country.

"Care home staff put the needs of residents first and put their own needs and their family's needs after. They responded in a way that demonstrated the very best values of care and compassion and kindness."

He believes that HC-One's staff showed leadership at every level.

"My definition of leadership is behaviour that inspires people to do something that they might not have otherwise done. I've seen many people demonstrate that leadership – the cooks, the housekeepers, the care assistants. These are not people who have leadership in their title, but they have demonstrated it by coming to work every day and sacrificing their own needs for the needs of residents."

One of the biggest issues the leadership team faced was the evolving understanding of the virus. HC-One had to adapt to 31 different sets of guidance from the government. This meant company policies and procedures were constantly reviewed.

"We have been learning as we go. Our knowledge of the nature of the virus was so incomplete. It wasn't until the second or third week in April that we were clear about asymptomatic staff taking the virus into care homes. That was one of the biggest challenges. The virus was hidden.

"Staff, residents and relatives all wanted clarity on how the organization should be responding, supporting staff and treating residents. The last thing we were able to provide was clarity. Even now we're still learning about this virus and how it operates."

For several years, Sir David served as the Department of Health's director general of social care. He knows the inner workings of Westminster and he's seen the sector from every angle. At the age of 64, he says he has "never felt more independent." But he's reluctant to criticize the government.

"I have been invited on several occasions to be critical of government and I took a decision not to do that. Hindsight and retrospect are wonderful things."

The initial government guidance claimed it was "very unlikely" that residents in care homes would become infected. Sir David's view is, "With the value of hindsight was the government guidance in early March sufficient? No, it wasn't. Did I think that in March? I didn't know."

On the other controversial issues that emerged in the crisis, Sir David is candid. He believes HC-One coped well in ensuring staff had the right PPE. "When there was a national debate over PPE, we ensured we had sufficient supplies."

He acknowledges that discharging elderly residents from hospitals back to care homes accelerated transmission of the virus but adds, "It had multiple entry points. Residents returning from hospital was one of them but staff, contractors and visitors were another. This virus entered care homes in numerous different ways."

He is adamant on the importance of putting in place regular and routine testing for staff and residents. "I have been saying that for the best part of three months. I am convinced that was what was needed. We are just getting those arrangements in place now." It may rankle with him that this didn't happen sooner, but he accepts that "there is always a gap between government policy being announced and it being delivered on the ground."

He does bristle a little when I raise the English Health Secretary Matt Hancock's claim that a "protective ring"[58] was placed around the care sector from the beginning of the crisis.

"It really did not feel like there was a protective ring around these care homes in March, April and May," he says definitively.

Of course, it was not just the UK that saw a high death toll in care homes. The situation was replicated around the world. "We knew from Wuhan it hit older people. We knew that where there was the greatest concentration of older people was in care homes," Sir David says. "Yet all governments missed it."

So, what of the future of the care sector? COVID-19 has brought to the surface issues that have been swirling around for decades. In recent years governments of different hues have all judged reform to be too difficult.

When Sir David led on social care in the Department of Health, he produced two white papers proposing change – one for Labour Prime Minister Gordon Brown and one for the Conservative and Liberal Democrat coalition of David Cameron and Nick Clegg. Then, when he was CEO of the sector's regulator, the Care Quality Commission, he once again addressed the need for change in a statutory report to Parliament. "I said the social care sector was approaching a tipping point and my message was this service is becoming so precarious and so fragile that a long-term solution was required," he tells me.

"The virus has proven just how fragile the sector is. It's also proven there's an urgent need for reform. If I wasn't clear before – and I think I was brutally clear – I am now. What do viruses do? They find the weakest part of the body. What has this virus done?

It has found the weakest part of our public services and that is the care system."

So, what is the solution?

"A risk pool based on the whole population and based on taxation is the most effective way of providing care for older people. If I contract cancer, I will be cared for under the NHS. But if I develop Alzheimer's, I will receive social care through a means-tested system. This is the basic unfairness that sits at the heart of the debate."

Social care has been means-tested since the NHS was founded in 1948. In order to develop a system similar to the NHS, one of the political choices is to use public money to end the means-tested system and make social care free at the point of delivery for everyone. Sir David sees that as "the fairest way to do it" but adds, "You would have to spend billions to buy out the means test." There's also a pressure to extend the care system to include the unmet needs of more than a million further people. Sir David frames the quandary as follows: "If you have finite resources, do you buy out the means test, or do you offer care to more people?"

He describes these as "very difficult political choices." Ironically, they might have been choices that a newly elected Conservative government would have been willing to take on with its healthy majority in Parliament achieved in 2019. But now COVID-19 has made the affordability of a solution more difficult and the social necessity more urgent.

"It is a huge political challenge at a time when we are going into the biggest shrinkage in our economy since the 1700s. We need political courage. We need political vision to make a difference. We need that political courage now."

As the virus recedes in the UK, challenges for the sector grow. Inquiries will look at the systemic issues and, no doubt, interrogate judgements made by governments and care providers. The reputation of care homes has been hit hard. Sir David believes there are two essential ingredients to restoring public confidence – the regular testing of residents and staff, and ensuring homes demonstrate the very best standards of infection and hygiene control.

"This is not just for the next few months. This is with us permanently. This is a marathon, not a sprint," he says.

"We are months and months away from a vaccine and treatments. We are going to have to continue to work through uncertainty and continue to harvest the evidence about what works in managing this virus and what doesn't. That means as leaders we need to continue to be agile, nimble and adaptable in the way we respond."

Throughout my conversation with Sir David Behan, he frequently returns to the concepts of service, duty and values. He believes that these are the attributes that give leaders the strength to continue in the very worst of circumstances. They've been the bedrock of resilience for him and his colleagues.

"What we have gone through over the past four months have been the toughest times in my 42 years in work. But we are judged as leaders not on what we are like when the going is good; we are judged as leaders on what we are like when the going is tough."

CHAPTER 20

CLEMENT KWOK, CEO, THE HONGKONG AND SHANGHAI HOTELS

LOCKED DOWN IN HONG KONG, 18 MAY 2020

The Peninsula Hotel in Hong Kong is an icon of luxury. Some say it's the best hotel in the world. Its fleet of 14 green Rolls-Royce Phantoms are the epitome of style. In the 1970s, it played a starring role in the Bond film *The Man with the Golden Gun*, as Roger Moore and Britt Ekland tangled in its silk sheets. The Peninsula is a global brand with ten hotels around the world. COVID-19 has hit them hard as international borders closed and high-net-worth guests were told to "stay at home."

"The impact on our business has been very severe. There is no secret about that," The Hongkong and Shanghai Hotels CEO Clement Kwok tells me. "We're at the forefront of the industry, bearing the brunt of what's happened."

When Bond was surprised by a naked Mary Goodnight slinking out of his shower in The Peninsula, Roger Moore delivered the memorable line, "I was trained to expect the unexpected."[59] The same could be said of Clement.

"Over history these things happen," he tells me of the current crisis. "Don't go out and think you are a long-term investor – say over 100 years – unless you have the stomach to live through the ups and downs. If the moment a down comes along you run scared, you are not a long-term investor."

The Hon Sir Michael Kadoorie is chairman of The Hongkong and Shanghai Hotels. He owns more than 50% of the company. His grandfather founded the business and his family has been at the heart of it for three generations. He takes an "amazingly robust view on long-term investment," says Clement. The Peninsula Hong Kong is testimony to that. It was built in 1928 for HK $3 million and is now worth around HK $12 billion.

Clement has been CEO for 18 years. He's steered the group through SARS, the global financial crisis and every bump along the way. "The players that are more committed, are more passionate and have the financial resources will be the survivors," he observes.

The dapper chartered accountant has served as an independent non-executive director of Swire Pacific, which owns Cathay Pacific, and as a non-executive director of Orient Overseas, one of the world's largest container lines. He has the clarity that comes from experience. "The balance sheet is often forgotten until a crisis comes along," he tells me. His balance sheet is robust.

He describes the current focus as "managing costs and looking after our people." In the SARS pandemic no one was let go. This time some of the 7,500 staff have been furloughed. None has been laid off permanently. "We will be a survivor that has been able to look after our staff and will come out at the top end of any comparison."

The Hongkong and Shanghai Hotels has been trading for more than 150 years. It is the oldest international hotel group that's stayed in continuous operation. There are ten Peninsula Hotels around the world. Six are temporarily closed. Four have remained open – Beijing, Beverly Hills, Hong Kong and Shanghai. The hotels still operating have seen low occupancy.

As a global leader in the luxury hotel sector, Clement is well placed to predict the future. "I don't have a crystal ball, but it is not impossible that we are going to see quite a disruption to travel for two to five years. During that time, it is likely that there may be changes in the supply side. Some operators may not survive or choose to do something else. Some hotels may be converted into something else. To what extent will airlines be disrupted? We have got used to a world where we have taken for granted that we have instantly at our fingertips everything we want in terms of travel.

"I do believe fundamentally people will still want to travel. For business travel, relationships of trust only come through face-to-face contact. Once people have had the experience of luxury travel, they want more."

The Hongkong and Shanghai Hotels operates the Peak Tram – the world's steepest funicular railway. Six million visitors normally use it each year to get up to Hong Kong's most famous viewpoint. The shops, restaurants and the Sky Terrace at the top are also run by the group. It has just embarked on a HK $684 million (US $88 million) upgrade of the tram and the facilities. But tourist numbers and revenues have plummeted in 2019/20. Before COVID-19, the city was hit by months of protests and unrest, which stopped many tourists visiting. In the company's 2019 annual report, Clement said that "the violence and destruction was heart-breaking to witness." It was a stark contrast to what he described as "Hong Kong's usually peace-loving, family-oriented society."[60]

As COVID-19 receded, the democracy protests returned. It is a double whammy for many of the international businesses in Hong Kong. "We were affected by the protests quite materially. Without getting into any political views, for our business we benefit from stability. So, that sort of uncertainty and concerns over violent protests are very much against our interests."

Just a few days after Clement and I talked, China announced that it would impose a controversial new national security law on Hong Kong. Thousands of protestors poured back onto the streets. They were met by police with water cannons and tear gas.

This will not encourage tourists back to Hong Kong and is another economic concern on the back of COVID-19. But Clement is a resilient leader whose view is that in the hotel business you just have to get on with your job.

"We can't offer solutions but at the moment we are going about our business the best we can. In our planning we are taking into account the speed at which our recovery might be further affected by this."

The Hongkong and Shanghai Hotels is a global business. Clement and his team are building three new Peninsula Hotels – in Istanbul, London and Yangon in Myanmar. They were due to open in 2021/22 but construction has been temporarily disrupted by the COVID-19 lockdown.

There will be a need to put in place operational changes to protect staff and guests but Clement believes that measures will have to be proportionate.

"Some people say hotel guests might not want to interact with other humans. I don't subscribe to that. People tend to overreact when there is a threat. I can't imagine we're all going to live in some disinfected sterile hotel environment."

Building the London hotel at Hyde Park Corner will cost £800 million in addition to the purchase of the land. The company's strategy remains intact despite COVID-19 but its operating tactics are where the focus of the immediate future will lie.

"Once you have built a hotel with 300 rooms you can't take it anywhere else," says Clement. "The nature of the asset means you can't really put it to an alternative use. We believe in the long-term viability of the business." There is even the possibility that changing behaviours after COVID-19 mean some people will prefer a spacious hotel room. "It is about managing whatever the recovery period is in a way that is flexible and adaptable and looking after the staff in the best way we can."

In mid-May 2020, things started to open up again. "Hong Kong is starting to feel normal," says Clement. "If the only economy that mattered was Hong Kong as a closed economy, we wouldn't worry too much. But we are very dependent on international trade and international travel and tourism. It is difficult to predict when the borders will be reopened."

Looking back on the COVID-19 crisis, Clement provides his own insight into what matters when a business is being rocked to its foundations.

"During a crisis is when the importance of human relations and communications becomes very apparent," he says. "When you are under the pressure of crisis that really becomes key. Keeping the close relationships and the trust in each other – because you have to have trust in your colleagues."

In Clement Kwok's office is a rack that holds more than 400 golf balls. He's collected each one from the many great golf courses he has played around the world. There are 25 from the great links of Scotland, including one from the course outside my own home. Right now, he has little time for golf. The future of The Hongkong and Shanghai Hotels comes first. There's a history, a legacy and a brand to be nurtured.

"We don't know what the new future is," he concludes. "But I believe if you're good at doing something and you commit to the thing that you're good at, then the fundamental of what you do will continue to be in demand and your product will be sustainable."

RESETTING THE SUPPLY CHAIN

Several of our leaders in lockdown believe there will be a seismic shift in the shape of supply chains because of COVID-19. The pandemic exposed weaknesses that had developed over decades of corporate decision-making based on efficiency and the lowest cost. But when national borders are closed, when global cargo is halted and when whole populations are locked down, businesses lose the ability to function. Add to that geopolitical tensions and the threat of further health emergencies in the future, and it is easy to understand why this issue goes to the top of the corporate agenda.

Supply chains will become simpler, closer to home, and less at risk of disruption due to politics or pandemics. This issue will also be shaped by the geopolitical friction between China and the US.

Some see a game-changing acceleration of robotics and automation. This could drive manufacturing back from Asia towards Europe and the US but without the need for human workers.

In the next four chapters we hear from leaders who – as well as having great insights on coping with the business fallout from COVID-19 – all have views on how supply chains should change.

Christian Lanng is a disruptor. His business promises a supply chain revolution through digital. He describes what happened as a "massive breakdown of the global order." He's in the vanguard of change.

Martin Gilbert is a grizzled City of London veteran. He ponders whether globalization really works and says he "would love to see us return to greater support for local products, communities and economies."

Mike Cherry champions the small business. He urges that in our post-COVID-19 reset these smaller entities need to be valued more and put at the heart of any economic recovery. They are the real engine of the global economy.

Li Tong is looking to the future and the role that robotics and automation can have in transforming the way we make things and the way we serve customers. His robots had a crucial impact on how the health sector coped with COVID-19. Now robots can play their part in reimagining manufacturing.

Our leaders in lockdown were adamant on this theme – supply chains will be reset post-COVID-19. They will never be the same again.

CHAPTER 21

CHRISTIAN LANNG, CEO, TRADESHIFT

LOCKED DOWN NEAR SAN FRANCISCO, CALIFORNIA, US, 22 MAY 2020

In early April 2020, Christian Lanng and his colleagues at the digital supply chain business Tradeshift were getting set for a long, cold economic winter as COVID-19 froze the business world. "We were preparing to not sell anything for the rest of the year," he tells me.

Then the phones started to ring. "They all asked us the same question: 'How can we get to digital now?'" In the next six weeks, Tradeshift signed up more suppliers and digitized more supply chains than they'd done in the previous five years.

"A lot of our customers simply found out overnight that they thought they were digital but all they had truly done was put a glossy digital layer on top of 30 years of business crust. That was a massive wake-up moment," Christian tells me.

One customer had three million invoices sitting in a shared service centre that they couldn't process because the staff had all gone home. "They didn't have a clue what their costs were," Christian reveals.

Eight years ago, the Danish CEO moved Tradeshift from Copenhagen to the shadows of San Francisco's Golden Gate. The company was founded in 2010 in a garage by three Danes – Christian Lanng, Mikkel Hippe Brun and Gert Sylvest. That was their first lesson: "If you want to start a company in a garage, you should probably do it in California because it's really cold in a garage in Denmark in winter."

In 2018, Goldman Sachs raised a $250 million round of funding for Tradeshift. That valued the company at more than $1 billion. The Vikings had become unicorns.

They're doing for procurement what Tinder did for singletons. They're a supply chain matchmaker, digitally connecting businesses and their suppliers – two parties who need each other but have never found it easy to get together. They aim to end paperwork, automate payments and banish manual processes.

Christian's attitude to change sets a high bar. "Disruption and change don't happen in a linear curve," he tells me. "We've had very little change for the last 10 to 20 years."

It's only 45 miles on Route 101 from Tradeshift's headquarters to Apple's headquarters. For many, Apple's iPhone is iconic of how the world has changed. But Christian believes we could have done so much more to realize the potential of this technology. "Truly, the impact of that hasn't been as revolutionary as you'd think. The phones are cool, and we can do a lot of stuff. The software looks better on your screen. The screen is bigger. But if you look at what the impact has been in the enterprise world, it's largely the same buttons that were there 20 years ago doing exactly the same things. Beneath all of that is a lot of paper and a lot of manual processes and people in service centres. What happened with COVID-19 is all of that came to a stop."

Tradeshift now connects 2.5 million businesses across 190 countries and operates half a trillion dollars of trade. It employs a team of 1,200. COVID-19 has accelerated growth. Christian believes it compelled people to make major mindset changes. "Change is forced at first, then that resets our expectations about everything else we can do. With COVID-19, every single long-held belief has been thrown out of the window and people are very open to change."

The Tradeshift founders are supply chain revolutionaries. They've spent their lives trying to solve supply problems digitally. When Facebook and Twitter were making it so easy to connect the world, all the three Danes saw were barriers between suppliers and their customers. That's when they imagined a social network for invoices.

"For a lot of small companies before Tradeshift, if you needed to become part of the GM or Unilever supply chain and connect with them digitally, you would easily spend a million dollars for starters. Now it's free."

They're now also a payments fintech. Christian wants to help suppliers get paid more quickly – especially at times of crisis, when cash is king. He imagines, "Can we help companies get paid on day one?"

During the crisis Tradeshift worked with Danish Export Finance to open up $55 billion of liquidity for large companies. The company estimated that COVID-19 trapped $9 trillion of working capital in supply chains globally as they ground to a halt.

He describes countries panic buying PPE as "a massive breakdown of the global order." He adds, "Why were countries fighting for the same resources? Because the only thing that happens is the price goes up. The world had enough production capacity to make this stuff. We had the technology to solve the problem."

He claims when COVID-19 first struck there were only two and a half weeks' supply of aspirin left in the whole of the UK. "You need to ask some pretty hard questions," he says. "Is it right to run a healthcare supply chain the same way as you build cars? The outcome of failure is vastly different. It would have cost the UK 1% of the current stimulus package to have had enough PPE up front. Who made the decision that that was too costly? Now we are paying ten times the price for the same masks. In weeks, we've spent 20 years of PPE budget. We need to move away from just-in-time supply chains. We need to move to just-in-case and that's a cost decision."

Christian believes that the behaviour of businesses in the past is now the root cause of the environmental issues and trade wars of today – not least moving so much manufacturing from the US and Europe to Asia and China for short-term gains.

"I say to CEOs, you made decisions in the 1980s and 1990s that kick-started the trade war you are having now that is killing your business. If you think this is something political that has nothing to do with you, go back to the decisions you made decades ago. History has a very long lens and people forget that when they are making short-term decisions."

Tradeshift has a research and development centre in China. That informs Christian's take on the China-US trade war. "China is the largest market in the world. We need China. But China doesn't need us so much. That is a tough pill for the West to swallow." He's seen for himself how China defines the long term. "In China, they think in the context of 100 years. We think in the context of six months."

A conversation with Christian is like a top game of tennis – one good point and then another. On leading in a crisis, he believes the most important attribute is empathy. "It separates the leaders that understand and can do it from those who can't. Empathy is one of the things that is truly needed right now."

He sees offices as optional in the future, describing what happened during COVID-19 as the largest change in office life since the Second World War. "Being together is going to come at a premium," he tells me. "Zoom is going to do the same thing to professional services as the container did to physical trade."

He imagines greater flexibility in the world of work, with smaller business units closer to employees' homes – places where people can drop in for a while. Christian is acutely aware of the growing importance of mental welfare at work. "You need to manage your mental health very actively and not take it as a given." He's been working from home, locked down north of San Francisco.

Throughout the crisis, he's taken a break most days to go for a cycle ride. He's taken more time to play with his young son. These are habits he hopes to continue. He's convinced himself to live with the new world of COVID-19 and "stop holding your breath for this to be over."

In the future, he thinks robotics and automation will accelerate bringing manufacturing back to the US and Europe but not the jobs. "The operators of the robots will stay in India. One human can manage four robots from a shared service centre. There is no need for the people to be in the factory."

Equally, employees can be located anywhere there's a Wi-Fi signal. That sets companies free to recruit talent from anywhere they want. Recruiters can cast their nets wider and wider. Customers and suppliers need know no boundaries as geography becomes history. "Right now we are learning to consume any service possible over Zoom that involves people. So, it stops mattering where those people sit."

On the geopolitics of rising protectionism and nationalism, Christian sets a lofty ambition: "A sizeable chunk of the world's economy is running through our pipes. No matter what happens politically, our job is to try to keep the global business cohesiveness. The opportunity is massive."

A conversation with Christian Lanng redefines the definition of ambition. From a garage to a unicorn, and there's more to come.

"Our overall mission is to create economic opportunity for *all* the companies in the world – for them and us. The more connection there is between companies, the easier it is to help companies to grow and create jobs. We are the connective tissue."

CHAPTER 22

MARTIN GILBERT, FOUNDER, ABERDEEN ASSET MANAGEMENT; CHAIRMAN, REVOLUT; CHAIRMAN, TOSCAFUND AND NED GLENCORE

LOCKED DOWN IN ABERDEEN, SCOTLAND, 28 APRIL 2020

This was supposed to be a time to celebrate for Martin Gilbert – champagne and speeches. The end of an era. A moment to look back at a 40-year journey that started with only three men in an office. They bought a £50 million investment trust and turned it into an asset management company controlling billions.

"The time has come to close the door. That chapter is over," he tells me. But the party will have to wait. Martin is locked down, like the rest of us. He's been at his home in Aberdeen for five weeks – the longest period he's been there since he founded the company back in 1983.

Martin grew Aberdeen Asset Management into a business operating in 40 countries. He propelled the company into the FTSE 100. Through major acquisitions, it became the second largest listed fund manager in Europe – behind only Schroders.

Then, in 2017, Martin navigated a merger that created Standard Life Aberdeen, the company he's now about to leave.

He's a man who thought he'd seen it all. "This is my fifth or sixth crash. The shock of the market move on Black Monday in 1987 was huge. I remember as a young man, the US went down 30% that evening. But the economic effect of this will surpass that in multiples. This is going to be the most dramatic since the 1930s. It will be a long, long recovery."

Martin is a chartered accountant, so it is not surprising to hear what he believes matters most every time a crash comes. "It shows the need for a strong balance sheet," he tells me while stroking his newly acquired beard.

The three businesses that he is now involved in all pass muster on the capital count. Standard Life Aberdeen has £2 billion in cash. He is chairman of the digital banking giant Revolut, which just completed $500 million of fundraising. He also sits on the board of the multinational commodities giant Glencore. It has £10 billion available should it be needed. No one has been furloughed in these businesses.

Martin is the very definition of a City veteran. But that doesn't mean his views follow convention.

"I am a great believer that the world is going to change. Globalization has made us better off, but better for whom? Better off for only 10% of the population. I would love to see us return to greater support for local products, communities and economies."

COVID-19 has exposed issues with the supply chain that he believes will need to be addressed in the aftermath of the crisis. The international wrestling over the purchase of PPE and testing kits brought to the surface issues that have been festering for a while.

"After this, there will be much more interest in the supply chain. We'll need to look at where we get things from. In the UK we've lost the manufacturing base for so many things. The whisky companies had to produce sanitizer. The PPE had to come from China or Turkey.

"We have devolved too much manufacturing. When it comes to the public inquiry into COVID-19 in the UK, it will show the frailties of the supply chain."

Martin predicts a period where countries will look inwards. "We may well see a rise in protectionism where countries act to ensure they have more control of their supply chain."

He takes a middle road on the length and depth of the recession. Some have optimistically claimed it will be a V-shaped bounce-back from the bottom. The more pessimistic predict an L-shaped recovery. "There's no doubt it's going to be really tough. I think, on balance, the comeback will be a mix between the V and the L."

It's the asset management sector that Martin knows best, having spent most of his working life there. He believes it is an even more vital part of the financial services sector in a world of low interest rates. "Asset management is such an important industry because we have this huge responsibility towards society to encourage people to save. Then we have the responsibility to manage their money in a cost-efficient and effective way so they can have a successful life after they stop earning money.

"They say the rich need to make money. Actually, the rich just want to preserve what they've got. I'm much more in the area of wealth preservation – in the current climate – than wealth creation."

A conversation with Martin involves a whirlwind of opinions and insights. On Rishi Sunak, the UK Chancellor, he says, "All in all, I think he's done a pretty good job. The economic packages have been pretty all encompassing. He's stopped businesses laying off their entire staff. When he did see an anomaly with his initial measures, he was sensible enough to correct it."

On the asset management sector he says, "Revenues in asset management will be down 20% to 25% off the top line and COVID-19 may accelerate consolidation in what's a fragmented industry."

On the insurance sector he notes, "This might turn out to be the biggest insured loss ever." Turning to the banks, "Not paying their dividends was a sensible thing to do." On the regulators, "They've been better coordinated than in the last crisis."

On the new Governor of the Bank of England, Andrew Bailey, who had only been in the job ten days when the crisis hit, "A good man for the job – facing up to one of the greatest crises in the last 100 years."

On purpose, which has been a word on many leaders' lips, "There is no point having a purpose if you're not going to survive. Our purpose was always to do as well as we can for the clients."

Coming out of COVID-19, Martin will be entering a new era. For the first time in his life, he will no longer have an executive role in asset management. Much of his time will be focused on chairing the digital finance business Revolut.

"We will hopefully be applying for a banking licence and going global with our great customer experience." He'll also take on the role of chairing Toscafund. "Most of all I want to enjoy the roles I do and help make these businesses grow. It will be tough in this environment, but it will be exciting."

There are two things that Martin has missed most in his weeks of lockdown. No golf and no salmon fishing. The courses have been closed in Scotland and the salmon beats have been out of bounds. The only salmon he's seen for a while are on the painting on the wall of his home office. For those two sporting reasons, the end of lockdown can't come quickly enough, although he acknowledges these are necessary precautions for the most unprecedented of circumstances.

When COVID-19 is all over, much in the world will have changed. Much in Martin Gilbert's business world will have changed too. The start of another chapter for this veteran of the City.

CHAPTER 23

MIKE CHERRY, CEO, WH MASON AND CHAIRMAN, FEDERATION OF SMALL BUSINESSES IN THE UK

LOCKED DOWN IN BURTON UPON TRENT, ENGLAND, 29 APRIL 2020

In 1897, Mike Cherry's forefathers decided to go into the timber business. They've been on the same site in the world-famous beer town of Burton upon Trent ever since. Five generations of his family have nurtured the business over those years.

But they closed their doors on 23 March 2020 and haven't opened again. They had survived a century of change and two world wars before they were laid low by COVID-19. "I am quietly confident we'll get through this, but we are likely to be one of the last groups to emerge," Mike tells me.

When Britain's pubs, restaurants and hotels closed, the country's independent brewers lost 80% of their sales overnight. Mike's company makes a range of traditional wood products, mainly for the beer business. They include the taps on the casks and the shives[61] that are used as stoppers.

The chances are that if you've had a pint of English bitter, it's been secured in a cask with one of Mike's products. Some of you may have had your pint pulled by a WH Mason pump handle.

But overnight a world with no pubs and no beer had no need for Mike's products.

"We had no option but to shut."

Mike's is a shining example of the resilience of small business-people in the face of the crisis. "Our hope is that there might be a huge bounce in 12 months' time. Provided there is a treatment or a vaccine, people will, once again, have the confidence to gather like humankind wants to do and socialize in their local with a drink of beer. But it's a virus that humanity will have to live alongside for quite a while."

Mike is also the chairman of the Federation of Small Businesses in the UK. Throughout the crisis he has been meeting the UK Chancellor, Rishi Sunak, to put the case for government support of the country's small enterprises. "I can work constructively with him. We highlight the evidence our members provide. We make the case and show a constructive way forward."

One of the early battles Mike took on was the lack of support for the self-employed in the various UK government interventions that had been announced. "I had a robust conversation with the Chancellor, and we were very pleased with what he came out with and how he was willing to adapt. Additional support is always welcome but there are still far too many businesses that are unfortunately likely to fail."

That change of tack by the Chancellor meant grants of up to £2,500 per month for self-employed people who earned less than £50,000 a year – a substantial sector of the economy.

There are nearly six million small businesses in Britain.[62] They account for 99.9% of the business population. Globally, there are 400 million small and medium enterprises. That's 95% of firms in the world and around 70% of employment.[63] The problems these businesses faced in the crisis were similar wherever they were.

"It is devastating, especially for newer businesses. Small businesses are cash light. They do have some cash reserves, but they can't survive for long without support when you effectively stop so much of the economy. What you tend to see when a major crash comes along is that many people may well say 'I am not prepared to do it any more' and they just shut."

A great frustration for small businesses has been the time it took to get the money pledged by government into their bank accounts.

"The value of these interventions depends on the speed at which funding is received. While some local authorities have stepped up and delivered, others have not. A laser-like focus on delivery is essential," according to Mike.

He sighs a little when I cite the system in Switzerland, which takes an hour from a business applying for support to the money being received in its bank account. He believes the time has come to put something similar in place in the UK.

"I have been arguing for years that we need a central database of businesses. This shows we need it."

But Mike recognizes that there are also opportunities that emerge from such moments of disruption.

"If you look back at previous recessions, this is often the best time to invest. This is where small businesses and entrepreneurs really stand out. They are key to facilitating new ways of going forward."

Mike also realizes that the range of loans, grants and reliefs provided by the UK government and other governments around the world has just bought us all a bit of time. "They can't continue forever. We need to get out of lockdown in a confident way. How you do that is the real dilemma."

The true tsunami of business closures will come when lockdown ends. As one business leader put it, "We will get back on our bikes to discover that the bikes have just fallen over."

Mike is acutely aware of the scale of things to come. But he believes that one positive to come out of COVID-19 should be a major reappraisal of the environment needed to encourage small businesses.

"We need to value much better the contribution that the self-employed microbusiness brings to the economy. Small businesses are great at just doing things.

"We need to move away from political short-term vision. We need to think longer term. We need to create the right environment post-COVID-19 for our small businesses to flourish. We are the people who will provide the employment to help the economy bounce back.

"The bigger issues we need to tackle include a fundamental reform of the tax base in the medium term. We need to simplify the tax code. Everyone should pay their fair share of tax. There is an unfair and disproportionate burden on small businesses," says Mike.

Part of this anomaly, which clearly irks small businesspeople, is how to tax multinational internet traders. "It doesn't make sense. If you make a sale in a country, you should pay tax in that country.

"We need to change so much, from reducing the burden of business rates to creating the right tax infrastructure to maximizing the skills base. We need younger people trained better in vocational skills and new technology. We need to get it right for our future and our children's future. Now is the time to do it."

Brewing in Burton upon Trent goes back to the Middle Ages, when monks made ale to sate the thirst of pilgrims. In more recent years, the town has been famous for beers such as India pale ale and brewers such as Bass, Ind Coope and Worthington.

These famous names have all been consigned to history. With more than a century's tradition behind him, Mike Cherry is determined that his business won't suffer the same fate. As we finish our videoconference, we both agree to raise a pint of real ale to that.

CHAPTER 24
LI TONG, CEO, KEENON ROBOTICS

LOCKED DOWN IN SHANGHAI, CHINA, 30 APRIL 2020

"I believe that anything a human can do can be done by robots in the future."

That's the bold prediction of Li Tong, a CEO whose mission is to make science fiction become reality.

"Technology is always overestimated in the short term but underestimated in the long term," he adds with the simplicity of Confucius. He is the CEO of Keenon Robotics, a Shanghai-based innovator in robots and automation. This is not the world of hopefully dreaming inventors. It's serious business.

It is predicted that the robotics market in China will be worth more than $100 billion by 2023. At the peak of the COVID-19 crisis, robots took a place in the front line of fighting the virus and saving lives. Keenon donated more than 200 units into 80 hospitals over the Chinese New Year in early 2020, when the virus was threatening to overwhelm the public health system.

Other Chinese robotics manufacturers also sent their inventions into the heat of battle. Robots fitted with infrared thermometers were able to take the temperatures of patients, visitors and health workers. That helped to identify those with symptoms of COVID-19 and acted as an early warning system.

Keenon's main product is a robot called Peanuts. It can talk. Facial recognition means it can remember and recognize customers. Previously, its main job was as an electronic waiter delivering food in restaurants. Peanuts's surprise presentation of a birthday cake was particularly popular! But in the COVID-19 crisis, it was pressed into service to avoid putting hospital workers in the way of infection.

Tong's view is that when it is a matter of life and death, robots can save lives. The future potential for them to be used in pandemics is considerable – whether that's for delivering food or medicines, or for sterilization. "The epidemic has accelerated the development process," he tells me.

Keenon has now developed a $40,000 version of the product that can use ultraviolet light and disinfectant to clean and treat areas where COVID-19 might be lurking. The US military has bought some to use in mess halls and barracks.

Speaking from his headquarters in Shanghai, Tong tells me, "With the outbreak of the COVID-19 crisis during the Spring Festival, our robots officially landed in the medical market. In the areas where the epidemic was most serious, the medical staff faced the risk of being infected at all times, due to the shortage of protective equipment. They also faced exhaustion and tiredness because of the multi-day working.

"The use of unmanned delivery robots relieved the work pressure of first-line medical staff to a certain extent. It saved the scarce protective equipment and the most important thing was that it reduced the contact between medical staff and patients, greatly reducing the infection of medical staff."

Keenon's robots are in 400 cities across China, as well as overseas markets in Canada, Germany, Italy, Singapore, South Korea, Spain and the US. The company posts videos of its robots on the platform Douyin, the Chinese brother of TikTok. Before the outbreak, they were only watched by a few thousand people. Now one of the more popular videos has attracted more than 60 million views.

"Everyone in the company is a person who believes that technology can change lives," Tong tells me. "I think that in the future there will be multiple robots in every household, responsible for simple tasks. That will leave people to be increasingly engaged in more creative work."

Tong, like many of his colleagues, first became involved in robotics when he was at university. "I formed a team with my classmates. Everyone participated in the Challenge Cup and the National Electronic Circuit Design Competition. There was also the Smart Car Competition. For myself, the experience of striving for a dream is full of passion and it is still unforgettable. At university, I also met others who went on to form start-ups. Everyone forged a profound revolutionary friendship in cooperating on the projects and in the competitions."

Robots have come a long way in Asia in recent years. When a tsunami and earthquake damaged the nuclear reactor at Fukushima in Japan in 2011, robots were sent in to try to clean up the highly contaminated toxic mess. However, there were a series of failures that took six years to overcome. That set back confidence in the sector's value in disaster situations.

Before COVID-19, the level of exposure to service robots on the market was not high. But the success robots have had in helping to deal with the pandemic may accelerate growth in both health and hospitality.

Keenon's goal this year is to sell more than 10,000 robots. They will also focus more on moving into the health market. It remains to be seen whether COVID-19 will help or hinder that goal. Li Tong believes we should never underestimate the power of the robot in dealing with a pandemic. He also thinks that medical workers and patients found them reassuring.

"Perhaps this idea is influenced by various Hollywood science fiction movies. When robots appear in reality, people imagine that they are omnipotent."

MAXIMIZING POTENTIAL

The final theme that ran as a thread through the interviews was a focus on exploring new methods and behaviours to maximize the individual potential of our leaders and their teams.

There was a strong feeling that COVID-19 had seen the triumph of the empathetic and compassionate leader and the death of the 'Superman' leader. A new style is needed to maximize the potential of virtual and remote teams – different skills, a different mindset, a different approach and different structures are required for that.

Our leaders also talked of a new era of greater awareness of mental and physical wellbeing in maximizing potential. Some championed a far more proactive approach to looking after themselves and their colleagues – not just because it was the right thing to do, but also because it was the way to improved performance.

Coaching senior executives during this highly stressful period was also seen as a key to success. Developing a true coaching culture in business is now seen as essential to maximizing potential. In the future, an executive coach may be deemed a necessity, just as it is in the world of elite sport.

In the next four chapters, we hear another wealth of stories and insights on leadership. Will Ahmed is at the forefront of innovating around executive performance. His 24/7 wearable health tracker is increasingly used by senior executives. Will tells us that to maximize their own potential, executives must develop "the same mindset that an Olympian has."

The importance of communication in maximizing potential has never been more obvious than in COVID-19. Sally Osman, who used to advise the Queen, picks up this theme as she dissects one of the most infamous episodes in the crisis. She also wonders about corporate crisis communication plans: "Did anyone envisage events that came close to what actually happened?"

Derek Deasy has huge experience maximizing the potential of individuals and teams. His challenge to leaders in the crisis was, "Can you role-model empathy, compassion, transparency and collaboration?" Now he believes we will only create a new world of business if we focus with clarity on what effective leadership really is.

Pinky Lilani's take on maximizing potential is that kindness is at the heart of the issue. She believes kindness should now become an essential leadership behaviour. She tells us how she aims to "build a new status quo" around kind leaders.

The evolving theme of leadership post-COVID-19 will be maximizing potential – focusing on new ways for individual leaders, their teams and their businesses to be the very best they can.

CHAPTER 25

WILL AHMED, CO-FOUNDER AND CEO, WHOOP

LOCKED DOWN IN BOSTON, MASSACHUSETTS, US, 1 MAY 2020

"I fundamentally believe that this moment in time will shift the way humanity thinks about health."

That's 30-year-old Will Ahmed's view of the COVID-19 crisis. His 24/7 wearable health tracker, WHOOP, has gradually been growing a cult following in recent years. Now this might be the moment when a much wider audience discovers what it can offer. The company was created with the intention of providing game-changing research for elite athletes. Now it's also helping business executives. Post-COVID-19, it hopes to help reimagine the way public health works.

I met Will via videoconference. He's locked down at home in Boston. First, I learn that when he's in the office, he doesn't have to go far for his sporting inspiration. The WHOOP team look out over one of the best-known citadels of American sport, Fenway Park – the home of the Boston Red Sox.

Will was an elite squash player. He captained the men's team at Harvard. But he freely admits he overtrained and didn't understand his body. That was when he realized that what gives elite athletes the winning edge is not measured in training sessions. The real difference is what you do in the other 22 hours of the day.

"Sleep and recovery are more important to performance than measuring performance itself," he tells me.

He set up the business eight years ago. His co-founders are John Capodilupo and Aurelian Nicolae. Capodilupo studied maths and statistics at Harvard before dropping out to create WHOOP. Nicolae is another Harvard scholar. His sweet spot is mechanical prototyping and engineering. Their mission is "to unlock human performance."

When I spoke to our leaders in lockdown, I normally got clues to their character from what else I could see in the frame of their laptop's camera. A bookshelf, ornaments or paintings on the wall can reveal a lot. Will's background gives nothing away. But his words reveal a lot.

"When you get something that might affect 7.5 billion people, you want to do your part."

Early in the crisis, Will focused the WHOOP team on reorientating their tech. The aim was to get their wristband to collect data that might give people an early warning that they were infected by COVID-19. "At WHOOP we are very interested as to whether respiratory rate can be a predictor and there is evidence to show it may be."

In a short space of time, the WHOOP team were able to add this as a feature on their app and start presenting potentially life-saving data to their members. "If you knew that someone had COVID-19 before they showed symptoms and you quarantined that person, think how many fewer people they would infect."

Will described his company's transition to helping with the health crisis as a huge morale booster for this team. "It was WHOOP fighting back." After just five weeks they had data from 1,000 members who got COVID-19. This gave their researchers a unique view of what was happening to these victims' bodies moment by moment from when they caught the virus. This was valuable insight that wasn't available elsewhere.

But how did Will and his colleagues manage to develop the respiratory feature in such a short space of time? "We have a smaller team and less resources [than many companies]. So, we move a lot faster. Things that can seem like a disadvantage can often be turned into an advantage.

"We consider the pace that we release features and update our features and update our product to be a core differentiator. It goes back to our business model being a subscription. So, you're paying every month and therefore we are fighting for your dollar every month."

Celebrity sports stars who endorse WHOOP include the champion golfers Rory McIlroy and Justin Thomas, basketball star Kyle Lowry of the Toronto Raptors and the CrossFit champion Katrín Davíðsdóttir – dubbed the fittest woman in the world.

These role models are used to motivate WHOOP's members. Now COVID-19 might be another inspiration. "People who are healthier and fitter have more confidence in this moment of time than people who are at risk for whatever reason. That is going to create a lasting memory. After this pandemic more people will think, 'Wow. I really need to think about my health and understand my body.' My hope is that it could make humanity at large healthier and fitter.

"It goes back to our deep belief as a company that human performance is not something you solve in one day. It's something you want to solve for the rest of your life."

Since 2015 the number of units of wearable technology in use around the world has shot up from 84 million to 245 million.[64] The competition to WHOOP is fierce. Google now owns Fitbit. Biostrap and Polar are also in this space, while Apple and Amazon are developing products in a rapidly growing market. WHOOP has a tough fight on its hands. It's a relative minnow compared to the big fish of the tech majors.

But WHOOP can boast Fortune 500 CEOs and top politicians – all now proud wearers of the strap – as it grows its following from the playing field to the boardroom. Will says he has seen a gradual shift in the attitudes of senior executives in recent years. Now more and more are realizing that understanding their health leads to improved performance and better business decisions.

"We have super-high-performing individuals who are making incredibly important decisions every day and they recognize, 'If I have an earnings call[65] tomorrow or in two days, how am I going to peak for that?'

"It is the same mindset that an Olympian has to how they are going to peak for a competition. The reality is that there is a lot about measuring your body, measuring behaviours and measuring lifestyle decisions that can either position you to succeed and be the best version of yourself on that day or position you to be run down."

Will sees other positive possibilities. "One optimistic point of view is that there is going to be a feeling of rebirth coming out of this. There is going to be a deep level of appreciation across humanity for things where previously there wasn't.

"There is probably this recognition that a lot of people are having that they were on a treadmill of 'Go, go, go' and they never really paused to stop and look at all of it. It could lead to a happier society."

But the really big change that wearable tracking can bring about involves a rethink of how public health works. Across the world, as people are living longer, the strain on medical services is growing at a rate that no one can match.

The scale of that challenge was captured in 2018 by *Forbes* magazine. "Between 2015 and 2030, the number of people in the world aged 60 years or over is expected to grow by 56%, from just over 900 million to nearly 1.5 billion. By 2050, the global population of people older than 60 is expected to jump to two billion. In the United States, the number of Americans over the age of 65 is expected to double from roughly 50 million to nearly 100 million by 2060."[66]

The policy response is to shift from cure to prevention. Technology is the key to opening that door. "I am optimistic that COVID-19 is going to pull our healthcare system in the United States forward by a decade," says Will.

He believes wearable health tracking like that offered by WHOOP could be a major part of that game changing. "It can empower doctors to see the people they really need to be seeing. You are wearing technology. It's on your body. Over time it will be in your body. It is collecting everything you need to measure and understand your health. It's pushing you to be a better version of yourself and to be fitter and healthier.

"It is also identifying that moment in time when maybe you do need to see a doctor or an emergency is about to happen. To me that is so much more cost-effective than the way our existing health-care system functions. Everything around medicine is cheaper and more effective if it is preventative rather than curative."

WHOOP has also been able to gain insight into what happened to the health of its community during lockdown. People slept longer – swapping commuting time for bedtime. Stress levels rose as people dealt with the anxiety of COVID-19 and its impact on their personal and business lives. There was a big increase in people going running, walking and hiking. As gyms closed and team sports were suspended, weightlifting, basketball and football decreased.

The biggest change to Will's own personal health scores through the crisis might have been sparked by the curtailment of business travel. He hasn't been on a plane for 40 days. That's not happened since he was in his early twenties, before he founded WHOOP.

"As an entrepreneur I always told myself 'Get on the plane. Close the deal.' Could I now be even more thoughtful about that? Should I travel as much coming out of this? How can I be more purposeful when I do travel?"

Will has become an avid devotee of meditation to help his own karma. He exudes the confidence and calm of a high-performing tech exec. But the strains of running WHOOP must be many. The company raised $55 million in new funding in November 2019. So, it has thirsty investors to keep happy. His advisory board looks like the A-Team. It includes mathematicians, professors, cardiologists, engineers, marketing executives, pro sports ambassadors and designers.

For WHOOP, COVID-19 has been both tough and invigor-ating. The company's strategy has been tested. Costs have been cut. But, if anything, WHOOP's purpose may be emerging all the stronger and clearer.

"This is accelerating what we have been saying for years. Understanding your body and understanding your health is really important."

With that thought, Will Ahmed sleeps soundly.

CHAPTER 26

SALLY OSMAN, FORMER DIRECTOR OF ROYAL COMMUNICATIONS, THE ROYAL FAMILY

LOCKED DOWN IN LONDON, ENGLAND, 2 JUNE 2020

Sally Osman is no stranger to a crisis. She spent eight years heading communications at the BBC. Then she became a senior adviser to the Royal Family with The Queen as her boss. Now she's a consultant to the global CEO of the advisory firm Teneo.

Her analysis of the UK government's communications during lockdown pulls no punches. "The government started with such good will. The messaging was so clear. People thought, 'We had better do what we are told.'" But as the crisis went on, she believes the communications went from competence to chaos. "It was like they were down a rabbit hole from a communications point of view. It seemed it was being done on the hoof. The way it waxed and waned over the ten weeks was quite extraordinary."

Sally identifies four key communications moments in lockdown. First, the initial announcement that the country was to stay at home – which she believes was done well. Then the moment Boris Johnson was released from hospital. Act Three was the announcement of the relaxing of lockdown and the final key moment was the Dominic Cummings affair. Years of communicating in a crisis have taught Sally the golden rules.

"In a crisis you need to be absolutely honest about what you know and what you don't know," she tells me. "You need to show empathy, be authentic and be clear. You also need to be visible. You can't hide. Those are the basics."

Some have questioned why we didn't see more of the prime minister for long periods, especially in the latter part of the crisis. In the early weeks he had good reason to be absent. He was ill with the virus and admitted to intensive care. When he emerged from hospital, he told the nation, "The NHS is the beating heart of this country; it is unconquerable; it is powered with love."[67] Sally thinks this was Boris at his best.

"When he came out of hospital, you thought this was a man who had faced death. You could feel the authenticity in his voice about what he had been through. He was reassuring the nation and it felt like a piece of communication that came from the heart. That was incredibly powerful. But it went rapidly downhill after that."

Sally has spent many years carefully observing the impact of individual stories on the public mood. She thinks deeply about how particular moments can alter perceptions and damage reputations. The prime minister's television address on 10 May 2020, when he announced how the country was to exit lockdown, was a first for her.

"That was the worst piece of public communication I have ever witnessed, just at a time when you need real clarity and certainty and honesty with the public. It was just a mess. There were mixed messages. It wasn't clear. It wasn't delivered well."

Then there was the Dominic Cummings affair, when the prime minister's special adviser was revealed to have travelled 250 miles from London to Durham to isolate at his parents' farm. This seemed to be a clear breach of the spirit of the lockdown rules he had written. He held a media conference in the gardens of Downing Street where he refused to apologize, said he had no regrets and declined to resign.

"I just thought am I really seeing this – an unelected official being given the privilege of a press conference in the Downing Street Rose Garden, normally reserved for high-level ministers and visiting dignitaries. What the hell is going on? No sense of contrition and bizarre answers. It was very weird.

"When somebody becomes the story who isn't the leader, it is such a distraction from the main issue at hand. You have to lance the boil. Some would resign out of duty. Others would be sacked by strong leaders who know what's at stake. You have to get them out."

But Cummings doesn't play by the normal rules. His position was that he had not and would not consider resigning.

"It speaks to his personality and a degree of arrogance. There he is saying he's a man of the people. He has shown he's absolutely not. Because if he was, he would truly understand how furious and angry and upset people were – people who did abide by the spirit of the law under much more difficult circumstances than he was facing. To treat people with such contempt and to treat people as if they are stupid was the most remarkable moment."

When history reflects on the UK government's handling of the COVID-19 crisis, the Dominic Cummings affair may be seen as a defining moment.

"I cannot believe they allowed it to happen like that. The polls immediately showed the public had lost trust in them – Boris in particular. If he'd sacked Cummings, he would have shown backbone and leadership. I'm afraid it ended in a dog's breakfast, which undermined any residual authority or trust they had."

Sally sees the communications of the UK government in sharp contrast to the way that the Royal Family connected with the nation throughout the crisis. She points to their use of social media and video messaging as a watershed moment for the Royals engaging with the public.

"The Queen and other members of the Royal Family have been clear and reassuring. They absolutely hit the mood. They were relevant and rallying whether they were talking to front-line workers, nurses or farmers. They showed so much empathy. You've had these complete contrasts between government and monarchy."

Sally also sees The Queen's address to the nation on 5 April 2020 as a key moment in the early days of the crisis. "I think she got the pitch of it absolutely right. The Queen has very sound judgement when it comes to the mood and what will resonate with people. One of The Queen's most important roles is as 'Head of Nation', to wrap her arms around the nation in good times and bad."

Sally reflects that the mission for royal communications is the same now as it was when she was in charge. "The challenge is about demonstrating the role and relevance of a modern monarchy. Events sometimes help or hinder. The Royals are at their best when they show public support and empathy. They are at their best when they say, 'We're in this together.' Most of all, they are at their best when they are true symbols of fortitude and duty."

The crisis was also a huge challenge for how businesses behaved and communicated.

Sally points to examples of companies that did 'the right thing'. Burberry made PPE for health workers. McLaren Formula One helped to develop ventilators for intensive care units. "These are great signals of what companies can do more of in the future – delivering for the public good."

She believes post-COVID-19 will see another step change in corporate behaviour. "There has been so much talk of purpose in recent years. This is a reckoning, a moment of truth when organizations will be judged on giving purpose real meaning through action not words."

Sally is strongly of the view that COVID-19 will make the business world reassess its crisis communications. "All the big businesses had corporate crisis plans. It will be fascinating to see – whose plans were good? How well did the plans stand up? Who resisted the temptation to over-communicate? Whose internal communications plans worked? Did anyone envisage events that came close to what actually happened?"

Sally also sees the crisis as a moment when social media played a more positive role in the national conversation than we might have imagined. She applauds the creative way that many used it to capture the mood and help to lift public spirits. She asks, "Could this be the coming of age of social media – as a force for good?"

The shining example of that was the story of Captain Sir Tom Moore, the 99-year-old military veteran who initially decided to try to raise £1,000 for the NHS. His aim was to do 100 lengths of his garden before his 100th birthday. Cheered on by social media and then adopted by the mainstream media, he ended up raising £32 million. Sally says, "His story was just amazing. He was a lightning rod for people who wanted to do something and didn't know how."

Sally Osman has one more tip for communicating in a crisis. It's also her hope for changed behaviour in politics and business as the world emerges from COVID-19. "Leaders need to really listen in a crisis.

"As we go through the different waves of concern and worry, leaders need to listen to what people are really feeling and where they are emotionally. Then you can calibrate and craft your communications."

Communicating is about listening, not transmitting.

CHAPTER 27

DEREK DEASY, PROFESSOR OF ORGANIZATIONAL BEHAVIOUR, INSEAD

LOCKED DOWN NEAR FONTAINEBLEAU, FRANCE, 24 APRIL 2020

Derek Deasy is an Irishman in France. He lives in a picturesque village in the forest not far from the historic town of Fontainebleau. It's only 45 minutes from Paris on the fast train from the Gare de Lyon but seems like another world.

I find him today turning his executive coaching upon himself. He's at home with his wife and three young sons and trying to come to terms with his current situation. His work habitat is normally the amphitheatres of INSEAD, one of the world's leading business schools. That's his stage. It's where he feels fulfilled.

He works with MBA students and has recently pioneered the groundbreaking INSEAD Coaching Certificate (ICC) for executives. The experiential learning approach employed on the ICC has been highly praised by the executive coaches who have trained under Derek's challenging and watchful eyes. Over many years, he's worked with a wide range of corporations and senior leaders, helping them to maximize their potential.

At the heart of Derek's work is the systems psychodynamic coaching model. It pays attention to unconscious forces at the individual, interpersonal, group and organizational levels. It regards emotion as data that opens the window on these unconscious forces. This approach holds at its centre the dynamic relationship between the person, their role and their organization (PRO). It advocates working below the surface with clients – attending to the virtuous as well as the shadow side of life. This helps people better understand their relationships with themselves and with others. It encourages courageous conversations. It sees the coach as an accompanist rather than a director.

Today Derek is reflecting on how so many people's roles and their organizations have changed so dramatically overnight. He knows from his own experience how unsettling that must be.

"The social stresses of being confined are quite large. At an identity or 'P' level, the usual reinforcement from 'working' is lost, which brings into question, who am I in all of this? Then there are the multiple roles – breadwinner, father and home schoolteacher. There used to be clear lines between them. Not now. There is no break from it. It is always on and trying to be sensitive to which role my children and family need in any moment is demanding."

Decoding these interactions in the PRO system is crucial to understanding the impact on individuals in this current crisis.

"The dilemma is how people get reassured about their own utility. You question, do I have value? People become preoccupied with individual survival. That brings levels of fear and issues of ambiguity around organizational identity."

He sees a lot of people trying to structure their way out of uncertainty. His own avoidance tactics have focused around "lots and lots of gardening." Now he wonders what's going to happen when the garden is done – a long-term worry!

Derek's background means he can bring several perspectives to his view of COVID-19. He spent many years working as a director in healthcare. His particular area of expertise was child sexual abuse, leading a team that offered forensic and therapeutic services to vulnerable children and their families. Even that tough experience hasn't prepared him for this.

"The amount of death is so difficult to bear," he tells me. "There is a number where people stop becoming people and start becoming statistics. We've gone way beyond that number. Why are we actively ignoring the scale of deaths? The number of people who are dying is devastating. People are going through unfair loss, which possibly could have been avoided. Where is their anger going to go? What is the future for governments who will eventually have to face up to and contain that anger?"

In the first ten days of the crisis, Derek carried out around 60 short coaching sessions with individuals and teams. He found these sessions on Zoom "surprisingly fatiguing." They are much less renewing than meeting face to face. As this way of working continues, he's sure we will realize how much our social health is being compromised.

So, what has been the common ground in these numerous coaching conversations?

Derek sees two quite different trends. There have been the 'rush to action' people. They feed off the need to be resilient and get everything structured and organized. Then there have been the more thoughtful people, who are asking themselves, 'What is the meaning of all this?' The risk, of course, is that they will do nothing – but, equally, doing something will be renewing only if it connects well with our values.

So, what would he say to our political and corporate leaders if he were one to one with them at the height of the crisis?

"I would be drawing their attention to several questions – how do you want to be remembered at a time when the world is paying attention? How do you want to be seen living your values at a moment in history? How can you role-model empathy, compassion, transparency and collaboration?"

Like many others I spoke to, Derek is despairing about the lack of international cooperation and the absence of foresight. "It wasn't that we couldn't *see* it would happen – we couldn't *believe* it would happen. Then it very quickly became political. How are my interests going to be impacted? Things might have been different if we'd had true global leadership. But, instead, it became about looking after your own and countries fighting over plane loads of face masks."

He finds any debate framed as a choice between health or economics intellectually bereft. "What's the use of having a thriving economy when all your people are dead or grieving the dead?"

So, is he hopeful that this terrible situation may lead to a new world of business? Derek explains, "I am reminded of Churchill, who said, 'If you're going through hell, keep going.' That makes me think that this is a bad time to be making new plans for the future. The best time for that is probably at the time of the transition to the new normal.

"But we will be back to the way we were unless there is a fundamental change about the things we value. At the moment it is like the world is having a heart attack and we say we'll give up cigarettes. Once the scare is over, there is a great danger we will just go back to smoking again.

"The longer it goes on, the greater the possibility of change. And you know this is a terrible thing to say but maybe the virus isn't dramatic enough. Ebola and SARS scared the hell out of people. Some people see COVID-19 and hear there's an 80% chance they'll be okay, and they say, 'I'll take that chance.'"

But if change can be nurtured, where should it bloom? To answer that, Derek believes people should consider what it was they valued when they didn't have their freedom. What of that will they want to hold on to?

He would like to see political and business leaders being more mindful of the impact of what they stand for. He believes a new world order must bring greater collaboration between the public and private sectors. He applauds Google and Apple for working together to create a COVID-19 contact-tracing tool. The drugs companies Sanofi and GSK have joined forces to try to find a vaccine. If the new world order saw a plethora of corporate cooperation, that would be a positive step forward.

He believes growing consumer activism in the future will keep big corporates truer to their purpose. A trend towards supporting local businesses as "doing our civic duty" would also be a good thing. Perhaps even a return to the high street, where shopping was a community exercise rather than the individual consumption priority it has become.

He also sees an opening for a new currency of exchange – a kind of corporate bartering. Already he has been carrying out pro bono coaching in a way that he hasn't done before.

The post-COVID-19 period will be a tough time for business schools. Most rely on global travel for executives and students flying in from around the world for MBAs and personal renewal. Some predict that this will never be the same again as virtual learning replaces air miles. The learning and development budgets of big corporations are normally slashed in the wake of financial shocks. This is a false economy. It's at times like these when you need a corporate culture of progress over performance, the courage to challenge and refine your assumptions, and leaders whose habits and behaviours offer holding and purpose, helping others to be at their most effective.

If there is to be a new world of business, it will only be created by effective leadership. Coaching our best people to become even better will be a way to progress from the carnage of COVID-19. Derek Deasy's advice to them is simple but powerful.

"What was effective in leadership 1,000 years ago is still effective today. Leaders can't lead if their followers don't shape them. But they can't be subservient to their followers. This is the dance."

These are the gems of insight he throws like pebbles in a burn.

CHAPTER 28

PINKY LILANI CBE DL, ENTREPRENEUR, FOOD GURU AND KINDNESS CAMPAIGNER

LOCKED DOWN IN LONDON, ENGLAND, 28 MAY 2020

Pinky Lilani is different. She's the only person in the world who uses a wok, coriander and turmeric to develop business leaders.

"Cooking is a lot like leadership," she tells me. "Because if I give four people the same ingredients, all the dishes will taste different. They will all apply them with different energy and different passion. It is the same with leading big companies. The leaders have the same ingredients, but they bring them together in different ways. Sometimes it tastes good. Sometimes it doesn't," she warns.

Pinky started with small teams from some of the UK's best-known brands. They came to the kitchen in her London home to learn the ingredients for success. Since then her unique brand of leadership development has gone global. "The wok has travelled a lot," she tells me. Aviva, EY, Shell, all the major business schools and the Bank of England have all had the pleasure of the sweet smells of Pinky's curries wafting through their meeting rooms. Their boards have all had the benefit of her insights. "It is interesting to see which leaders are up for putting in that little extra piece of chilli," she observes. "They are the risk takers!"

In 2015 she was awarded a CBE for her work with women in business. She now focuses her time on inspiring the next generation of leaders. Her Women of the Future Awards and her Kindness and Leadership initiatives have just expanded to 11 countries in South East Asia.

If there were an Olympic event for networking, Pinky would be a gold medal contender. Her friends and contacts help her create moments that inspire the potential stars of the future. She regularly takes her young leaders to tea at Buckingham Palace, drinks at the Palace of Westminster and networks at the American Embassy. "It has grown naturally but we have a voice now," she tells me.

Throughout the crisis, Pinky has been talking to senior leaders across global business. So, she has a good insight into what they have been through.

"It has been a real challenge for every single leader," she reveals. "Everyone I have spoken to has been pushed to the limit. The strain on their mental health and the worries about the physical safety of their teams and families has been immense. Some have become quite insular as they focused on helping their own business to survive. Some have pulled the shutters down. For the few whose businesses are booming, the strain has been huge. People need to have a balance but here there have only been extremes."

The younger leaders and entrepreneurs whom she works with have had to cope with a different set of pressures. Several days each week during the crisis, Pinky has been holding virtual coffee mornings. They bring together young female leaders from around the world. This week they've connected female entrepreneurs from Myanmar with the next generation of women leaders in the City of London. Pinky says it has been a powerful and hugely valuable experience.

"It has been a real roller coaster. Some feel very lonely working from home, especially the young female high-flyers, who have been used to working long hours in the office. Several of the entrepreneurs have had their business models challenged. Everybody wants good, positive energy right now. The virtual coffee mornings help give them that."

Pinky is less positive about our political leaders.

"I think in the UK the politicians haven't handled it well and in America it's just crazy," she tells me.

Pinky was born in Kolkata, India, and moved to the UK more than 40 years ago.

"I grew up in a country where we respected our leaders. We thought they knew more than us. They would make the wise decisions. What the crisis has shown is that they don't know more than anyone else. They are clutching at straws and flying by the seat of their pants, which is quite worrying because we are all depending on them. Some really bad decisions have been made and we have some leaders who just don't listen."

Post-COVID-19, Pinky believes people will hold their leaders to account even more. "I hope we will be a more caring and kinder society. We have experienced it during the crisis. In the past a lot of leaders were quite brutal. It used to be they need to be feared rather than loved. In the future we want to show that to be a really successful leader you have to be a kind leader."

Pinky describes herself as a "kindness campaigner." She aims to showcase 50 kind leaders every year in an attempt to "build a new status quo." She wants to share their stories and their styles and the impact they have had on their organization and industries. She sees kindness as a quality that should be recognized as critical in "empowering change."

Pinky likes to quote her friend Professor Lalit Johri of the Saïd Business School, who said: "When you are kind you go from being a successful leader to being a significant leader."

She adds, "As a leader, you have to have a mantra. Mine is 'you have not lived the perfect day unless you have done something for someone who can never repay it'. Kindness is something that everyone can practice. It is universal. There is huge reciprocity in it. It is the gift that keeps giving. It has a huge domino effect. Being unkind brings so much negative energy. People want to work with kind people."

She would love to see kindness on the criteria in role profiles and executive searches. She's considering research that could prove the link between the kindness of a leader and the financial success of their company.

When she recognized the former Unilever CEO Paul Polman for his kind leadership, he told her, "I have many accolades, but this is the most meaningful."

Pinky believes she has seen more kindness in the COVID-19 crisis than ever before. "The real challenge is to maintain and preserve it. It will be needed even more in the recovery.

"None of us want to do business with people who are duplicitous. Sometimes people keep silent when they see bad behaviour in a position of power – like Harvey Weinstein. Not so in the future. I believe in karma.

"The young leaders see collaboration and giving back as hugely important. They want to be part of an environment of giving and caring."

So, if Pinky were going to cook up a curry to help us emerge from the crisis, what would it be? She reminds me of a quote from Hippocrates: "Your food shall be your medicine." Then she points me to the Indian concepts of Ayurveda – 'the science of life'. They were created 5,000 years ago and attach special emphasis to the medicinal properties of spices. They also discuss the meaning of life in general and the importance of mental as well as physical health.

According to Ayurveda, it is important to prepare food in the right frame of mind – with love and enthusiasm – and to eat in an atmosphere of tranquillity. During lockdown, Pinky believes there was much scope to follow the Ayurvedic principles.

"There are so many health-giving spices and herbs that are beneficial to keep fit but also build immunity. Tranquillity with families living under stress was harder to practice."

For her post-COVID-19 curry, Pinky Lilani invents karahi chicken with spinach, dill and fenugreek. She describes it as "a new world combination, which is healthy, exciting and different. Cooked with positive energy. Topped off with a huge sprinkling of coriander and, for you, Atholl, washed down with a chota peg of whisky."[68]

True leaders never stop learning. The COVID-19 crisis has shown us that the human species has a lot to learn about a lot of things. The final pages of this book are dedicated to challenging our readers to learn from the insights which have gone before. The hope is that the stories of those at the forefront of leading the business world's response to the pandemic will be a catalyst to encourage others to pause, consider and change the way they lead. In order to do this, individual leaders must consider what are the behaviours which they personally need to change and which their businesses need to change to deliver better outcomes in the future. In these last two chapters we look at the personal behaviours of leaders and we summarize what may change in the external environment as we emerge from COVID-19. If everyone just reads this book and sets it aside, we will have failed. My challenge is to now consider what are you going to change? What new habits are you going to embrace? How are you going to change behaviours and deliver results?

CHAPTER 29
LEADERSHIP LEARNINGS

JUNE 2020

My interviews with the leaders in lockdown were all carried out over a remarkable 100-day period. As lockdowns began to be lifted in Asia, Europe, the UK and the US, it was only the end of Act One of COVID-19. As the virus ebbed in these regions, it was growing worldwide, wreaking its pain in Africa, India and South America. It was also escalating in the southern states of the US. When you read this, the story will have moved on, but the leadership learnings from lockdown will remain just as relevant. The insights of these leaders should be applicable to any change, any crisis, and anyone who chooses to lead now and in the future.

So, what can we learn from COVID-19 and the way these leaders in lockdown handled it?

For my executive coaching, I mainly use the systems psychodynamic model taught at INSEAD – considering the person, the role and the organization (PRO). But for coaching leaders in a crisis, I have developed the LEAD model for senior executives to provide another prism. Each letter in LEAD depicts a vital set of behaviours for crisis leadership. The 'L' is for looking like a leader, the 'E' is for empathy, the 'A' is for awareness and the 'D' is for delivery. Let's consider the leaders in lockdown against this model.

LOOKING LIKE A LEADER

So, what does a leader look like? The leaders in lockdown distinguish themselves through their words, their presence, their actions and their mindset. They are people who have mastered 'the inner game'. As Leena Nair of Unilever put it, "Leaders who strengthen their inner game deliver high performance and get the business to grow."

My first observation is that they all had an aura of calm when quite remarkable things were happening around them. They led by example. As General Stan McChrystal told us, "Act how you want others to act." They brought a clarity to chaos. They were clear about what needed to be done to get through. Mark Thompson of *The New York Times* said, "It is the subtle, flexible, responsive ones who will survive and thrive. People who are too slow to respond are going to be toast."

They looked for the opportunities. They championed the power of purpose. Leena Nair of Unilever epitomized this when she said, "This time has elevated purpose like no other." Nupur Singh Mallick of Tata said, "We know why we exist. ... What comes from society should go back to the people." Ho Kwon Ping of Banyan Tree mused, "Purpose is at the very heart of living." Sally Osman, a former adviser to The Queen, called it "a moment of truth when organizations will be judged on giving purpose real meaning through action not words."

They all prioritized communicating with employees, customers and stakeholders. That meant saying what they didn't know as well as what they did. George Hongchoy of Link Asset Management told us about his 3Cs – collaborate, communicate and care. He said, "You can never communicate enough."

The leaders in lockdown displayed a mindset that demonstrated they could think in a way that others might not. Sir Brian Souter of Stagecoach worried about social unrest when no one else was talking about it. "I fear this may turn into public revolution and disorder," he said. Weeks later there were riots in the streets. The murder of George Floyd unleashed public protest about racial inequality and much more.

Former Grant Thornton CEO Sacha Romanovitch told us, "The one thing this proves is that trickle-down economics doesn't work." Clement Kwok of The Hongkong and Shanghai Hotels was crystal clear about what the long term meant for him: "Don't go out and say you are a long-term investor ... unless you have the stomach to live through the ups and downs."

They had big, challenging thoughts about society. Alison Martin of Zurich asked, "What is that world we want to aspire for our children to live in? Can we try and build that one rather than the one we were destroying six months ago?" Ho Kwon Ping observed, "We are seeing an entire paradigm shift in civilizational relationships now." Will Ahmed at WHOOP told us his mission was "to unlock human performance." Vivienne Artz from Refinitiv asked why, if we can do the unthinkable and shift battalions to home-working, we cannot fix inequality: "Women shouldn't have to do two things to succeed while a man only has to do one." Martin Gilbert threw his spanner in the works with, "Globalization has made us better off, but better for whom? Better off for only 10%." Osvald Bjelland challenged us to find a new generation of leaders who could bring people together, saying, "We may never get this moment again in our lifetimes."

When we talked about the search for a vaccine, Pocket Sun said, "Society shouldn't be saved by billionaires." Gary Liu of the *South China Morning Post* observed, "Conviction is going to become central to quality leadership in the future in a way that it hasn't been before." Through their words, their presence, their actions and their mindset, they looked like leaders.

EMPATHY

The leaders in lockdown emphasized the need for empathy. Leena Nair proclaimed that this was the end of the 'Superman' boss and the beginning of a new era of the compassionate leader. Sally Osman's formula for crisis leadership was, "You need to show empathy, be authentic and be clear." Marian Salzman gave good examples and said, we need to "inject humanity back into leadership." Nearly every leadership interview stressed prioritizing care for the people we work with.

The art of listening was a common theme. As Leena Nair observed, "The first thing [leaders] do is listen and acknowledge the pain and the answers will follow." Sally Osman said, "Leaders need to listen to what people are really feeling and where they are emotionally."

Along with empathy comes the empowerment of teams and individuals. The crisis exposed the weakness of command and control. As Richard Bevan from the world of sport said, "The really exciting companies are those that manage from the bottom up and that has been accelerated by this crisis." Pinky Lilani grounded us in empathy. She quoted a friend who believes, "When you are kind you go from being a successful leader to being a significant leader."

AWARENESS

Awareness comes in two parts. It is a heightened awareness of what you are doing and how you are perceived by others. It is also an acute awareness of what is going on around you – seeing what others don't see. Several of our leaders were planning for COVID-19 well before governments moved into crisis mode. They saw it coming.

In my private conversations with the leaders in lockdown – which I have not included in the book – I saw an abundance of self-awareness. Several leaders quite willingly volunteered what they had got wrong and how they could have done better. One told me, "I wasn't as prepared as I should have been for this crisis. Next time I will be much better prepared." That leader's company had excelled, but he was still trying to learn through challenging himself.

At Black Isle Group, we are increasingly asked to help clients with psychometric personality assessments. These help individuals and teams to understand themselves better. They're a starting point to maximizing performance. They are also gold dust in selection and recruitment.

INSEAD professor Derek Deasy made a good challenge to any leader's self-awareness when he asked, "How do you want to be remembered at a time when the world is paying attention?"

Increasingly, a major part of self-awareness is knowing your own mental and physical states and being able to keep tabs on your own energy. This is especially important in periods of prolonged stress, such as the COVID-19 crisis. Will Ahmed, CEO of WHOOP, summed that up when he told us that business leaders need to adopt "the same mindset that an Olympian has" so that they can be "the best version" of themselves.

Self-improvement cannot begin without awareness.

DELIVERY

Throughout these conversations, the leaders in lockdown demonstrated delivery in a way that few would have thought possible in normal times. There were different phases to the crisis. First, they had to move their people to remote working. Then many had to take action to ensure their financial sustainability going forward. Then they moved to adapting to working in the crisis and to mining opportunities. Many quite rapidly began to reset and rethink their operations and business models to come out of the crisis in a better position to face the new world of business.

In the first phase, Nupur Singh Mallick and her colleagues shifted 600,000 people to homeworking. Christian Lanng, Alison Martin, Mark Thompson and several others had similar stories to tell. Leena Nair delivered across countries and continents. Pocket Sun told us, "It is about evolving with agility and embracing change."

I observed two types of leader in the crisis. There were the rescuers and there were those who hoped to be rescued. The leaders in lockdown were very much driving the lifeboats. Others were flailing thrashing around in the sea.

Pocket Sun was all about opportunity. She had stories of how her entrepreneurs had seized the day. They hadn't wallowed in self-pity as the crisis hit. They weren't frozen in the headlights as their cash ran out. They were drawn to where there was a commercial need. They did this in a way that showed agility, innovation and ambition. The leaders in lockdown displayed delivery by the lorryload.

LEADING

In more normal times, you can add to the LEAD model and turn it into the LEADING model – where the 'I' stands for impact. Through this, at Black Isle Group we often work on communication styles and personal presence. We like to help people understand the power of brevity, clarity and impact. The 'N' stands for nurturing. This is about how we inspire and grow the people around us. The 'G' in LEADING stands for game changing. We don't want our leaders to just maintain the status quo. We want them to deliver transformational change and new ambitions. Take Christian Lanng, CEO of Tradeshift. He felt there hadn't been that much change in the past 20 years. He shared his ambition for the future: "Our overall mission is to create economic opportunity for *all* the companies in the world – for them and us."

Wherever you are in your executive career, it can be cathartic to consider how you show up against the seven behaviours of our LEADING model. Ask a friendly colleague to give feedback on where they see you. As well as being a good measure of self-awareness, it's a good place to start your post COVID-19 journey towards maximizing your potential.

CHAPTER 30

THE NEW WORLD OF BUSINESS

How much will change because of COVID-19? How quickly will it change? These are the key questions to consider as we try to predict the shape of the new world of business.

The 9/11 attacks were the deadliest terrorist event in history. Nearly 3,000 died and 6,000 were injured.[69] In the aftermath many sure-fire predictions were made around the end of business travel and the reluctance of workers to return to skyscraper offices. These forecasts did not come true. In the wake of the global financial crisis in boardrooms, in academia, the media and dinner parties many waxed lyrical about the end of the capitalist system, the death of globalization and the urgent need to address inequality. Little changed.

So, is it different this time? There is a lot to suggest that maybe it is. For a start the pandemic has had a personal and emotional impact on nearly everyone in the world in some way or another. The economic fallout will do the same. The extreme nature of this crisis is what makes me believe it will precipitate a greater degree of change than the crises of the past.

In the end the question of 'how much will change' will be answered only by the actions of leaders through time. The scale and pace of change will depend on effectiveness, mindset and ambition. The conditions are ripe for leaders to do something totally different. That may be to reposition their business for where the market will be in one, five, ten or fifteen years' time. Or, more importantly, it may be to lead in a way that helps to solve the existential issues in society that have been highlighted by the shared global experience of COVID-19.

Some will use the crisis to make changes that they should have made before. They didn't make them because their skills as change leaders were not good enough to overcome the forces of opposition to change. Should the education sector have embraced virtual learning more than it has before now? Should the corporate sector have adopted more flexible working before now? Should many sectors have further advanced their digital capability before a pandemic forced them to make more change in ten weeks than they might have in ten years of normal business?

Through interviews with 28 thoughtful leaders, this book has identified that change is most likely, and most needed, in seven key areas. They are the seven themes of the leaders in lockdown:

1. The new age of purpose
2. The new world of work
3. Tackling inequality
4. Global cooperation
5. Resilience
6. Resetting the supply chain
7. Maximizing potential

There were other key changes that flowed through their insights. Most of all, the suggestion of further major advances in digital ran through everything we discussed. We could think of this as entering an era of 'supersonic digital'. It's like in the past 20 years all we did was learn how to fly. Now we have discovered Mach 2 digital is possible.[70]

Ho Kwon Ping captured this when he told us he expects that the new advances in technology would be in "terms of life expectancy, prolongation of life, cures for cancer, immunotherapy, cloning, DNA – the COVID-19 crisis has pushed much of this forward."

Christian Lanng of Tradeshift said that all many corporates had done in recent years was add "a glossy digital layer on top of 30 years of business crust." Now is the moment for real digital transformation.

What the COVID-19 crisis highlighted is that it is not the new technology that is the barrier. It is humans' caution about adopting new things that has stopped progress. When we were forced to change by the pandemic, the world found virtual communications a breeze. Businesses and sectors that fail to make major advances in digital and automation may be consigned to gradual or sudden extinction.

All our leaders in lockdown agreed that COVID-19 had brought society to a crossroads. We can choose one path or another.

We owe it to our children and our grandchildren not to go back to the way we were. We owe it to the millions who were infected and the hundreds of thousands of people who died. We must use the memory of the experience of COVID-19 to improve our world and to improve the lives of the eight billion people who inhabit this planet. How successful will we be in this endeavour? In the end, as always, it all comes down to leadership.

ENDNOTES

1. Johns Hopkins University Coronavirus Resource Centre, accessed 27 July 2020, https://coronavirus.jhu.edu/data.

2. Stephanie Nebehay, *Reuters* Business News, "Nearly Half of Global Workforce Risk Losing Livelihoods in Pandemic – ILO," last modified 29 April 2020, https://uk.reuters.com/article/uk-health-coronavirus-ilo/nearly-half-of-global-workforce-risk-losing-livelihoods-in-pandemic-ilo-idUKKBN22B1LO.

3. *COVID-19 Financial Assistance and Debt Service Relief* (International Monetary Fund, 2020), accessed 13 July 2020, https://www.imf.org/en/Topics/imf-and-COVID19/COVID-Lending-Tracker.

4. "Squawk Box" (CNBC, 22 January 2020).

5. "Wuhan Coronavirus," HC Deb, 23 January 2020, vol. 670, col. 432, accessed 13 July 2020, https://hansard.parliament.uk/commons/2020-01-23/debates/38D462B1-70F8-4CC6-AABD-2CCF4E271C34/WuhanCoronavirus.

6. Chen Wang, Peter W. Horby, Frederick G. Hayden and George F. Gao, "A Novel Coronavirus Outbreak of Global Health Concern," *The Lancet* 395 (2020): 470–473.

7. Tony Munroe and Roxanne Liu, "Xi Says China Faces a 'Grave Situation' as Death Toll Hits 42," *Reuters*, last modified 25 January 2020, https://www.reuters.com/article/us-china-health/xi-says-china-faces-grave-situation-as-virus-death-toll-hits-42-idUSKBN1ZO005.

8. Macer Hall, "Nerves of Steel – Rishi's £30 Billion War on Virus," *Daily Express*, last modified 12 March 2020, https://twitter.com/Daily_Express/status/1237868184343961602/photo/1.

9. Rishi Sunak, "Budget Speech 2020," Gov.uk, last modified 11 March 2020, https://www.gov.uk/government/speeches/budget-speech-2020.

10. Boris Johnson, "Prime Minister's statement on coronavirus (COVID-19): 12 March 2020," Gov.uk, last modified 12 March 2020, https://www.gov.uk/government/speeches/pm-statement-on-coronavirus-12-march-2020.

11. Harry Robertson, "Corona Crash: Global Markets Suffer Worst Day Since 1987 as Virus Spreads," *City AM*, last modified 13 March 2020, https://www.cityam.com/corona-crash-global-markets-suffer-disastrous-day.

12. Kevin Breuninger, "Trumps Says Businesses Could Reopen – Soon – While Fighting Coronavirus," CNBC, last modified 23 March 2020, https://www.cnbc.com/2020/03/23/coronavirus-trump-says-businesses-could-reopen-soon-while-fighting-COVID.html.

13. Ernest Hemingway, *The Sun Also Rises* (London: Arrow Books, 2004) 119.

14. Peter Tchir, "What if Buffett is the One Swimming Naked?" *Forbes*, last modified 4 May 2020, https://www.forbes.com/sites/petertchir/2020/05/04/what-if-buffett-is-the-one-swimming-naked/#63c3d2166e36.

15. "Insolvency Practioners," Wikipedia, accessed 30 July 2020, https://en.wikipedia.org/wiki/Insolvency_practitioner.

16. Oli Ballard, "Is Business Debt Set to Double to More Than £8.6 Billion Due to COVID-19?" Business Leader, last modified 6 April 2020, https://www.businessleader.co.uk/is-business-debt-set-to-double-to-more-than-8-6bn-due-to-COVID-19/82527/.

17. Rishi Sunak, "The Chancellor, Rishi Sunak, Provides an Updated Statement on Coronavirus," Gov.uk, last modified 20 March 2020, https://www.gov.uk/government/speeches/the-chancellor-rishi-sunak-provides-an-updated-statement-on-coronavirus.

18. Boris Johnson, "Prime Minister's Statement on Coronavirus (COVID-19): 23 March 2020," Gov.uk, last modified 23 March 2020, https://www.gov.uk/government/speeches/pm-address-to-the-nation-on-coronavirus-23-march-2020.

19. Danny Boyle, "Tuesday Morning News Briefing: The End of Freedom," *The Daily Telegraph*, last modified 24 March 2020, https://www.telegraph.co.uk/news/2020/03/24/tuesday-morning-news-briefing-end-freedom.

20. "UK Economy Takes 25% Hit from COVID, Recovery Seen Slow," *Reuters*, last modified 12 June 2020, https://uk.reuters.com/news/picture/uk-economy-takes-25-hit-from-COVID-recov-idUKKBN23J0V0.

21. "She's the Bee's Knees," *The Guardian*, last modified 29 June 2003, https://www.theguardian.com/books/2003/jun/29/society.

22. Marian Salzman's personal website, accessed 27 July 2020, https://mariansalzman.com/meet_marian/.

23. Marian Salzman, *Chaos: The New Normal* (Marian Salzman, 2019), accessed 13 July 2020, https://mariansalzman.com/wp-content/uploads/2019/12/CHAOS-THE-NEW-NORMAL_HD.pdf.

24. Osvald Bjelland, "A Message from Our CEO: Forging Our Future Together in the Heat of the Crisis," Xynteo, last modified 23 March 2020, https://xynteo.com/insights/latest/message-our-ceo-forging-our-future-together-heat-crisis.

25. Johns Hopkins University Coronavirus Resource Centre, accessed 27 July 2020, https://coronavirus.jhu.edu/data.

26. Richard Milne, "Coronavirus Leaves Wealthy Norway Facing Tough Spending Choices," *Financial Times*, last modified 2 April 2020, https://www.ft.com/content/e1117528-5c8f-47ee-86bd-e7cce7bf3382.

27. "The World's Most Powerful People," *Forbes*, last modified 11 November 2009, https://www.forbes.com/2009/11/11/worlds-most-powerful-leadership-power-09-people_land.html#56c0c260624d.

28. "Chairman Ratan N Tata's Statement on Tata Trust's COVID-19 Strategy," BW Online Bureau, 28 March 2020, http://bwpeople.businessworld.in/article/Chairman-Ratan-N-Tata-s-Statement-On-Tata-Trusts-COVID-19-Strategy/28-03-2020-187582/.

29. N. Chandrasekaran and Roopa Purushothaman, *Bridgital Nation* (London: Penguin, 2019).

30. Nikhil Inamdar, "Coronavirus Lockdown: India Jobless Numbers Cross 120 Million in April," (BBC News), last modified 6 May 2020, https://www.bbc.co.uk/news/world-asia-india-52559324.

31. Lam Ka-sing, "Hong Kong's Link Reit Announces Entry to Europe With US$487.5m Acquisition of Morgan Stanley's London Home," *The South China Morning Post,* 27 July 2020, https://www.scmp.com/business/article/3094824/hong-kongs-link-reit-announces-entry-europe-us4875-million-acquisition.

32. Mike Carson, *The Manager: Inside the Minds of Football's Leaders* (London: Bloomsbury, 2014), 152.

33. Mike Carson, *The Manager: Inside the Minds of Football's Leaders* (London Bloomsbury, 2014), 294.

34. Alex Ferguson with Michael Moritz, *Leading* (London: Hodder and Stoughton, 2015) 235-242.

35. Alison Andrew, Sarah Cattan, Monica Costa Dias, Christine Farquharson, Lucy Kraftman, Sonya Krutikova, Angus Phimister and Almudena Sevilla, "Parents, Especially Mothers, Paying a Heavy Price for Lockdown," (Institute of Fiscal Studies), last modified 27 May 2020, https://www.ifs.org.uk/publications/14861.

36. Kate Clarke,"US VC Investment in Female Founders Hits All-time High," Techcrunch, last modified 9 December 2019, https://techcrunch.com/2019/12/09/us-vc-investment-in-female-founders-hits-all-time-high/.

37. A burr is a distinctive aspect of the local accent in some parts of England and Scotland.

38. Hilary Mantel, *Wolf Hall* (London: Fourth Estate, 2009), 458.

39. Shan Ross, "Sir Brian Souter Makes Massive £109m Donation as Charities Experience Perfect Storm," *The Scotsman*, last modified 22 October 2019, https://www.scotsman.com/news/politics/sir-brian-souter-makes-massive-ps109m-donation-charities-experience-perfect-storm-1404544.

40. "Data Can Be a Powerful Tool against Coronavirus," *Financial Times*, last modified 7 April 2020, https://www.ft.com/content/48739142-735c-11ea-95fe-fcd274e920ca.

41. "Coronavirus: Track and Trace System in Place from June – PM," BBC News, last modified 20 May 2020, https://www.bbc.co.uk/news/uk-5274133.

42. Edward Thicknesse, "Health Minister Admits NHS Coronavirus App Might Not Be Ready before Winter," *City AM*, last modified 17 June 2020, https://www.cityam.com/health-minister-admits-nhs-coronavirus-app-might-not-be-ready-before-winter.

43. Ofcom Communications Market Report, 2 August 2018, https://www.ofcom.org.uk/about-ofcom/latest/features-and-news/decade-of-digital-dependency.

44. Gaëlle Ferrant, Luca Maria Pesando and Keiko Nowacka, "Unpaid Care Work: The missing link in the analysis of gender gaps in labour outcomes," OECD (2014): 2.

45. Circuit breakers is a term used in Asia to describe measures brought in to break the community spread of COVID-19.

46. Oliver Ralph, "UK Companies to Shun Business Interruption Insurance," *Financial Times*, last modified 4 May 2020, https://www.ft.com/content/ba7b8321-73a0-442d-ac85-74ad09019223.

47. "Zuck" is the nickname of Facebook founder Mark Zuckerberg. Lord Beaverbrook was a British Canadian newspaper publisher who was one of the most influential figures in the media in the first half of the 20th century.

48. Johns Hopkins University Coronavirus Resource Centre, accessed 27 July 2020, https://coronavirus.jhu.edu/data.

49. Sisk, Richard, "Gates Wanted McChrystal to Fight for His Job," Military. com, last modified 3 February 2014, https://www.military.com/daily-news/2014/02/03/gates-wanted-mcchrystal-to-fight-for-his-job.html.

50. Sean Loughlin, "Pentagon: 'Major Combat' Over, but Smaller Fights Remain," CNN, last modified 14 April 2003, https://edition.cnn.com/2003/US/04/14/sprj.irq.pentagon/index.html.

51. Matthew Stern, "How the NFL Can Help The Theatre Through COVID," Broadway Symposium, last modified 23 July 2020, https://www. broadwaysymposium.com/post/how-the-nfl-can-help-the-theatre-through-COVID?postId=5f18f9ec1bf601001704b0ce.

52. Kevin Quealy, "The Richest Neighborhoods Emptied Out Most as Coronavirus Hit New York City," *New York Times*, last modified 15 May 2020, https://www.nytimes.com/interactive/2020/05/15/upshot/who-left-new-york-coronavirus.html.

53. Jeffrey C. Mays and Andy Newman, "Virus is Twice as Deadly for Black and Latino People than Whites in NYC," *New York Times*, last modified 8 May 2020, https://www.nytimes.com/2020/04/08/nyregion/coronavirus-race-deaths.html.

54. Doree Lewak, "NY Women Are Coronavirus Crushing on Andrew Cuomo: 'Is He Single?'" *New York Post*, last modified 21 March 2020, https://nypost.com/2020/03/21/new-york-women-are-coronavirus-crushing-on-andrew-cuomo-is-he-single.

55. Amy Julia Harris, Kim Barker and Jesse McKinley, "Nursing Homes Are Hot Spots in the Crisis," *New York Times*, last modified 13 May 2020, https://www.nytimes.com/2020/05/13/nyregion/nursing-homes-coronavirus-new-york.html.

56. Jim Mustian, "NY Nursing Home Reports 98 Deaths Linked to Coronavirus," (NBC New York), last modified 1 May 2020, https://www.nbcnewyork.com/news/local/ny-nursing-home-reports-98-deaths-linked-coronavirus/2399097/.

57. "Coronavirus: Twitter Allows Staff to Work from Home Forever," BBC News, last modified 13 May 2020, https://www.bbc.co.uk/news/technology-52628119.

58. Valentina Romei, Gill Plimmer and Laura Hughes, "Hancock Claim of 'Protective Ring' Round Care Homes Questioned," *Financial Times*, last modified 15 May 2020, https://www.ft.com/content/6afb06d6-abd6-4281-ac16-74f500f096d0.

59. Guy Hamilton, dir., *The Man with the Golden Gun* (United Artists, 1974).

60. *The Hong Kong and Shanghai Hotels, Limited: Annual Report 2019* (The Hong Kong and Shanghai Hotels, 2019), 27, accessed 13 July 2020, https://www.hshgroup.com/-/media/Files/HSH/Financial-Reports/2019/2019-Annual-Report---English.ashx.

61. A shive is a wooden fitting in an ale cask.

62. "UK Small Business Statistics," FSB, accessed 27 July 2020, https://www.fsb.org.uk/uk-small-business-statistics.html.

63. "Small and Medium Sized Enterprises," National Action Plans on Business and Human Rights, accessed 27 July 2020, https://globalnaps.org/issue/small-medium-enterprises-smes/.

64. Nida Rasheed, "Top Wearable Technology Trends and Health Apps to Look for in 2020," Smartercx.com, last modified 2 January 2020, https://smartercx.com/top-wearable-technology-trends-and-health-apps-to-look-for-in-2020.

65. An earnings call is a conference call between the management of a company and its investors, analysts and media to discuss the company's financial results.

66. William A. Haseltine, "Aging Populations Will Challenge Health Care Systems All Over the World," *Forbes*, last modified 2 April 2018, https://www.forbes.com/sites/williamhaseltine/2018/04/02/aging-populations-will-challenge-healthcare-systems-all-over-the-world/#493c47ee2cc3.

67. Boris Johnson, "Prime Minister's Statement on Coronavirus (COVID-19): 30 April 2020," Gov.uk, last modified 30 April 2020, https://www.gov.uk/government/news/prime-ministers-statement-on-coronavirus-COVID-19-30-april-2020.

68. A chota peg is an Indian expression for a small measure, normally of whisky.

69. "Casualties of the September 11 Attacks," Wikipedia, accessed 13 July 2020, https://en.wikipedia.org/wiki/Casualties_of_the_September_11_attacks.

70. Mach 2 is named after the Austrian physicist Ernst Mach and is a measure of twice the speed of sound.